GOA 2011

Reviewing and Recovering Fifty Years

About the Editors

Dr. Savio Abreu is Director of Xavier Centre of Historical Research (XCHR), Goa. His PhD from Indian Institute of Technology, Mumbai was a sociological study on New Christian movements in contemporary Goa. He has published articles in various Journals such as Indian Church History Review, Seminar, Social Action, etc. He has published papers in edited volumes, the last one being on "Social Development of the Christian Community in India" in, *India Social Development Report 2012: Minorities at the Margins* (Oxford University Press, 2013). He is visiting faculty at Jnana-Deepa Vidyapeeth (JDV), the Pontifical Athenaeum in Pune since 2012. E-mail: savioasj@gmail.com.

Dr. Rudolf C. Heredia is an independent researcher residing at Campion School, Mumbai. His doctorate in Sociology is from the University of Chicago (1979), and he was the founder director of the Social Science Centre, St. Xavier's College Mumbai, 1980-1992 and director again from 1994-2003. From 1992-94 he was director, department of research, at the Indian Social Institute, Delhi and edited the institute's journal, Social Action, 1993-95. His publications include *Changing Gods: Rethinking Conversion in India*, Penguin, N. Delhi, 2007 and *Taking Sides: Reservation Quotas and Minority Rights in India*, Penguin, N. Delhi, 2012. He has also published in various journals such as the Economic and Political Weekly, contributions to Indian Sociology, New Frontiers in Education, etc. E-mail: rudiheredia@gmail.com

XCHR Studies Series No. 12

GOA 2011

REVIEWING AND RECOVERING FIFTY YEARS

Edited by

Savio Abreu

Rudolf C. Heredia

CONCEPT PUBLISHING COMPANY PVT. LTD.

NEW DELHI-110059

ISBN-13 : 978-93-5125-070-8

First Published 2014

Published and Printed by

Concept Since 1974

Concept Publishing Company Pvt. Ltd.
A/15-16, Commercial Block, Mohan Garden
New Delhi-110059 (India)
T: 25351460, 25351794, *F*: 091-11-25357109
E: publishing@conceptpub.com. W: www.conceptpub.com
Editorial Office: H-13, Bali Nagar, New Delhi-110 015, India.

Cataloging in Publication Data—*Courtesy:* D.K. Agencies (P) Ltd. <docinfo@dkagencies.com>

"Goa 2011 : Reviewing and Recovering 50 Years" (Seminar) (2011 : Alto Porvorim, India)

Goa 2011 : reviewing and recovering fifty years / edited by Savio Abreu, Rudolf C. Heredia.

p. cm.

Includes bibliographical references and index.

ISBN 9789351250708

1. Goa (India : State)—History—Congresses. I. Abreu, Savio. II. Heredia, Rudolf C. III. Title.

DDC 954.78 23

Dedicated
to
Late Jenny Abreu
and
Late Dr. Sharon D'Cruz

Preface and Acknowledgements

As this volume goes to press I share the excited feelings of a mother delivering her first born baby. Putting together this volume has taken a long time, as it is with all edited ventures. I first spoke to Rudolf about the project of publishing this volume a few months after the seminar but due to various factors beyond our control the timeline for the project kept extending. I am grateful to Rudolf for accepting to co-edit the papers and for his continuous encouragement. It is because of Rudolf's constant support and timely reminders and the interest of some of the paper presenters that I was able to complete this maiden editorial venture. Balancing my duties of running a research centre with writing and editing has been a taxing job, but this assignment was made easy and enjoyable by the help I received from various persons.

I, along with Rudolf, would like to express our appreciation to all the participants of the seminar and the other scholars who have contributed to this volume. I wish to thank Dr. P.D. Xavier who carefully went through the papers, making corrections and giving valuable suggestions. I am grateful to Ms. Anjali Dar Sen Gupta who painstakingly copy-edited the papers. My gratitude goes out to Fr Anthony da Silva, former provincial of Goa Province, for his generous support. I cannot forget the hard work and reassuring support of the staff of Xavier Centre—Vanessa, Arti, Thomas, Tari, Urmilla, Fr Rinald and Fr Anand—in organising the seminar and in the editorial work. I wish to thank Concept Publishing Company Pvt. Ltd., New Delhi-110059 for the trouble taken to ensure that the entire publication process went smoothly. Since this is my first editorial project I wish to dedicate the volume to the memory of two women—my late sister Jenny Abreu and Dr Sharon D'Cruz, a bright young historian, who was closely associated with the Xavier Centre, and who passed away recently.

Goa
September 2013

Savio Abreu

Contents

Contributors' Profile

Agnelo Paulo Fernandes (Dr.) is a senior History Researcher based in Goa. He presently works for National Centre for Documentation and Research, Government of Abu Dhabi on Portuguese Documents for History of Arabia from Archives of Goa as well as from Europe. His Ph.D. thesis 'Portuguese and the Mughals 1627-1707' is based on original Portuguese Documentation from Archives in Goa and from Europe which he visited in 1984 on a scholarship from *Calouste Gulbenkian* Foundation, Lisbon. He has published several articles on Indo-Portuguese history. He can be contacted on E-mail: dr_agnelofernandes@yahoo.com.

Cláudia Pereira (Dr.) is an anthropologist and her PhD thesis is an ethnographic research on the meanings of caste and tribe, among a Catholic and Hindu group of Goa, India (translated from the Portuguese: *Caste, Tribe and Conversion, the Gaudde of Goa*, 2009). For two years she has done fieldwork in Hindu and Catholic Goan villages. Cláudia held a photo's exhibition titled "Goa: (Non) Convert Gaudde", at the Portuguese Consulate in Goa. She was a Visiting Scholar at Brown University, USA, and a Visiting Student at the University of Amsterdam, The Netherlands. Currently she's a postdoctoral researcher at ISCTE, CIES-IUL, Centre for Research and Studies in Sociology, Lisbon, Portugal. She can be contacted on E-mail: claudia.pereira@iscte.pt

Frederick Noronha (Mr.) has been a journalist for the past three decades—both in Goa and working for the outstation media. He has been active in promoting many alternative online communication ventures in cyberspace. Currently he heads the Goa,1556 book publishing alternative venture which he founded in 2007, and which has published more than 65 (Goa-related, mostly non-fiction) books till date. He is also a PhD research scholar at the Department of English, Goa University, where his topic is related to book publishing in Goa in the 20th century. He can be contacted on E-mail: fredericknoronha1@gmail.com

Maria Bernadette Lia Gomes (Dr.) finished her Ph.D in Sociology from Goa University, in 1994. She has taught in the Rosary School, Mira-Mar, in CES College of Arts and Commerce, Cuncolim, and in Government College of Arts Science, Commerce, Quepem, Goa. She has presented research papers in the area of folklore, culture, ecology and ethno-medicine at various seminars in the state. She has prepared a monograph on the pastoral tribe, the *Gouly,* the first tribal (*Gawda ,Kunbi, Velip*) census report and a documentary *Sons of the Mountains:. The Goulys of Goa*, for the Government of Goa. She was the Vice-Chairperson of the Goa state traditional occupations accreditation Council. She can be contacted on E-mail: abolemgoa@gmail.com

Prajal Sakhardande (Mr.) has been teaching History at the Dhempe College of Arts and Science (Miramar, Goa) since 1993. He is President of Goa Heritage Action Group (which completed 13 years in September 2013). He is also the Convener of History, History Forum, and President of Goa's Movement for Special Status Heritage Cell Utt Goenkara. He writes a column, 'Pages from the Past', for The Navhind Times. He has penned books on 'The Muslim History and Heritage of Goa', 'Matanhy Saldanha: The Legend', and 'Walking In and Around Panaji'. He is currently doing his PhD. He can be contacted on E-mail: hertiageprajal@rediffmail.com

Pratapananda Naik (Dr.) is one of the founding members of Thomas Stephens Konkani Kendra (TSKK), Alto Porvorim, Goa and associated with it as Asst. Director, Director, Researcher, Editor of Sod (TSKK Research Bulletin) from 1980 to 2012. His Ph.D. in Linguistics is from University of Poona. He has written many Konkani books in Kannada, Devanagari and Roman scripts related to linguistics, anthology of poetry, play, folk literature and textbooks, besides many research papers and other articles related to Konkani. He has presented papers at National and International seminars in India and Japan. He has also written lyrics for Konkani songs and has presented Radio and TV programmes in Konkani in Goa and Mangalore.

He can be contacted on E-mail: pratapnaiksj@gmail.com

Remy Dias (Dr.), Associate Professor in History at Govt. College of Arts, Science and Commerce, Quepem-Goa. Also holds currently the Additional Charge as Dy. Director of Higher Education, Directorate of Higher Education, Govt. of Goa. Area of specialization is Agrarian and Consumption History, Population Studies of Goa (pre- and post-liberation period), etc. Organises regularly various State and National Level Workshops, Seminars, Conferences on History (Indo-Portuguese),

Education, Research Methodology, etc. Has presented research papers at various National and international Conferences. A number of papers have been published in Journals and Books (National and International). Co-Edited a book (Pius Malekandathil and Remy Dias, 2008. Goa in the 20th Century—Its History and Culture, Panaji: IMB). He can be contacted on E-mail: remy_dias2002@yahoo.com

Ricardo Cabral (Dr.) is presently working in the State Council of Educational Research and Training (SCERT) for the Government of Goa. His publications include '*The development of teacher education in Portuguese Goa (1841-1961)*' (Concept 2009) *and 'Primary Education in Portuguese Goa' (Concept 2013)* besides many articles and papers. He can be contacted on E-mail: rcabral@sancharnet.in

Rowena Robinson (Dr.) is Visiting Professor at the Department of Humanities and Social Sciences, Indian Institute of Technology Guwahati and Professor at the Department of Humanities and Social Sciences, Indian Institute of Technology Bombay. She has also taught at Delhi University and Jawaharlal Nehru University. Among other publications, she is author of Tremors of violence: Muslim survivors of ethnic strife in western India (Sage, 2005) and Christians of India (Sage, 2003), editor of Minority Studies (OUP, 2012), and co-editor of Religious conversion in India: modes, motivations and meanings (OUP, 2003) and Margins of Faith: Dalit and tribal Christianity in India (Sage, 2010). She can be contacted on E-mail: rtbrobinson@gmail.com

Rudolf C. Heredia (Dr.) is an independent researcher residing at Campion School, Mumbai. His doctorate in Sociology is from the University of Chicago (1979), and he was the founder director of the Social Science Centre, St. Xavier's College Mumbai, 1980-1992 and director again from 1994-2003. From 1992-94 he was director, department of research, at the Indian Social Institute, Delhi and edited the institute's journal, Social Action, 1993-95. His publications include *Changing Gods: Rethinking Conversion in India*, Penguin, N. Delhi, 2007 and *Taking Sides: Reservation Quotas and Minority Rights in India*, Penguin, N. Delhi, 2012. He has also published in various journals such as the Economic and Political Weekly, Contributions to Indian Sociology, New Frontiers in Education, etc. He can be contacted on E-mail: rudiheredia@gmail.com

Sachin Savio Moraes (Mr.), Asst. Prof. of Sociology, Parvatibai Chowgule College, Margao, Goa. He is busy with his Ph.D research at the Goa University, titled '*The Goan Diaspora: A study of socio-cultural dynamics in Goa*'. He can be contacted on E-mail: sachinsaviomoraes@gmail.com

Sandra Ataíde Lobo (Dr.) has recently finished her *Ph.D in Theory and History of Ideas, and the title of her thesis* was 'O desassossego goês: cultura e política em Goa do liberalismo ao Acto Colonial' (2013). She was Librarian and Archivist until 2005 at ANTT, Center of History of Culture, Historical Archive of the Diocese of Cochin. Since 1994, she has been a member of the Free Seminary of History of Ideas; she has also participated in collective researches and publications related to the history of Portuguese liberalism and republicanism, intellectual history and history of magazines. Since 2005, she has been focused on Goan cultural, political and intelectual history, and has published several related papers. She can be contacted on E-mail: sandralobo@netcabo.pt

Savio Abreu (Dr.) is director of Xavier Centre of Historical Research (XCHR), Goa. His PhD from Indian Institute of Technology, Mumbai was a sociological study on New Christian movements in contemporary Goa. He has published articles in various Journals such as Indian Church History Review, Seminar, Social Action, etc. He has published papers in edited volumes, the last one being on "Social Development of the Christian Community in India" in, *India Social Development Report 2012: Minorities at the Margins* (Oxford University Press, 2013). He is visiting faculty at Jnana-Deepa Vidyapeeth (JDV), the Pontifical Athenaeum in Pune since 2012. He can be contacted on E-mail: savioasj@gmail.com.

Sharmila Pais (Ms) is teaching history at St. Xavier's College, Mapusa, Goa for the last 14 years. She has presented several papers at both state level and national level seminars. She has registered for her PhD at the Goa University.
She can be contacted on E-mail: shamipais1000@yahoo.com

Sushila Sawant Mendes (Dr.) is Associate Professor and Head of Department of History, Govt. College of Arts, Science and Commerce, Quepem, Goa for the past twenty-five years. She was the Vice-Principal of the college from 2000-06. She was awarded PhD in History by the Goa University in 2012 for her research on *'Luis de Menezes Braganca (1878-1938) and the emergence of political consciousness in Goa'*. She has presented several research papers at State and National level seminars and has many publications to her credit. She is the author of the book 'Luis de Menezes Branganca–Nationalism, Secularism Free Thought in Portugese Goa".
She can be contacted on E-mail: sawantmendes@yahoo.co.in

Victor Ferrao (Dr.) is professor of philosophy at the Diocesan Seminary of Goa at Rachol, Goa. He also teaches at Jnana Deepa Vidyapith, Pune. He has published several books and many articles in reputed journals. His recent book titled "*Being a Goan Christian: The Politics of Identity, Rift and Synthesis*" has raised interesting questions on the issues of culture, religion and identity. His area of interest is the intersection of philosophy, religion and science.
He can be contacted on E-mail: victorferrao@yahoo.co.uk.

Introduction

On December 19, 2011, Goa celebrated fifty years of liberation from Portuguese rule. Fifty years in the crucible of history may seem like a drop in the ocean. These brief but momentous years, however, have been shaped by a long chain of events spread over hundreds of years and at the same time are a precursor to 'history in the making'. Thus any analysis of post-colonial Goan society leads us back to both the colonial and pre-colonial periods of Goan history. Jubilees are not just occasions to celebrate, but are, more importantly, opportunities to take stock, to re-discover one's heritage and to analyze the numerous by lanes and twists and turns of the post-1961 thriller.

The historical event of 1961 associated with the jubilee is itself disputed. Some call it the Indian annexation or invasion of Goa; others refer to it as the liberation of Goa. Similarly, the events in post-colonial Goa, whether it be rapid industrialization and urbanization accompanied by infrastructural development and decline in agriculture, or the large scale in-migration with the resultant issues of Goan identity, language and culture, or the real estate boom and growing environmental concerns, are viewed and judged from different perspectives. Post-colonial Goa has also seen the emergence of various subaltern groups and communities that have lobbied and protested vociferously for recognition of their rights and their unique identity.

Most of the articles in the book were presented at the national seminar, "Goa 2011: Reviewing and Recovering 50 years", organised on the occasion of the golden jubilee of Goa's liberation from Portuguese rule. The seminar intended as the first of a series of multi-disciplinary seminars on Goan themes and issues, was convened by the Xavier Centre of Historical Research (XCHR) and the Thomas Stephens Konknni Kendr (TSKK) to begin a process of self-education and knowledge-creation to comprehend how the people of this state have shaped and directed their post-colonial history and how specific socio-political and cultural contexts have influenced that contemporary history. This was a process of rewinding and recovering post-colonial Goan heritage and culture and analyzing the complexities of multiple historical contexts to arrive at a mosaic of Goa in 2011 and to create a knowledge base on contemporary Goan society and culture. Organised at the XCHR-TSKK complex from September 29 to 30, 2011 and funded by the Directorate of Art and Culture, (Goa Government), this seminar was not only restricted to the influence of the colonial and pre-colonial periods on contemporary Goa but also analysed the impact of the socio-political and economic developments in independent India on Goan society.

The first chapter by Rudolf C. Heredia was the inaugural address at the seminar setting the context for the others to follow. He looks at the larger national context in which Goa is embedded. The dialectic between the dividend and deficit of democracy at the national level is reflected at the state level, and Goa is no exception to this. He articulates his perspective to the multiple crises the state experiences and the challenges it must face. According to him the future of Goa and its people will be assured when the democratic dividend outweighs the democratic deficit and for this the contribution of all citizens is vital.

The chapter by Victor Ferrao on "Between Two Communities: Past Disruption and Present Inter-relations" squarely confronts the inter-communitarian impasse between the Hindus and Christians in Goa. The communal divide between Christians and Hindus has its roots in the colonial era, even though the two communities still share cultural codes and ways of mediating difference. However, increasingly the everyday inter-communitarian intercourse in Goan society is being subverted by an identity politics exploited for partisan gain. Antagonistic histories of the two communities are constructed on the 'trauma of colonisation' and in particular that of religious conversion for the Hindu and privileging of Christian neophytes. To cope with this trauma, he proposes an ethic of compassion to precipitate a healing catharsis and reconstruct an inclusive, tolerant Goa society. His hope is for "a new spring time of peace and harmony."

Such a therapeutic process must be grounded in a history that is committed to a project of truth and reconciliation rather than redress and retribution. Agnelo Paulo Fernandes sets out the local resources in his chapter on "History Research in Goa (1961-2011)". In this "Short Survey" he sets out the research done, the materials available, the centres involved and, finally, the ways of preserving and enriching this historical heritage.

Civil society issues are addressed in the next three chapters. Savio Abreu introduces the theme of civil society movements in "Civil Society Movements in Contemporary Goa: Themes, Issues and Perspectives". He examines the themes of post-coloniality, locality, identity and culture, modernisation and issues related to development, environment and ecology that emerge from the various movements in post-colonial Goa. By analysing the fishermen's struggle, as well as the Nylon 6,6 and Meta Strips struggles, he has attempted to construct a socio-cultural theory of civil society movements in Goa. The social ferment in post-liberation Goa indicates people cannot be imprisoned in a fossilised social structure and any study of social movements in Goa needs to take into account the historicity of colonial rule, the attempts in post-colonial Goan society to deal with the fissures of the past, and the role and place of 'outsiders' in contemporary Goa.

Sushila Sawant Mendes then gives us "An Insider's Story" of "The Student Movement in Goa of the Early Eighties". Beginning in the 1970s it went beyond what might be regarded as a 'student movement' involving students who had no allegiance to a political party of communal ideology; but were more concerned with 'social consciousness' than 'career consciousness' which has now become the priority with the new generation. Mendes analyses how study circles, conferences, cultural workshops, street plays, village and slum programmes were used to conscientise and empower people.

Savio Abreu in "The struggle against SEZs in Goa" describes the successful people's movement against SEZs in Goa. He mentions various reasons for the success of the anti-SEZ movement in Goa, such as, the role of the middle class intellectuals, the extensive use of RTI to get information and expose land frauds, the collaboration and working together of different Non-governmental Organisations, etc., which served as a catalyst for similar people's movements against SEZs and other forms of land grab by the government and big private players in other parts of the country.

The subaltern cultural heritage of Goa is represented in the next two chapters. "Sons of the Mountains: the Goulys of Goa" is the result of some painstaking documentation by Bernadette Gomes of some of the aspects of the life and culture of a little known semi-nomadic pastoral tribal community in the Western Ghats of Goa. Even today the Goulys are the least developed community in the state. They suffer from a loss of self-image due to the traumatic changes they are subjected to. With just 7,000 members they are not a significant vote bank. Yet their plight is an indictment of so much that has gone away with a political class that cares less and less for our marginalised peoples.

The subaltern Gaudde community shares a rich cultural heritage of song and dance common to both Christians and Hindus. Claudia Pereira's fieldwork on the music of the Catholic and Hindu Gaudde demonstrates how dances and songs performed in specific religious rituals, once repressed in colonial times for not being Catholic, have now-a-days, become marketing initiatives in tourism, "voicing the unheard through heritage", as an authentic cultural form of Goa's heritage that resisted its colonial past. Reinforced by external confirmation, it attracts the young Catholic Gaudde who now have come to celebrate it. This has contributed to the conservation, restoration and reinvention of the so-called traditional practices. However, the consequences of commodifying and packaging this cultural genre for a market have still to be assessed.

Language has long been controversial in Goa even in pre-liberation times. Pratapananda Naik in his chapter on "Konknni: a Language at the Crossroads" makes a plea to retain both the Roman and Devanagri scripts in which Konknni is still written, since each represents a distinct dialect with its own specific cultural nuances, each associated with one of the major religious communities in the state. Turning from language politics to Goan nationalism, Sandra Ataíde Lobo's discussion on "The return to Indianness: Goan nationalism in the 1920s" argues that after the First World War there were two currents of thought among the Goan intelligentsia as regards the future of the territory. The autonomist current, predominantly

Catholic, argued against a colonial relationship and for a federal solution for future relations with Portugal and her overseas territories. The other viewpoint favoured a future integration of Goa in the Indian federation, and this was more representative of the Hindus. With the dictator, Salazar's Acto Colonial of 1930 and the hardening colonialist discourse, it was the second that finally came to prevail.

Post-liberation Goa underwent much rapid change. The press in Goa has continued to evolve its role in post-liberation Goa. Frederick Noronha's overview of the "Post-1961 Press in Goa, Its Politics and Processes" traces the demise of Portuguese newspapers in the 1960s, the growth of the Marathi-English language media, the sole Konkani daily in the 1980s, and the changes in the media in recent decades. These changes in the media have been quite significantly, even if imperceptible. Today media ownership by industrialists and wealthy politicians does not augur well for a free and active press, but Goa is not unique in this.

Another major change in post-liberation Goa that Remy Dias reviews is "Tenancy Reforms in Goa since Liberation: 1961-87". The Goa, Daman and Diu Agricultural Tenancy Act, 1964, by the Goa Legislative Assembly initiated land reforms in order to reduce poverty, accelerate economic growth and equity in pursuit of social justice and dignity for a large section of the people. However, its implementation, like elsewhere in the country, has not been smooth. Suitable amendments are required to effectively implement full rights to those tenants who still do not enjoy fully secured rights to the land that they hold.

Historically one of the main supports for the villages in Goa has been the money migrants have repatriated to their families there. Goa has a long history of male migration among Catholics both on and off shore. Sachin S. Moraes looks at "Negotiating Male Migration" through "The Experience of Women in Goa". The histories of women in Cuncolim reveal the various ambivalent processes and the multiple coping strategies among these women, for whom cooperation with other women is critical. The changes in gender relationships, both at the personal and social level due to male migration, may not always provide emancipator potentials for women.

The evolution of elementary education system in colonial Goa is covered in the chapter "Elementary Education in Goa during its Colonial Period (1821-1910) and its Impact on Goan Society" by

Richard Cabral. He argues that the period from 1821 to 1910 laid the foundations for healthy educational indices in Goa today.

Sharmila Pais sketches the history of public transportation in Goa in the 20th century: "From *Caminhão* to *Avião*: A Study on the System of Public Transportation in Goa." With the conversion of the 19th century metre gauge running from Londa to Vasco to broad gauge, and the Konkan Raliway in 1998, not to the mention the expansive inter-state bus system and the expanding air traffic, Goa is fairly well connected to the rest of the country. But within the state most people have to rely on public transport, which is overcrowded and expensive, less than adequate, and not always reliable.

History is not just recorded in the written manuscripts, as Prajal Sakhardande demonstrates with his contemporary historical discussions of "The Goa Ancient Monuments and Archaeological Sites and Remains Act, 1978". This was intended to preserve ancient heritage monuments and archaeological sites of historic value. Hopefully the Goa Heritage Action Group founded in 2000 to spearhead a heritage movement in the state, will create an awareness of the recent Amendment to the Act in 2010 with regard to "reconstruction and re-erection" of monuments, which is detrimental rather than helpful to its intended purpose.

Taken together, these papers underline the rapid and at times traumatic social changes Goan Society is undergoing today. Whether it be in regard to the construction of their past or the preservation of their culture, including that of the subalterns and the marginalized; whether in controversies over their collective identity as Goans, expressed in their language or their politics, whether in relation to the land and its commodification by the market or its objectification with unsustainable development; whether in the search for a relevant education or the struggles of civil society movements—everywhere there is evidence of the complex and multiple impact of rapid change at various levels. What surely is the need of the hour is now to find a horizon of hope within which to understand our world so as to be able to change it as subjects, rather than just coping with it as objects of our own history.

Goa
September 2013

Savio Abreu
Rudolf C. Heredia

CHAPTER 1

Goa 50 Years after Liberation

Light and Shadow

RUDOLF C. HEREDIA

Introduction

This inaugural address is a brief introduction to the overriding theme of the seminar, "Goa 2011: Reviewing and Recovering 50 Years". Goa is the smallest state in the Union of India. After 50 years of liberation from five centuries of colonial rule, its challenge now is be a beacon of light for the rest of the Union rather than a replication of its shadow side.

The Political Trajectory

The democratic experience in Goa since liberation can be divided into four periods (de Souza, 2004). The first, from 1963 to 1977 was the two-party system, with the Maharashtra Gomantak Party (MGP) and the United Goan Party (UGP). The former had the support of the Bahujans, the latter that of the Christians. This two-party system seemed to work to for a while.

However, with the breakup and collapse of the UGP the Congress made its entry into Goan politics, first as Congress (Urs) and then as Congress (Indira). This changed the political scenario from a regional two-party system to a 'national *versus* a regional party' one. This was the second period from 1977 to 1989, which saw the politics of manoeuvre being played out on the political stage even as the centre of decision-making began to shift to Delhi and North India. This weakened the bond between the people of a local constituency and its elected representative.

The third period, from 1989 to 2003, began with a surfeit of defections and chief ministers playing musical chairs. Goa has had the largest number of chief ministers in the shortest period of time. In assembly elections during this period, Goa had 44 defections although they were only 40 members in the legislative assembly (MLAs). Three very important decisions at the national level were taken in this period: the anti-defection law was passed by Parliament in 1985, but it was subverted and had to be corrected through the 91st Amendment; statehood came to Goa in 1987. By now another national party, the Bhartiya Janata Party (BJP), made its entry in the state politics in Goa. In the Congress *versus* BJP contest the decision-making was even more focused on Delhi and the politics of manoeuvre increased further.

The fourth period, from the 91st Amendment in 2003 till today, was marked with an amendment to anti-defection law to make it even more stringent. Now a defector had to resign and be re-elected. But even this could not end defections—in a small constituency ways were found of subverting this, as happened in the by-election of Poinguinim in 2005. (de Souza 2010).The candidate defecting to the opposition party resigned but was re-elected in by-elections with that party's support.

The factional politics of manoeuvre focuses on short term partisan gains that compromise long term state objectives. This results in a revolving door scenario in state politics. Between from January 1990 and December 1994, Goa had seven governments, some Chief Ministers lasting eight months, or 19 days, or even as little as two days (de Souza, 2004).

Some pertinent questions now need to be considered further: is it true that the representatives of our democracy lack the requisite moral fibre for good governance? The only thing that controls them seems to be the legal system. But legality can never govern all of human conduct. Again, are small constituencies better or worse? Smaller constituencies were thought to bring the representatives closer to the people, but this has hardly happened in practice. Is the overall impact on political behaviour positive or negative? Is it encouraging more participation or more manoeuvring? Certainly, in Goan politics, small is not politically beautiful!

Multiple Crises

We must read the multiple social crises of the state against this background of "democracy's inconvenient fact" in the murky political meddle of Goan politics since liberation. The first is the political crisis of subaltern inclusion. The broader participation in a more inclusive political process does have its ambiguities. For the subaltern classes their moment in history has arrived. After being marginalised for ages, at last they see their chance for a place in the sun. Their politics is played by improvised rules. The elites, however, perceive this as an institutional decay. The new politics has taken away many of their taken-for-granted advantages and privileges. Forced to play the game by the new rules, they are perhaps more subtle and less crude in their manoeuvres.

Yet none of this has reversed the unequal class relations between the haves and the have-nots even as new players assume the old roles. The politics of rent-taking and the politics of patronage continue with other rent-takers and new patrons. The changes turn out to be more positional than structural. Eventually, a broader inclusion and more active participation do yield a 'democratic dividend'. This is the positive aspect of democracy in our country. But this can also be overwhelmed by the democratic deficit, the negative aspect of democracy—the cynical and self-seeking politics of power. When democratic institutions are thus corrupted from within they must lose credibility and finally collapse. In the resulting uncertainty and confusion, the disconnect between government and people is an invitation to majoritarian and populist regimes that are only too willing to step in and bridge the gap.

The second is the economic crisis of Goa's development. What is the economic model of development we want for Goa? Though the country itself is struggling with this question, Goa is a small state and it could decide for itself rather than follow on other states or wait for an answer at the national level. Some states have begun ruthlessly exploiting their natural resources, but this may well damage their environment to the tipping point of un-sustainability, if they have not already gone beyond the point of no return in places. Himachal Pradesh, on the other hand, has decided quite clearly to focus on agro-industry, a far more sustainable and egalitarian development. Can this be a viable choice for Goa? Will the mining lobby destroy the natural beauty of Goa and drive the state into an environmental disaster?

What is the future we envisage for Goa? Should it be urban-industrial or agro-industrial, high-tech or service oriented, capital intensive or employment oriented? Should tourism be a priority sector and so, should it be high-end or low-end tourism? These are policy decisions that have to be made for the next 50 years. But we may be too preoccupied with immediate gains to balance the development of Goa between progress and sustainability.

There is a civic crisis in Goa of rising expectations of the subaltern and the new social equations this brings about. People have to adjust to a whole new society in which the roles and status of individuals is being redefined. Unfortunately, this could lead to mere positional circulations of elites rather than an egalitarian society. We see this in politics: at election time voters are free to throw out one set of rascals, only to see them replaced by more of the same, *plus ça change, plus c'est la même chose.*[1]

There is the religious crisis that derives from the legacy of Western colonial Christianity. How do we cope with the wounded memories of religious conversions in Goa? We must come to terms with our past. Merely condemning or condoning it does not heal our present wounds or lighten the burden we carry into our future. How do we heal the hurt and redeem the guilt that still remains? There is today a religious revivalism, fundamentalism and even extremism that opens old wounds and exacerbates them. Rather than healing these wounded memories, these are exploited for partisan political purposes. This precipitates communal tensions that are tearing apart the fabric of Goan society.

Yet would it be chauvinistic to claim that Europe gave nothing to Goa. Part of the positive colonial legacy in Goa is the European Enlightenment that came to Goa much before it reached the rest of the subcontinent. An example of this is inheritance law. Goa has a common civil code imposed by the colonial rulers. This remains a Constitutional ideal for the rest of the country but is still a long way from being realised. Personal laws must be made more gender-just, in the face of opposition from conservative leaders in the name of their religious tradition. A small state like Goa be an exemplar in this and in other ways for the rest of the country as well.

The cultural crisis of collective identity in Goa is evident in the rapid change it is undergoing. This leaves traditions and institutions crumbling while the new ones are not yet in place. This creates a collective identity crisis. In a globalising world the winds of change will inevitably blow about our house, but we need not close our windows and shut our doors for fear of being blown off our feet, if only we had them firmly on the ground. However, when cultural crises get politicised, another dynamic begins to play out, as has happened with the politics of language. The on-going controversies on the medium of instruction in schools, on the script to be used for Konkani, are less concerned with the practicalities involved than mobilising people to affirm linguistic identities.

Once collective identities are embedded in language, then they spill over into a politics of passion. What is the language of Goans, and what ought it to be? How far is the cultural identity of Goans embedded in their language? These are questions best taken forward by the social sciences and the creative arts, not defined by politicians and used for an electoral payoff. A common language is a crucial component of identity for a community but it is not the only one.

Some identities have prevailed with a borrowed foreign language, not a local one. Urdu is not indigenous to any of the provinces of Pakistan. Hindi has superseded many regional languages in North Indian states, like Bhojpuri, Maithili, Magadi, Kadhiboli.... Yet regional identities still survive. In the British Isles English has displaced Gaelic and Welsh, but the Scots, the Irish and the Welsh still have their own identities. The early emigrants brought English across the Atlantic with them and made it official for all who came later, but Americans are not English.

Goan identity could be positioned as an Indo-European interface, a Janus-faced construction looking both East and West. With its ancient pre-colonial history, and five centuries of Portuguese rule, Goa is uniquely placed on the subcontinent to be the bridge between the two, representing an Enlightened Europe for India and presenting an incredible India to Europe. Goans would have to construct such a unique identity, through its welcoming openness and its sensitive tolerance, once a traditional component of Goan culture now under increasing stress.

The National Context

The multiple crises in Goa must be seen in the larger context of the contemporary situation in the country where similar contradictions and dilemmas are even more evident. Our Parliament is failing, our democratic institutions are corroding. After being carefully nurtured by Nehru but later manipulated by his daughter, these democratic institutions have by now lost much of their credibility and legitimacy. They are increasingly perceived to be manipulated by corrupt politicians and their partisan and short-sighted politics.

This is not unusual when the democratic base is broadened to include the excluded. It is a process that must be pursued as vigorously as it must be carefully monitored and corrected to be put back on track. Or else, in the resulting confusion, such a democratic inclusion may be co-opted by authoritarian leaders and majoritarian politics. We already have some waiting to project themselves on the national stage from the shadows of their divisive state policies that favour some and rubbish others.

As a people we seem to be divided on our vision for the country. Do we want to be a powerful nation, a major player on the world's stage, or a just and decent people, a model for all of enriching unity in our multiform diversity? Are we still inspired by the ideals of our freedom struggle and the Constitution our founding fathers gave us or are we exchanging these for a mess of pottage of affluence and consumerism? The frequent comparisons we make of ourselves with China are a revealing indicator of this ambiguity. There is danger that our impatience with the very oblivious democratic deficit may bring us to compromise and not build further on our equally real democratic dividend.

Democracy is like trench warfare with incremental gains rather than major battles and victories. Every country that has put democracy in place has gone through such crises and some have lost out with them as well. The peoples who have won their freedom from colonial rule have so easily submitted to dictatorships and authoritarianism. The countries on the fringe of the South Asian Subcontinent are evidence of this and might well presage our own future if we do not stem the rot soon.

India was the first country in the non-Western world to promulgate a democratic constitution as the sun set on the British Empire. In spite of a brief intermission with Indira Gandhi's Emergency, 1975-77, its popular endorsement explains "India's unusual record as a robust, non-Western democracy" (Sen 2005, 13). The active, and at times even chaotic participation of *The Argumentative Indian*, accounts for "the tenacious persistence of that system, in contrast to many other countries where democracy has intermittently made cameo appearances" (ibid.).

We are justly proud of our electoral democracy and it is indeed a great achievement. India is the only country ever to have universal suffrage from the beginning of its democratic republic. No other democracy started thus. The democratic right to vote was always restricted at first to property owners, then gradually expanded to other male citizens, and lastly to women. And even then indirect ways of restricting the vote to 'our kind of people' was widely practiced.

India's electoral democracy is a lesson to the world. The sheer size of our electorate and the logistics involved dwarf any elections elsewhere. There are electoral abuses and subversions by corrupt and criminal politicians that need urgent electoral reform and better and more stringent electoral laws. Yet by and large our elections are acknowledged to be free and fair, even though admittedly there is surely room for making them more so.

But our real problem is substantive democracy, the values and norms that are the basis of democratic procedures. These cannot be legislated; they must be socialised in an alert and active citizenry. Without this we will forfeit our democracy, our democratic rights will be compromised and our civil liberties will not last. As Lord Acton said, "The price of liberty is eternal vigilance." This is even more so when we are constitutionally committed to pursue liberty with equality and fraternity.

This is an immense challenge to our hierarchical and patriarchal society, still so feudal and riven with caste and factionalism. But we do have a tradition of discussion and debate. Traditionally, in village panchayats all had a right to participate, though all were not treated equally. Persons denied a hearing could legitimately protest by going on a *dharna* (a sit-in) to draw attention to their cause. Discussion was the way of building a consensus for addressing a problem, but it is a slow and even fragile process. This perhaps is why democracy has taken root in India to the extent it has, for democracy can be perceived as "government by discussion" (Buchanan 1954, 120).

But lest we focus too exclusively on the democratic deficit it is appropriate to recall some recent successes of our democratic dividend. The Right to Information Act, 2005, has forced a certain transparency on our governance. A Constitutional Amendment in 2009 has made education a fundamental right for children between six and fourteen years. The right to food to provide food security to the poor, is on the anvil as is the right to work. A Lokpal Bill once enacted into law will empower an ombudsman against corruption across the board.

Conclusion

This is the larger national context in which Goa is embedded. The dialectic between the dividend and deficit of democracy at the national level is reflected at the state level, and Goa is no exception to this. To perceive Goa thus lends perspective to the crises we experience and challenges we must face. Our future will be assured when the democratic dividend outweighs the democratic deficit. After 50 years of liberation we must realise that the way forward depends not just on our leaders but on all of us as citizens as well. As we make demands on our politicians and leaders, we must also make corresponding demands on ourselves as citizens. Tempting shortcuts in dealing with the scenario just sketched only become disastrous short circuits once taken.

REFERENCES

Buchanan, James M., 1954. "Social Choice, Democracy, and Free Markets". *Journal of Political Economy*, 62 (2): 114-123.

de Souza, Peter Ronald, 2004, "Democracy's inconvenient fact". *Seminar*, (543). http://www.india-seminar.com/2004/543/543%20peter%20ronald%20desouza.htm

de Souza, Peter Ronald, 2010. "Dynamics of a Working Democracy: Representative Politics in a Goa Constituency". *Economic and Political Weekly*, 22 April, 41 (16): 1574-83.

Sen, Amartya. 2005. *The Argumentative Indian, Writings on Indian History, Culture and Identity.* London: Penguin Books.

CHAPTER 2

Between Two Communities

Past Disruption and Present Inter-relations

VICTOR FERRAO

Does the trauma of the colonial past afflict Goan Society today? Does the distress of the past live in the present? The answers to these questions seem to be in the affirmative. But there is a kind of discomfort to admit it. The situation is similar to what Michel Foucault called 'discursive episteme'(that is, objective spirit) which determines that which we know but about which we have to talk and act as if we do not know, and that which we do not know and about which we have to talk and act as if we know. It conditions what we know but have to pretend that we do not know (Zizek 2010, 4). Perhaps, here I am going to utter the unutterable and say the unsayable with regard to the already fragile communal harmony in Goa. I shall make an attempt to listen to the background noises that often go unheard and strive to hear the unsaid and express the unexpressed.

This study attempts to unlock the inter-communitarian impasse, especially between the Hindus and Christians, which we notice in Goa. The issue under our scrutiny is complex and reaches exponential levels as I do not have the luxury of studying it from a safe distance. It directly and intimately involves me both as a Goan and a Christian. Hence, I approach the study with humility and profound awareness of my fallibility as well as deep sensitivity and respect to my Hindu brethren.

This study attempts to be attentive to the politics of identity that played between the Christians and Hindus of Goa and tries to narrative in conscious memory, is opening new vistas to an understanding on the politics of identity brewing among many communities. On one side we have become profoundly conscious of the unfathomable depths of human suffering while, on the other, we can feel its affliction in the present. It is as if the past is still adamantly persisting in our present. Cathy Caruth points out that 'trauma is not simply a destruction but also, fundamentally an enigma of survival' (Caruth 1996, 58).

Trauma, being a tragic event outside the normal range of human experience, makes a profound mark on the person subjected to it. Trauma is experienced when a person or a community perceives a certain set of events as life-threatening. A person can be traumatised not just by physically undergoing a tragedy but by also being the witness of a tragic event or even by hearing of some tragedy. The trauma exponentially compounds if one finds one's loved one as a victim of the horrifying event. Freud saw trauma as experience where, in a short space of time, the mind is forced to receive such a flood of stimuli that it is too powerful to be processed in the customary way, resulting in a permanent malfunctioning of the way we react to such stimuli. Later Freud saw it as stimuli that cross the tolerance limit of the person (Sari 2005, 15).

Trauma is experienced as a bolt from the blue with little or no time for the person or community to prepare itself to face it. It is said to produce new subjects and it is hard to separate the individual as well as collective impacts of trauma. Julia Kristeva argues that "the shattering of psychic identity" that accompanies even the periphery of such events has intensity that can afflict no less than those who experience trauma while being directly in the firing line (Kaplan 2005, 3-4).

Trauma and Compulsive Re-enactment

Victims cope with trauma through compulsive repetition. Trauma is repeated on behavioural, emotional, physiologic and endocrinologic levels. Many people expose themselves, seemingly compulsively, to a situation reminiscent of the original trauma. Freud thought that the aim of repetition was to gain mastery but clinical research has exposed that repetition only brings suffering for the victims and the people in their surroundings. In behavioural re-enactment the self may either play a victim or the victimiser.

Re-enactment of victimisation is the major cause of violence. Studies have revealed that criminals have often been physically or sexually abused as children. It has been extensively established that the children who were abused become abusers themselves. While trauma is often re-enacted through the victim turning into a victimiser, there is also a self-destructive manner of acting out of trauma. Studies have revealed a correlation between child abuse and indulgence into self-harm in later stages of one's life. Clinical studies have shown that self-mutilation is high among those who had trauma of violent self-abuse. This means trauma can re-enact through the process of re-victimisation. Hence, childhood trauma metamorphosises into high risk adults who might re-enact the trauma through victimisation of others or through the process of re-victimisation of self (Scaer 2001, 85-96).

Trauma and Embodied Translation

Post-colonial critics have drawn their attention to the experience of colonialisation and its impact on the colonised and the colonisers. Within the same framework, we can trace a psychoanalytically oriented trauma research. This research suggests that Western scholars may write from an unconscious guilt-ridden perspective of being descendants of colonial perpetrators of crime.

Nicolas Abraham and Maria Torok are considered to be pioneers in the study of what has come to be called transgenerational trauma. One might trace the origin of these studies in Freud's meta-psychology. Abraham believes that the unconscious passes from the parent's unconscious to that of the child's. Holocaust studies have revealed that trauma not only afflicts the victims of the traumatic experience but also their offspring. Scholars have attempted to study the principles of inter-generational trauma transmission. It was found that massive trauma is almost always pushed out of awareness. Thoughts, memories and feelings associated with the trauma are repressed and pushed into the unconscious. That is why trauma becomes an untellable, unspeakable black hole. Yet, no matter how far it is embedded in the unconscious, it springs forth and affects the conscious world under some precipitating circumstance reminiscent of the trauma. Traumatised persons thus become embodied vehicles of trauma that can explode at the first instance of provocation. Therefore, children of traumatised children get drawn into the trauma of their grandparents and in turn are traumatised by the same. In a way these children have to respond to double trauma: that to which their parents had been subjected and that of their own survival responses to the experiences of traumatised parents. Such children may also suffer from the guilt of not having rescued their parents or not having enlivened them sufficiently. That is why it is said that the grandchild carries more burden than the others. In the case of a grandchild the burden of the past can remain more innate and irrational as the sources of the trauma remain more hidden in the distant past (Scaer 2001, 85-96). Research in neuroscience reveals that the right hemisphere of the brain is dominant in early childhood and that it stores traumatic material. The right hemisphere is non-verbal and is often thought of as the unconscious. It is here that trauma is hidden from words, memory and knowledge but is coded in emotions, sensations, automatic behaviour and attitude patterns.

Understanding the Dynamics of the Past in the Present

Life does not just line up like words in a sentence or like clothes on a clothesline. There is no linear flow of time for humans. Somehow the past overflows into the present. Tragedies and trauma of the past almost always return to haunt the present. There is an afterlife of collective trauma. Colonial experience was a mixed bag for Goan society. It was a disruptive experience and its pain of the past still lingers on in our society.

The Dynamic of Loss and Recovery of Self

Many scholars such as Frantz Fanon (1952 and 1961) and Ashis Nandy (1983) have already studied how colonisation was a disruptive experience that brought about a condition of loss of self in the colonised and set in a dynamism of recovery that still reproduces itself today in myriad ways. Nishtha Desai (2000, 469-476) argues that Tristao de Braganza Cunha was the first to understand the impact of self, even before Fanon. Perhaps, the work of Jacques Lacan might illumine us as to how loss-recovery dynamism affects all Goans.

Lacan teaches that a child between the ages of 6 to 18 months goes to what Freud identified as a stage of primary narcissism. It is a stage when an individual is in love with the image of him/herself and his or her body. Lacan indicates that at this stage the infant begins to recognise his or her image in the mirror (this does not mean a literal mirror but a reflective surface, for instance, the face of the mother). This fascination with its own image brings pleasure to the child. During this stage, through seeing its image in the mirror, the child realises for the first time that his/her body has a total form. The infant governs the movement of its image through the movement of its own body. This sense of complete mastery is in contrast to the fundamental experience of the child's experience of its own body, over which it does not yet enjoy full motor control. The infant feels that its body is fragmented and yet united. Its mirror image provides it a sense of unification and wholeness. Thus, a sense of unified self is acquired at the price of this self being an-other, that is, its own mirror image (Homer 2005, 24-26).

Lacan himself applies his insight that ego is an effect of image, even to the adults. Many film critics have also applied Lacan's 'mirror stage' to the relationship between the spectators and the image that is portrayed on the screen. Within this train of thought, I propose to see colonisation as an experience of rupture felt by all Goans. The impact of rupture was articulated by Braganza Cunha as the denationalisation of Goans. Although the term was used by the Portuguese to refer to the Goans who have become hostile to Portuguese regime, the usage is revelatory from our point of view. Braganza Cunha referred to both Christians and Hindus as denationalised (although he seems to indicate that the denationalisation of the Christians was more pronounced). This denationalisation rendered both Christians and the Hindus incapable of responding to the tyranny of the Portuguese (Desai). Perhaps the Goans developed into master-slave dialectics (Homer 2005, 22-23) with the Portuguese as a result of loss of self that they experienced in the facc of white culture which they internalised as superior. A kind of mental enslavement produced the master-slave dialectic and Goans somehow got enchanted with 'the mirror image' and remained fascinated by it and thus let the Portuguese colonialism last four hundred and fifty years.

Recovery as Re-enactment

We have seen that trauma can become a pathological condition that manifests itself as a compulsion to repeat itself. Colonialism was indeed an experience of dislocation. It forced its subjects to breach 'the great divide' and relocate itself in space, time and language. Being affected profoundly, a post-colonial self can only feel a gap or a void (sense of original loss) that conveys an intoxicating feeling that things would be better if history had been different. This gap haunts as a continuous spectral presence of an absence. But the gap often opens and seeks to re-enact or materialise the lacuna by indirect means and embodies itself into inter-subjective relations in our society.

Lacan theorises the enigmatic presence of the absence with his notion of the real. The real is the unknown that exists at the limits of the socio-symbolic universe (that is, situates the symbolic and the imaginary in their respective position) and is in constant tension with it. It is a paradoxical concept that supports as well as undermines our social world. The real is not an object, a thing but something that is repressed and functions unconsciously, intruding into our symbolic reality as the unsymbolisable, profoundly associated with the trauma. Trauma arrests the movement of symbolisation and fixes the person in an earlier phase of development that keeps returning and repeating itself. That is why Lacan defined the real as that which always returns to the same place. The real never ceases to write itself. It is like a wound that refuses to be healed or a hole in the core of subjectivity that becomes visible in the desires of the person (Homer 2005, 81-94).

With Lacanian psycho-analysis, we can understand the politics of identity that is being pitched between the Christians and the Hindus in Goa. The trauma of the colonial experience can be seen as the matrix of the crises of inter-relations that we can discern among the two religious communities. It is the inexpressible presence of an absence that seems to adamantly persist and erupt into the inter-relations among them. The colonial burden has become a divisive yeast that has set in a chain reaction to reproduce suspicion, communication impasse and discord. As long as we do not come to terms with our past, the spell of the past will always remain in our present and re-act the trauma at different levels of sophistication.

Hence, the present relations among the Hindus and Christians of Goa testify beyond their knowing of the existence of a disruptive past. Thus, it somehow exists as the unsaid in the said, the forgotten in the remembered and the omission in the act of commission.

Within this framework, we can see how the identity politics that is brewing in Goa is mainly based on the essentialisation of a religion as a fundamental marker of identity, leaving out other markers such as language, gender, caste, specific aspects of culture, ideology, etc. Zizek's notion of master-signifier might illumine us. He teaches that the master-signifier is empty in content but pulls content form other signifiers that gravitate around it. Religion as a fundamental marker of identity pulls markers like language, caste, specific aspects of culture, ideology around it (Zizek 2009, 37). Such an ascription of core features of an identity is dangerously guilty of building identity on mere identifications.

The Dynamics of Translation of Trauma

Goan society is a community born out of the trauma of colonisation. Colonisation's impact still lives on and becomes visible in the way we have mediated difference in our society. The fact that collective trauma is inter-generationally transmitted within a community is established with the help of studies on the impact of the Holocaust on both the inflictors and as well as the victims. Homi Babha teaches that the past is encountered as an anteriority that continuously introduces otherness within the present. It implies that something went wrong in the past and it is for us to recover the lost 'future' of that past (Boheemen-Saaf 1999, 12). This loss recovery dynamism sets in a recycling of the disturbed past through a performative praxis that repeats the trauma.

One can find a ghostly void of the past operating among the historians of both communities. On the Christian side, we can trace historians such as Heras (1935) and D'Costal (1965) drawn into discourses that dispute the perspective of forced conversion. Both hold that the missionaries were 'humanist' in their approach and converted only those who exhibited genuine desire. On the Hindu side we can trace a sense of pain and loss in the writings of historians such as A.K.Priolkar (1961) and R.P. Rao (1968) (Robinson 2004,

179-181). Both sides attempt to interpret positively and materialise the unnameable trauma of the past. In this sense history becomes a presentation rather than a representation of the past. (There is no distanced or neutral representation of history.)

Thus, the simultaneous but hidden persisting presence of the disturbed past remains non-figural and yet acts like a piercing arrow that affects every aspect of post-colonial Goan society. Inter-communitarian relations among the Hindus and Christians manifest a figuration of an extreme trauma of the past. If we pay attention to the non-figural, we might get an insight into the presence of pathos and discern its impact on Goan society. Both Christians and Hindus 'stand' (inscribed) in a pathos of the past. This location into the pathos of the past is perhaps the chief reason of a discernible discomfort between the two. Although they might come from the same biological tree yet socio-political factors along with the trauma of the past brings about a sense of familiarity as well as alienness between them. Lack of direct social intercourse, as well as different shades of religious fundamentalism and communal politics, has brought about what I call the 'politics of outsidering'. Trauma seems to reproduce itself in the form of a new Hegelian master-slave equation through which the Hindu brethren appear to re-enact/materialise the trauma of their past by putting on the role of the victimiser and the Christians as the victims. This re-enactment has almost reached compulsive proportions leading to what can be called the geography of closure. The geography of closure marks the boundary between the two communities. With deep sensitivities to my Goan Hindu brethren, I theorise the geography of closure as a view that perceives Christians through the purity pollution principle and considers colonisation as contamination and the Goans who got converted to Christianity as contaminated. This perception makes Goan Christians 'outsiders' (resident aliens) in their own native land and, as such, they are deemed incapable of visualising what can be called the authentic aspirations of Goans.

The geography of closure is a unique response to the pathos of the past in Goa. The Hindu brethren as a community stand in the pathos of the past in the loss of a sizeable brotherhood to conversion into Christianity. This loss became an interrogation of all that they deemed as noble, sacred and holy. This sense of loss sets in motion a recovery dynamism and chain reaction thereof that has resulted into what we have called geography of closure. It is triggered by dual pain, the pain of the past separation as well a pain of hurting one's own in the present. Thus the geography of closure is hiding the pain of self-mutilation.

The Psycho-dynamics of Healing

Healing occurs if the communities are given an opportunity for catharsis as well as a deep insight into what is afflicting them. Within the context of Goan society, we need to engineer creative ways of what will become a therapy for the pain of the past. I suggest therapeutic awareness, examination of the mediating processes at work, seeking of ways of collective dealing with the trauma of the past and the development of a common collective story of Goa as ways of responding to the critical presence of trauma of the past in Goan society.

Therapeutic Awareness

Awareness and attention is a psychic energy. An awareness of awareness (meta-awareness) can become therapeutic for individuals as well as collectivities reeling under trauma. Awareness is the ability to see the light we are to ourselves and to the others. It is like waking up to the beauty and complexity of human existence. It is like growing up and taking responsibility for one's existence. But this awakening is not so easy. We resist getting out of our comfort zone. Recognition of this inner resistance is the first step towards a therapeutic awareness.

Therapeutic awareness can set in the process of healing of the trauma of the past. It will assist us in seeing through the disrupted past and lead us to discern how it is active in our present. Therapeutic awareness gives us the ability to filter information and reach a state of inner harmony. It just allows us to enjoy the ongoing stream of experience, in the process of living itself. It makes us mindful of everything that is going on within us, our emotions and longings as well as our pain and suffering.

Such awareness indeed has the possibility of transforming psychic entropy into inner equanimity. It engenders unity of purpose and directs psychic energy towards meaningful and realistic goals. Such awareness can become a therapeutic resource that can indeed become a central clearing house that builds the ability of mindfulness of our own fallibility and frailty and humbly we watch over our vulnerability of succumbing to the trauma of the past.

Examining the Mediating Processes of Difference

Mediation of difference and otherness can become a locus of the eruption of the trauma of the past. An honest look at the way we mediate our differences in Goa perhaps can assist us to find ways and means to heal the wounds of the past. Societies have evolved multiple ways of mediating differences. One can find a denial or absorption of otherness into the sameness in some societies. Some societies attempt to dissolve differences through monadic unity while others leave it to conflict to manage diversity. Some functionalise, others stigmatise, still others dissolve otherness into an *advaitic* relation. We can still find others who affirm plurality and celebrate diversity.

Goa seems to mediate differences through the exercise of power relations. Differences are arranged in hierarchies and are set into a universe of meaning of a caste-laden society. It appears that we leave it to conflicts to resolve our differences. Hence, the examination of the process of mediation of difference can lead us to a therapeutic understanding that can give us an insight into how the process of mediation of otherness often operates as sights for the surfacing of the trauma of the past.

The resources for mediating difference that have turned pathological can become a source of healing of the wounded past. If we leave conflicts to mediate differences in our society, we will further strengthen what I called the geography of closure, which will turn into a geography of enclosure as the unresolved pain of the past almost always refuses to allow a happy burial or closure. But pathos is therapeutic and the geography of closure can become an opening to dialogue and collective moaning of the pain of the past.

Dealing with the Pain of the Pathos

The geography of closure attempts to come to a closure of the pain of the past. But it belongs to the chain of re-enactment of trauma and becomes totally inefficient as it only succeeds in furthering trauma in our society. Hence, the geography of closure becomes only an enclosure that traps the Goan society into a collective reproduction and transmission of pathos. Hence, it is pathological and seeks its healing in the repetition of trauma. Antonius C.G.M. Robben calls this process 'transgenerational indigestible trauma' (Gampel 2000, 59).

This transgenarational indigestible trauma is naturally faced with a strategy of defence mechanism. Psycho-theorists teach that persons as well as communities often employ what they call 'affective anesthesia' and 'psychic numbing' that refuses to recall anything related to the trauma of the past (Ibid., 58). This strategy manifests in Goa as the geography of closure. But this repression only emerges through re-enactment and we are trapped into the *samsara* of pathos.

The indigestibility of trauma can be rendered somewhat digestible through a therapeutic process of collective talking and listening. This collective talking and listening can de-anchor several pathological identifications that we have innocently internalised. One of the obvious identifications is the blurring of the distinction between the colonisers and the Christians of today. Psychoanalysis and other therapeutic psychotherapies can assist us to resolve the pain of the past. Perhaps the reconciliation processes employed in South Africa and North Ireland can provide models that can be contextualised and reproduced in Goa so that we can allow the indigestible trauma to be healed collectively.

Restoring the Collective Story of Goa

We have seen a narrative turn in social sciences. Narrative is viewed as providing a hermeneutical horizon to our life. It is seen as a metaphor of life. We live our life as a story. The stories are first lived and then told. The stories that we live out, contribute a teleological character to our lives. Thus a human being is seen as a story-living as well as a story-telling animal. A story provides profound unity to our life.

Narrative provides congruency and consistency to our life. We experience our story as a shareable story. Narrative provides a pre-commitment to life. It provides a framework that allows us to see how we fit into the scheme of things. Contemporary society defines life as a loss of grand narratives. Goan society becomes a prime example of such a loss of a grand story. The collective story of Goa is fragmented by the interruption of colonisation; today Goans are encaged in the caves of their little stories. The fragmented story of Goa also fragments our Goan society.

It is a challenge for us to recover and restore the shareable collective story of Goa. A collective story of Goa will indeed be therapeutic as it makes room for all and will bring about a sense of belonging and provide a *telos* [an end or purpose] to life. As we live our story we will be enabled to live with the other in peace and harmony. As life and narrative intermingle, we shall be able to include every member of Goan society into the collective story of Goa and thus bring about community therapy that can heal the hurt of the past.

Conclusion

Our study has manifested how the disruptive past of Goa afflicts the present inter-communitarian relations between the Hindus and Christians of Goa and offers ways to understand its impacts and find creative means to respond to the same. This study indicates that a therapeutic process might break the geography of closure and bring about a new spring time of peace and harmony.

REFERENCES

Caruth, Cathy. 1996. *Unclaimed Experience: Trauma Narrative and History.* Baltimore: John Hopkins.

D'Costa, Anthony. 1965. *The Christianisation of the Goa Islands*. Bombay: St. Xavier's College.

Dessai, Nishtha. 2000. "The Denationalization of Goans: an Insight into the Construction of Cultural Identity", Losotopie, 469-476.Accessed on September 7, 2011 www.lusotopie.sciencespobordeaux.fr/desai.pdf.

Fanon, Frantz. 2004. *The Wretched of the Earth*, Translated by Richard Philcox. New York: Grove Press.

_______. 2008. *Black Skins and White Masks,* Translated by Richard Philcox. New York: Grove Press.

Gampel, Yolanda. 2000. "Reflection on the Prevalence of the Uncanny in the Social Violence". In *Cultures Under Siege: Collective Violence and Trauma,* edited by Antonious C.G.M. Robben and Marcelo M. Suarez-Orozco. Cambridge: Cambridge University Press.

Heras, Henry. 1935. *The Conversion Policy of the Jesuits in India*, Bombay: Indian Historical Research Institute.

Homer, Sean. 2005. *Jacques Lacan.* Oxon: Routlege.

Kaplan, Ann E. 2005. *Trauma Culture: the Politics of Culture and the Loss in Media and Literature.* London: Rutgers University Press.

Mink, Allen. 2010. *Trauma and Media: Theories, Histories and Images.* New York: Routledge.

Nandy, Ashis. 1983. *The Intimate Enemy: The Loss and Recovery of Self Under Colonialism.* New Delhi: Oxford University Press.

Robinson, Rowena. 2004. "Some Neglected aspects of the Conversion of Goa: A Socio-Historical Perspective". In *Sociology of Religion in India*, edited by Rowena Robinson. New Delhi: Sage Publications.

Sari, Salli. 2005. *Bolt from the Blue: Coping with Disasters and Acute Trauma.* Translated by Annira Silver. London: Jessica Kingley Publishers.

Scaer, Robert C. 2001. *The Body Bears the Burden: Trauma, Dissociation and Disease.* Oxford: The Haworth Medical Press.

Van Boheemen-Saaf, Christine. 1999. *Joyce, Derrida and Lacan and the Trauma of History: Reading, Narrative and Postcolonialism.* Cambridge: Cambridge University Press.

Van der Kolk, Bessel A. 1989. "The Compulsion to Repeat the Trauma: Re-enactment, Revictimization, and Masochism", *Psychiatric Clinics of North America,* June, 12 (2): 389-411.

Zizek, Slavoj. 2010. *Living in the End of Times.* London: Verso.

Chapter 3

History Research in Goa (1961-2011)

A Short Survey

Agnelo Paulo Fernandes

Introduction

I was very young when, on the morning of December 19, 1961, I witnessed, from the panoramic hills of Pilar, the bombing of the airport in Dabolim and the Goa Radio Station in Bambolim by fighter jets of the Indian Air Force, delinking any aerial communication with Lisbon. The Portuguese were forced to say goodbye to the Goans and a new era began for the Goans in the Union of India. Many of the events that followed, during the last 50 years, are fresh in my mind. There were numerous topics to choose from for this national seminar; I have selected the above title because, for over the last 30 years, I have been involved with documents and records of history lying in Goa, left behind from the Portuguese era, and they need to be preserved for future generations to see what Goa was.

The discussion in this paper has been divided into four parts:

1. First, a brief survey of the origin of research in Goa and the research works that followed.
2. Second, a few glimpses of the privileged position Goa enjoyed during the period of formation of these sources.
3. Third, a very concise description of the centres of research in Goa and Europe, housing this documentation.

4. Finally, it dwells on the present status of these sources, and the paper both suggests and solicits suggestions on how to preserve and utilise this vast and rich written heritage and save it from extinction.

1. Research and Researchers in Goa

Dr. Pandurang S.S. Pissurlencar has been called 'the father of Historical Archives of Goa' due to his great effort of reorganising this Archive as its Director, appointed by Governor General João Carlos Craveiro Lopes.[1] Not only did he gather thousands of State records in one place and had them bound, etc., he also studied some of its series and brought out original contribution to Indian History, particularly the political history of Marathas (Bibliography of Dr. Pissurlencar Collection, Vol. I).[2] In 1920, Dr. Pissurlencar published papers on history of Shivaji, in which he corrected Sir Jadunath Sarkar on some points and brought out original contributions on many aspects on the life of Shivaji. This brought him to the notice of historians of British India and Europe, many of whom became his friends and corresponded with him for documents from Goa Archives on topics of their interest.[3] Sir Jadunath accepted Dr. Pissurlencar's contributions as important research to fill in the gaps in not-yet-written history of India. For more than 25 years, Sir Jadunath maintained cordial relations and correspondence with Dr. Pissurlencar (Bibliography [Vol. III, Letter No. 120], 136),[4] and received from him documents from Goa Archives which he used for his writings—he wrote on July 13, 1953, "thanks for inestimate *[sic]* help which I have been getting from you ever since 1920, when the second edition of my Shivaji was published" (Bibliography [Vol. III, Letter No. 120], 197). He published several volumes of documents in Portuguese from Goa Archives,[5] as was done earlier by Cunha Rivara, A.B. Braganza Pereira, A. da Silva Rego, J. Wicki, etc. If one goes by Portuguese records in Goa Archives or other places of the world, it can be confidently stated that hundreds of aspects of the history of India and many other countries which are till now unknown can be brought to light.

Dr. Pissurlencar retired as Director of Goa Archives a few months before the Liberation of Goa. When University of Bombay started a post-graduate centre in Panaji, he took a keen interest in developing research in History. In 1964, he donated his large and valuable collection consisting of books, manuscripts, microfilms and photostat copies—more than 4,000 items—to the University of Bombay. He was soon appointed Professor and Research Guide in History by the University. Several students did research under his mentorship but health problems did not allow Goa's first research guide to achieve much.[6]

When I started research at the Historical Archives of Goa (henceforth HAG) in 1976, there were several Ph.D students from different universities who had used records from the HAG for the preparation of their theses. N.M. Pearson, T.R. de Souza, S. Mhamai Kamat and K.S. Mathew were some of them. Their contributions to research in History during the last 35 years are well known.[7] N.M. Pearson was privileged to film, for his personal use, as many documents from the HAG as he wished, free of charge, as C.R. Boxer and Antonio da Silva Rego were permitted earlier. The latter was responsible for the publication of many documents he microfilmed, in the periodical '*Boletim Filmoteca Ultramarina Portuguesa*' (c.60 volumes) and the films are preserved in Lisbon. C.R. Boxer was at the HAG for about two months in 1952. His works too are well known. He wrote a well known article entitled 'Glimpse of the Goa Archives' on 20 Series of the HAG, summarising more than 1,000 volumes of these 20 Series, pointing out the subject matter on one or two issues in a volume, when usually, each such volume contains hundreds of documents on hundreds of issues and topics. This article is primarily intended to serve as a reminder to historians about the importance of the documents in the HAG. He has followed *Roteiro dos Arquivos da India Portuguesa*, a HAG publication, with introduction and notes by Dr. Pissurlencar, and the Index Catalogue volume of the HAG. This *Roteiro* is a printed version in Portuguese of the main handwritten Index Catalogue volume of the HAG, which is also in Portuguese, and which researchers can use. It is more extensive than *Roteiro*. It is noticed that the titles in the said *Roteiro* sometimes do not match with those against corresponding number in the main Index Catalogue (Souza 2001, 1-10). Recent print of *Roteiro* follows the *Roteiro* of Dr. Pissurlencar without any improvements.

History research flourished in the post-graduate centre of the University of Bombay, the precursor of Goa University, under

Prof. B.K. Apte and later under Dr. B.S. Shastry. Several students made use of the documentation at the HAG, Central Library, Pissurlencar Centre, Xavier Centre of Historical Research (XCHR), etc. Since the formation of Goa University, several of its students have used records at the HAG for getting material for their theses. Besides its own staff, for a few years, the Directors of the HAG and XCHR (Dr. Celsa Pinto, Dr. Fatima de Silva Gracias and Dr. Filomena Sequeira Antony were the first three students of Dr. T.R. de Souza as its Director) were also recognised by the University as Research Guides.

Names of all researchers visiting the HAG, along with topics of research, were regularly published by the HAG in its periodical *Purabilekh Purutatva*.[8] This periodical was a good avenue for researchers in Goa to publish their articles but has currently been stopped. Another opportunity for Goan researchers to bring out their research work was the annual Local History Seminar (for several years, the contributions to these seminars were edited; copies of some of them are available at the HAG) conducted jointly by the University and the Directorate of Archives and Archaeology, which too has stopped. I hope these avenues are reopened. From 1979 onwards, a large number of research works have been published by individual researchers, Goa University,[9] the HAG and its Goa Gazetteer Department and XCHR.[10]

In 2001, due to keen interest shown in Portuguese records on History of Arabia at the HAG by H.H. Shaikh Mansour bin Zayed Al Nahyan, the President of the Centre for Documentation and Research (CDR), Presidential Court, Government of Abu Dhabi, Dr. Abdullah A.K. El-Reyes, the Director General of the CDR, had visited the HAG, and at the recommendation of Dr. S.K. Mhamai, then its Director, invited me to join that Institute and work on 'Portuguese Documents for History of Arabia'. In the same year, I was invited for the International Seminar on 'Arab History in the Archives of the World', where I presented the paper 'Goa Archives and Arab History'. This paper, after giving a brief description of the HAG, discusses the HAG Series *'Livros dos Regimentos e Instruções'*, analysing its first 14 volumes with subject-wise description of documents pertaining to the history of Arabia (Arab Documents 23, 124-137).[11]

Since then, during the last 10 years of my post-doctoral research[12] on over 16 Series of the HAG for CDR (now NCDR), at the Archives, has led to a collection of thousands of documents on the history of Arabia. I have over a score of volumes of handwritten notes with detailed indexes of different Codices I have referred to, in my office cupboards in Nizmar Centre, Panaji. This has resulted in over a dozen volumes, in book form, of documents on the history of Arabia of which only three[13] are edited until now. The microfilms of these documents are preserved in the NCDR, Abu Dhabi. The work of editing the remaining volumes will be done one by one.

2. Glimpses of Grand Goa

After the conquest of Goa, the Portuguese made it their metropolis in the East. Just as during the reign of Jayakesi I (1054 AD) of Goa Kadambas, Gopakpur[14] had become a prosperous international maritime interport centre, the Portuguese succeeded in raising the status of Goa to new heights. After its conquest in November 1510, Goa flourished as a prosperous port city due to the confluence of voyages linking it to maritime cities of the Atlantic, Pacific and the Indian Oceans (Boxer 1965, 216 and 224; Fernandes 1989, 61-68). The *Carreira* voyages (annual voyages between Lisbon and Goa and *vice versa*) brought it in direct contact with South and West coast of Africa, Eastern coast of South America and Atlantic ports of South Europe.

Their control of the Indian Ocean and their trade on the Pacific Ocean coasts and islands created new maritime connections. Goa was connected by trade with Japan and China and many of the islands of the Far East. After Malaka was captured and the sea route to the Far East shortened, the Great Ship of Amacon to Japan and later the voyages to China, Molucas, Timor, Siam, etc., brought various local goods[15] to Goa markets and to be redistributed through other voyages. Due to enforcement of *Cartazes* system, the Portuguese earned vast revenues in the form of duties at their Customs Houses.

Maritime trade in India came to be subjected to Portuguese *Cartazes* system. In the East, the Coromandel and Fisheries coasts up to Bengal and Arakan came under the influence of the Portuguese, under supervision from Goa. Ceylon came under Portuguese rule. Local trade on the West coast came to be run under the Southern

Cafilas and the Northern *Cafilas*, under their respective *Armadas*, which cruised from Goa to Cape Camorim, and to Surat and Diu, respectively. Goa as well as other centres on the West coast of India were connected to different ports in Western Indian Ocean, through very profitable inter-port voyages. There also started voyages to Mozambique and Mombaça and other centres on the East coast of Africa, trading in ivory, gold, slaves, etc. (Fernandes 1986), chiefly in exchange for textiles from India; as also voyages to Sindh, Hormuz (later Bandar Kung), Muscat and Basra; voyages to the Red Sea were chiefly to Mocha, Jiddah, Soaquem, etc.

There were voyages to the Red Sea and Persian and Arabian Gulfs from different Indian States: the Bahamanis, Vijayanagar, Sultanate of Gujerat, the Mughals, the Sultanates of Deccan, the Marathas, the Savants of Konkan, the Sundas, the Canaras, the Malabari kings, etc., from their respective ports. These voyages were subjected to Portuguese *Cartazes* system from the 16th to early 18th centuries.

In the early 17th century, rival North Europeans came to the Eastern seas challenging the Portuguese in Goa. The Dutch, in particular, captured many of the centres occupied by the Portuguese and were a great impediment for their voyages to the Far East, where only Macau and Timor with other islands remained with the Portuguese. They lost Ceylon and most of their centres in Fisheries coast and in Malabar to the Dutch.

The English were also trying to outwit the Portuguese. In the Persian Gulf, the Portuguese lost their most important centre of Hormuz to the Anglo-Persian alliance in 1622 (Boxer 1935, 46-129). But thereafter, the Portuguese occupied many Arab Coastal centres, from Rasal Kaima to Musandam to Muscat, some of which were under the kingdom of Hormuz. They enforced their *Cartazes* system on Persian Gulf shipping, including *Terradas* involved in pearl fishing (Fernandes 2009, 12-24). They developed Muscat as a great centre which continued with them till Imam Sultan bin Saif I unified Oman and ousted them from these coastal centres one by one and finally from Muscat in 1649. The Portuguese continued to function from their factory in the Persian city of Bandar Kung, their '*Armada* of the Strait of Hormuz and the Red Sea', mostly undertaking its annual visit to the Persian Gulf. They had good relations with the Shah of

Persia, always showing him their readiness for naval help against the Sultans of Oman. They also maintained an Augustinian Convent in Aspahan. They continued in Bandar Kung till the Persian revolution in 1730.

Portuguese relations with the rulers and States of the Indian subcontinent are different chapters of the history of India, which are only partially studied and written. Their four-and-a-half century rule in Goa had brought them in active contact with the different states of Malabar and Sri Lanka, of Coasts of Fishery and Coromandel up to Bengal and Arakan; then with the States of Canara, Vijayanagar, the Bahamanis, the Sundas, the Dessais and the Bhonsules of Konkan (Mhamai 1984), the Sultanates of Deccan, the Marathas, the Sultans of Gujerat (Pearson 1976), the Mughals (Fernandes 1986) and the rulers of Upper Gujerat to Sindh; and with the New States of 18th to 20th centuries; then with the Europeans including the Dutch, French, British India, etc.; finally, with Independent India and other States up to 1961.

The impact of Portuguese rule on Goa and Goans can be studied from the sources related to the impact. Despite the long Portuguese rule, basically Goans have remained with the same Indianness that the Konkan environment has made them, though thousands of them have left their birth place in search of means for 'better living'. A comprehensive history of Goa and Goans is yet to be written. The Portuguese have left ample sources on the conquest and formation of the present political boundaries of Goa, their democratic village set-ups (*Comunidades*), temples, coastal and inland trade and traders, religion, churches, castes, '*Camaras*', demography, mines, land records, legal disputes, '*rendas*' and '*rendeiros*', migration, freedom movement, to name a few aspects.

All the above topics have been elucidated to point out that the repositories and archives that are mentioned in this article and others not mentioned hold large source material on them.

3. Research Centres in Goa and in Europe

The HAG and the Central Library are two great centres of research left in Goa by the Portuguese. Other institutions that have good libraries for research in Goa are the Goa University and the XCHR.

The former, besides its library which has good number of printed works—including the Series such as *The English Factories in India 1618-1684* (edited by W. Foster and C. Fawcett, 17 volumes) and *The History of India as told by its own Historians* (edited by H.M. Elliot and J. Dawson, 8 volumes, etc.—has two other vast collections donated by Dr. Nuno Gonsalves (*Bibliography of Dr. Nuno Gonsalves Collection*, edited by V.R. Navelcar, Goa University, 1997) and Dr. Pissurlencar. The XCHR has a vast library with an excellent collection of books, periodicals, etc., and the Mhamai House Manuscript Collection (Souza 1982, 25-45) donated by Dr. S.K. Mhamai in the name of the Mhamai family of Panaji.

The Central Library has printed work as well as a few manuscript volumes. Most of the books, newspapers and journals of the Portuguese era are preserved in this Library, though a few of them are in brittle condition. The Library has also acquired a vast number of books and newspapers printed after Goa's liberation. Today, this Library is housed in a spacious new building situated in Patto, Panaji.

The HAG is a unique archive holding documentation formed from day-to-day administration from the 16th century to 1961 and later, but one does not know exactly what other materials it has as some of its volumes have translations of edicts on copper plates from the era of Goa Kadambas. The said documentation has been classified under different heads, some of which are: Correspondence of different types, Standing Orders, Service Records, Records on Customs Houses, Minutes of proceedings of different Councils, *Tombos* of Villages, Records related to *Comunidades*, Court records on Temple disputes, Registration of Sureties, Petitions to State Revenue Council, Treaties with other States, High Court of Goa, Senate of Municipal Council, on Oath Taking, on *Rendas*, on *Saguates*, on Awards, Book of Laws and Rules, Secret Correspondence, on Letters-Patent and Charters, Books of Royal Orders, Books of *Cartazes*, Books on Different Religious Orders, Books of Orders and Rules of His Majesty, Certificates, Demography, Land, Royal Tobacco Trade, Factory Correspondence, Taxes on Xendy, Arsenal of Goa, Agriculture, Market rules, Convents, Slaves, Sale Deeds, Military, Namoxins, Forts, Passports, 'Ranes', Salt and Abcari, Wills, Old Colleges, Records of Freedom Movement, etc.

To elucidate and explain how vast each subhead can be, let us see what the subhead 'Correspondence of different types' contains. It includes the Series of *Livros das Monções do Reino* (Books of Correspondence sent and answers received from Portugal or Spain through *Carreira voyages*). This Series has been wrongly translated as Monsoon Series for *Monções* meaning seasonal voyages and not monsoons. This Series has 456 volumes, having documents from 1560 to 1914. This Series is so vast that no one has yet gone through it. The Series *Livros de Alfandega*, that is, 'Records of the Customs Houses' has about 2,034 volumes. This Series is so vast that no one yet knows what it fully contains. Similarly, most of the subheads and their Series are so vast that they have remained unread fully till now.

Dr. Pissurlencar in his *Roteiro* points out 244 different heads/ Series under which this Archives is classified by him. This *Roteiro* was published in 1955 and is still the main reference index book. It, however, points mostly only to the Series that are up to 1955. There are also numerous other index pamphlets for reference to different other holdings of this Archive. This Archive holds hardly any deliberately written long reports. Therefore, these documents are very valuable for the purpose of writing History.

In 1973, when the Archive was housed in the new building, it had about 20,000 volumes. This new mega storage area comprised about 10-km linear length rack space in the Head Office and another 4-km rack space in Daulat repository in St. Inez, Panaji. Today stack rooms with standard steel racks house more than 200,000 Codices and files (Naik 2001, 165-177).

It is not possible to write about the total contents of the immense documentation of this Archive. My chief aim here, therefore, is to show the great importance of this vast repository and the need to salvage its documentation for the future. My regular visits over the last 10 years have indicated that the physical state of many of its Codices has deteriorated and that the white borer pest persists despite the hard work of its archivists and the preservation unit. This issue requires urgent attention, for the volumes this pest attacks are irreplaceable and their copies are not found anywhere else in the world. The uniqueness of this Archive calls for urgent solutions.

Access for researchers to this Archive is comparatively easy and the supply of Codices for reference is reasonably fast. The Archives has good facilities to issue digital copies of documents on request but as far as researchers are concerned, the new fees are considerably on the higher side. The State authorities could issue a corrigendum, reducing the same for promoting research as there is an agreement between this State Archive and the Centre to keep such fees to the minimum.

During my stay in Europe in 1984, under a scholarship from *Calouste Gulbenkan* Foundation, Lisbon, for Ph.D. research, I visited the following archives in Portugal: National Library, Archives of Overseas History, Archives of Academy of Science, Archives of Geography, *Ajuda* Library, National Archives of *Torre do Tombo*, Archives of Customs House of Lisbon, Archives of Municipality of Lisbon, all in Lisbon, District Archives of Évora, Municipal Library in Braga, Public Library of Municipality of Porto, Archives of the University of Coimbra. I also visited the British Museum Library in London, National Library in Paris, Jesuit Archives, Propaganda Fide Archives and Vatican Archives in Rome.

All these archives possess vast source material for the history of the Portuguese in the East and all of them are well preserved without any fear of being destroyed. While all these archives continuously refer to Goa and the East, some of them have special sections referring to Goa, particularly the Jesuit Archives. The Propaganda Fide Archives hold many reports sent from Goa, as well as letters and other documents by Goan Bishops, Dom Matheus de Castro Mahale (Fernandes 1986, 45-59), Dom Custodio Pinho and Dom Thomas de Castro, all of whom worked for Propaganda Fide in India and had pitched skirmishes against the *Padroado* men. The India section of the Archives of Overseas History (AHU) holds hundreds of *India Caixas* (boxes), each holding a variety of documents as per the concerned subject, sent to the Overseas Council in Lisbon for decision making, sometimes each *Caixa* holding about 1,000 folios. Similarly, other archives mentioned here have hundreds of volumes and reports on Goa and they mostly originated in Goa. There are also other archives in Lisbon and other parts of Portugal and other countries of Europe, particularly in Spain, which have material on Goa[16] but are not referred here.

4. Present Status of the Sources

Most of the Codices and files in Goa Archives are in Portuguese

(95%). Of the remaining, the bulk is in '*Modi*' language, a few are in Konkani and other languages. The paper of the documents, dated up to the end of the 18th century, is mostly good quality paper and there is no chance of its cracking; some documents are on thinner paper and the ink used appears to be corrosive (may be 5%). Documents are damaged because they are not touched for decades, there is no aeration of folios and the trapped humidity destroys them; most of the documents at the HAG get damaged because they are being eaten by white borers. The pest could be eliminated if all the Codices are cleaned and treated at a time, say within a period of three months. For this, the number of workers for this job must be sufficiently raised. It cannot be an easy job to clean and maintain 200,000 Codices and files. Temperature control and use of dehumidifiers could also help. The authorities of HAG must be aware of the modern methods of preservation but the fact is that the borers continue to destroy them and many documents are facing the danger of extinction.

When I was in Rome, I learnt that the vast documentation in Jesuit Archives there had been fully microfilmed and copies of the films were preserved in different parts of the world to save the documents, in case some mishap destroyed that Archives. Today, with easier processes of copying such as digitisation, the duplication of documents of the HAG is easier. I repeat that the documentation in the HAG is unique as there are no duplicates surviving in any part of the world. The Government of Goa should try to urgently seek Central assistance to save from extinction this vast and rich written heritage, holding our very own historical past. It is also important and necessary that heritage organisations in Goa and elsewhere in the world step forward and meet this challenge.

Conclusion

The chief aim of this brief survey is not only to bring out details of research carried out in Goa or elsewhere, but to state that the documents at the HAG, though they are in the Portuguese language, do not relate only the history of the Portuguese—90 per cent of these documents contain material on history of India, including that of Goa and of other countries. During my current research for the NCDR, I have so far collected original documents for about 20 volumes on

History of Arabia. Similarly, there are numerous documents on different topics I have elaborated in the sub-topic 'Glimpses of Grand Goa'. Has not Dr. Pissurlencar shown how Maratha history had to be written based on our records? Or similarly, have not other researchers mentioned in this article done the same?

Hundreds of theses can be written based on the records of the HAG which are on topics besides the history of the Portuguese. What is important is that these records are varied and should be saved from extinction and be preserved for the future. I sincerely wish that the Government of Goa or India or world heritage organisations should come forward to preserve them and prepare new scholars, training them in basics that are required to handle and use them, for which liberal scholarships must be instituted. A research centre of Indo-Portuguese Studies in Goa University or allied to the HAG is also recommended to fully utilise the gold mine in this mammoth documentation and records of the HAG and other centres.

Since the Golden Jubilee Year was in 2011, it is pertinent to refer to documentation on freedom fighters in the HAG. The index of T.M.T. (Military Tribunal) files shows that there are 1,766 files on different freedom fighters of Goa dating from the 19th century. The records in these files are in Portuguese but they contain the life histories of the freedom fighters and their brave deeds. Till today no serious study has been undertaken on this subject. Therefore, to honour the hard work of the men and women who suffered for the freedom of Goa, the Goa Government could immediately take up digitisation of these files and institute a scholarship for research on the subject.

NOTES

1. In 1925, Surendranath Sen, Officer in British service on Records of Bengal, visited Goa. He gave some advice to Dr. Pissurlencar in this work.
2. They are preserved in the Pissurlencar Centre in the library of the Goa University.
3. For letters received by Dr. Pissurlencar from Indian scholars, see: *Bibliography of Dr. Pissurlencar Collection*. Vol. III.
4. In 1928, Dr. Pissurlencar had been examiner for the D.Litt. examination in Allahabad University on the recommendation of Sir Jadunath Sarkar.

5. They are enumerated in: 'P.S.S. Pissurlencar', in B.S. Shastry, *Studies in Indo-Portuguese History*.
6. His only student who completed Ph.D. was B.S. Shastry. Besides his thesis on Portuguese-Canara relations, the latter has also contributed to several articles, some of which are published in his *Studies in Indo-Portuguese History* as well as in some Goa University publications.
7. All of them have published many research works. Prof. K.S. Mathew has his own Indo-Portuguese Centre in Cochin. A large number of contributions to history by T.R. de Souza are enumerated in "Metahistory", History Questioning History, Festschrift in honour of T.R. de Souza (on his 60th birthday) ed. Prof. Charles J. Borges, s.j. (USA) and Prof. Michael N. Pearson (Australia), published by Nova Vega, Lisboa, 2007, pp. 15-26.
8. The copies of this research periodical are still available at the HAG for sale. Most of the researchers who got their Ph.D. degrees are employed in different colleges of Goa and have themselves contributed to enrich the research literature.
9. In the past, besides some theses of the students, the University has published works such as Goa Wins Freedom, Bibliographies of Dr. P.S.S. Pissurlencar, and Dr. Nuno's Collections, the Series, Goa through Ages, some editions of Local History Seminars, etc.
10. The XCHR has its own series of publications and it has been responsible for initiating local and international Seminars, etc., which are well known.
11. In this paper, I have listed several publications and journals which can also serve as guidelines on how to use the records at the HAG.
12. During my research at the HAG in the last decade, I have met a large number of researchers who visited the HAG, from amongst whom two young Indian researchers, Dr. Paolo Aranha and Ms. Annanya Chakraborty from foreign universities, have impressed by their command of Portuguese and other related languages.
13. The documents in the volumes which are edited are selected from HAG Series, 'Livros de Concelho da Fazenda', 'Livros de Petições Despachadas no Concelho da Fazenda', and the Codice 'Livro de Provisões da Fazenda Geral'. Next to follow will be five volumes from HAG Series, 'Livros das Monções do Reino', documents selected, being from first 110 Codices of this Series, dating from 1600 to 1730. This Series has a total of 456 Codices dating from 1560 to 1914 AD.
14. Also referred as Govapuri or Gopakapattam, it was situated on the banks of river Zuari. Some of the archaeological remains of this era excavated in Pilar, soon after the liberation of Goa, are housed in the

Pilar Seminary Museum which is organised by Fr Cosme Jose Costa s.f.x. See his work *The Heritage of Govapuri,* Pilar Publications (2002); also see Gerald A. Pereira, *An Outline of Pre-Portuguese History of Goa,* Vasco da Gama, Goa (1973) and V. R. Mitragotri, *Social Cultural History of Goa from Bhojas to Vijayanagar,* Institute Menezes Braganza, Panaji, Goa (1999).

15. See "Cargoes brought from Macau to Goa in the Annual Voyage ships and their prices at Goa in 1716", HAG, Livro de Monções (1715-1717) Vol. No. 82, fl.10-16; also see my article "The Annual Goa-Macau-Goa Trade Voyages in Second half of 17th to mid-18th centuries" to be published in a forthcoming issue of *Revista Cultural,* Macau; the "Memorandum of the merchandise which the Great Ships of the Portuguese take from China to Japan" (1600)' Arquivo das Indias, Sevilla 1-2-1/13-R.31, published in C.R. Boxer, *The Great ship of Amacon,* Instituto Cultural de Macau (1988), pp. 179-184. This Memorandum also includes: (1) Cargoes from Macau to India; (2) Cargoes from Goa to China; (3) Shipping dues at Macao; and (4) Memorandum of the detailed selling prices at Canton at the end of the 16th century.
16. In different volumes of *Boletim Filmoteca Ultramarina Portuguesa,* A. da Silva Rego has published indexes of different Series of many archives in Europe and that of Macau in China.

REFERENCES

Arab Documents 23. 2002. The Historical Documents on Arab History in the Archives of the World, 124–137.Government of Abu Dhabi: Centre for Documentation and Research.

Boxer, C.R. 1935. "Anglo-Portuguese Rivalry in the Persian Gulf, 1615–1635". In *Chapters in Anglo-Portuguese Relations*, edited by Edgar Prestage, 46–129.

_______. 1965. "Portuguese was *Lingua Franca* of Coastal Asia for three centuries". In *Dutch Sea Borne Empire (1600–1800)*, 216 and 224. New York.

de Souza, T.R. 1982. "Mhamai House Records: Indigenous Sources for Indo-Portuguese Historiography". *The Indian Archives*, January-June, XXXI (I): 25–45.

_______. 2001. "The Vicissitudes and Growth of Goa Archives". In *Fourth Centenary Volume of the Goa Archives*, edited by S.K. Mhamai, 1–10. Panaji.

Fernandes, Agnelo P. 1986. *Portuguese and the Mughals, 1627–1707*. PhD thesis, Mumbai University.

_______.1986. "Portuguese Trading Company and its impact on Diu Trade". *Purabilekh Purutatva*, Vol V.

_______.1986. "Dom Matheus Castro e Mahale: the pioneer Goan Freedom Fighter". In *Goa Wins Freedom*, edited by B. Sheik Ali, 45–59. Goa University publication during Silver Jubilee Year of Liberation of Goa.

_______.1989. "Goa in the International Trade: 16th-17th Centuries". In *Essays in Goan History*, edited by T.R. de Souza, 61–68. New Delhi: Concept Publishing Company.

_______.2009. "Portuguese *Cartazes* System and the 'Magumbayas' on Pearl Fishing in Persian Gulf". *Liwa*, Journal of the NCDR, Government of Abu Dhabi, Vol I, 12–24.

Goa University. *Bibliography of Dr Pissurlencar Collection*. Vol I. Edited by B.S. Shastry and V.R. Navelkar.

_______. *Bibliography of Dr Pissurlencar Collection*. Vol III.

Mhamai, S.K. 1984. *The Savants of Wadi and the Portuguese*. Delhi: Concept Publishing Company.

Naik, Dilip B. 2001. "Development of Goa Archives during the past three decades and the problems". In *Fourth Centenary Volume of the Goa Archives*, edited by S.K. Mhamai, 165–177. Panaji.

Pearson, M.N. 1976. *Merchants and Rulers of Gujerat*. New Delhi.

Shastry, B.S. 1981. "P.S.S. Pissurlencar". In *Studies in Indo-Portuguese History*, 1–9. Bangalore.

CHAPTER 4

Civil Society Movements in Contemporary Goa

Themes, Issues and Perspectives

SAVIO ABREU

Introduction

The recent anti-corruption movement by Anna Hazare and the widespread media publicity it received has prompted several questions and debates on the theme of civil society *versus* the state. For example, the Centre for the Study of Social Exclusion and Inclusive Policy (CSSEIP), Goa University, organised a symposium on 'Civil society *versus* the state: Does it contribute to inclusive growth?' on August 23, 2011, to debate the changing relationship of state and civil society—two vibrant realms of social and political democracy in India—and to find out what kind of relations would contribute to the realisation of the nation's target of inclusive growth.

Civil society emerged in Goa only after the Portuguese left the shores of Goa. With the emergence of democracy and political institutions came also the need of those outside the mainstream political system to regulate and keep a check on those in authority. Along with rapid changes in the social structure, the emergence of new classes and rapid socio-economic development, several sections of society felt left out of the state-driven development process. Faced with the labour pains of the emergence of a new political entity and several post-colonial paradoxes, including the Goan *versus* Indian identity tussle and the fear of the outsider, many of the civil society movements were nothing but processes of coming to terms with the ever-shifting sand dunes of an increasingly modernised and urbanised Goan society. This paper attempts to undertake a socio-cultural analysis of the social movements in contemporary Goa and, in the process, contribute a theoretical understanding towards the rather scanty corpus of studies on social movements in Goa.

Definition of Civil Society Movements

In this paper an attempt will be made to derive the definition of 'civil society movement' from the common characteristics found among the local movements in Goa. According to the Oxford Concise Dictionary of Sociology, 'social movement' is an organised effort by a significant number of people to change, or resist change in some major aspect or aspects of society (Marshall 1994, 489). The term was first used by Saint Simon in France, in the beginning of the 18th century, to characterise the movements of social protest that emerged there and later elsewhere and was applied to new political forces opposed to the *status quo*. Thus a key characteristic that emerges regarding social movements is that they are connected to social change, either striving to bring about or resist some form of social change. Social movements also generally refer to groups and organisations outside mainstream political systems but they may penetrate quite deeply into political power circles as interest groups. They have specific goals, a formal organisation and a degree of continuity and are one of the basic elements, in fact the catalysts, of a living democracy. Under the broad banner of a social movement many individual social movements may operate in a relatively independent way, sometimes causing confusion and conflict within the movement itself.

Cohen (1987) made a critical distinction between 'resource mobilisation' theories and 'identity-oriented' theories. The former, particularly influential in North America, discuss movements as organisations and focus particularly on the needs of such organisations to mobilise resources. Within this perspective the term 'resources' takes on a wide array of meanings, including economic resources, ideologies, rhetoric and symbols. On the other hand 'identity-oriented' theories, more common in Western Europe, view movements as the central groups in the new and modern social politics, changes and realignments and as sources of new political identities.

Now coming to the first part of the definition, that is, 'civil society': it is even today an ambiguous and controversial term. The ambiguity has been brought to the limelight by the recent anti-corruption agitation which was portrayed as a civil society struggle against elected representatives. According to Heredia (2011), when elected leaders fail to deliver on good governance, the final guarantor of an effective democracy is an alert, critical citizenry in a conscientised, open society. Alexis de Tocqueville argued in the 19th century that a multiplicity of civic associations of engaged citizens is essential for the democratic functioning of a modern state, both to support it and contain it. Thus civil society refers to all social groups and institutions located between the institutions of the family (the individual) and the state. For thinkers like Hegel it was meant to be a temporary phenomenon to be transcended when particular and common interests combined, while for Antonio Gramsci it was the bastion of class, hegemony and, ultimately (though not unequivocally), supportive of the state (Marshall 1994, 55-56). Civil society thus implies the idea of a non-state autonomous sphere located in the social space between kinship and political systems, which is influenced by both sides. Civil society is always seen as dynamic (the dynamic side of citizenship) and embraces the notion of social movements.

While according to Heredia (2011), civil society is the social infrastructure on which the political edifice must be built, and civil society provides the software for the democratic hardware of political structures, quite often an alert and engaged civil society has to take an anti-establishment stance to correct the structural injustices and anomies of our political institutions. And T.K. Oommen (1990) argues that since any effort to question those in power, that is, to protest, is viewed with disdain and suspicion, the analysis of protest as a social phenomenon and its potentiality for change have been neglected. He points out that movements are often viewed as pathological aberrations and as anti-systemic enterprises, a view held not only by particular brands of theorists but also by the political, economic and cultural mainstreams. Movement studies are recent in India in general and in Indian sociology and social anthropology in particular. This is true not just of India in general but also of Goa in particular. Movement studies are not common in Goa and there are very few sociological and anthropological studies done on social movements in Goa. In 2008 I had published a study in *Social Action* on the struggle against Special Economic Zones (SEZs) in Goa and due to that article (which is published in this volume), I had got several invitations for seminars and conferences to speak on the SEZ struggle in Goa.

Themes Emerging from Civil Society Struggles in Goa

***A. Post-coloniality*:** Though the Portuguese left the shores of Goa in 1961, their legacy has left an indelible imprint on the post-colonial Goan society that continues to influence and impact decisions taken even today. The painful process of dealing with and attempting to heal the wounds of the colonial period has been a recurring and important narrative in the five decades of post-colonial Goa (Angley 1999, 5-10; Sinha 2002, 36-40). The voices of a small section of Goan society that lamented in 1961 the loss of the Golden Goa (Goa *Dourada*) image under the Portuguese due to the annexation of Goa by India (Newman 1999, 19), every now and then raise their heads, especially when fears are expressed over the ecological, cultural and economic damage due to the large number of migrants from other states (Sinha 2002, 16). According to C.H. Xavier (2004), Goan social movements, or organised non-governmental organisations (NGOs), have been the most visible face of a rediscovering of a distinct Goan identity, comfortable with its past and confident about its future. But the angst and emotional turbulence felt by the newer generation of Goans in confronting their past and dealing with the colonial remnants is visibly noticed in the works of Sinha (2002, 17), Angley (1999, 5-10) and Apte (1999, 11-16).

The birth pangs of the new state and its struggle with its colonial past was seen in the anti-merger movement, which was a tussle between keeping its so-called 'unique' Indo-Portuguese identity reflecting the Goa *Dourada* image and culture or rejecting centuries of Portuguese indoctrination and being integrated in the wider Indian identity. Since the anti-merger struggle or the Opinion Poll was basically a struggle between two political parties, the Maharashtrawadi Gomantak Party (MGP) and the United Goans Party (UGP), the question can be raised if it can be called a civil society movement. According to Heredia (2011, 642), civil society is located in the social space between kinship and political systems, and is thus influenced by both sides. In addition, the Oxford Concise Dictionary of Sociology mentions that social movements operate outside the regular political channels of society but may penetrate quite deeply into political power circles as interest groups. Though there was lot of mobilisation by the two political parties, the vote against merger was a decisive action of the civil society to deal with its colonial legacy by remaining a separate political and cultural entity. The Opinion Poll was also a precursor and defined several key issues that dominated many of the civil society struggles that followed in post-colonial Goa. So a brief analysis of the salient features of this event is necessary to arrive at a deeper understanding of the themes that emerge from civil society struggles in Goa.

In December 1962, general elections were held for 30 assembly and two Parliamentary seats with the regional party, the (MGP) emerged successful, winning 16 Assembly seats and both the Parliamentary seats. Since the MGP was voted on the election plank of 'immediate merger of Goa with the state of Maharashtra', the party along with the help of Congressmen in Maharashtra began agitating for the merger of Goa with Maharashtra. In the agitations that followed the Goans got crystallised into two camps, mergerists and anti-mergerists, Marathiwadis and Konkaniwadis, Hindus and Christians. To calm down the highly polarised situation, the Central Government decided to have a referendum on the political status of Goa.

The Church fully supported the stand of the Christians and the main opposition party, (UGP), demanding separate political status for Goa. In this campaign against merger the priests gave political speeches from the pulpits and marched in the streets with the laity, and often worked along with the Hindu Saraswat Brahmins who vociferously opposed merger. Though the MGP almost wholly concentrated its campaigning on the Hindu electorate its dream came crashing down with 54.20 per cent voting against the merger (Sinha 2002, 64). While the Christians and Saraswats opposed the merger along expected lines, the reason for the anti-merger victory according to Esteves was the fact that "the leaders of the Anti-Merger Front... saw to it from the very inception that its doors were kept open to

Goans of all religions, castes, sub-castes, Scheduled Castes and Tribes and also to citizens from all parts of the Territory... The Front included not only Congressmen, United Goans and others but also representatives of communities like *Mahar, Chamar, Kunbi* and *gaudde* (lower castes)" (Newman 1999, 29). This campaign against merger with Maharashtra was an initial attempt by Goan civil society to deal with the issue of its colonial past and link its resolution with the necessity of maintaining Goa's separate culture and identity.

B. Goan Identity and Culture and the Threat of the Outsider: Fears about the dilution and erosion of an ideal, romantic Goan identity and culture, which were linked to the Portuguese legacy and Golden Goa image, have triggered and acted as a catalyst to some of the civil society movements. Newman (1999, 31-2) traces a slow but steady change in the image and identity of Goans from 'oppressed or colonised people' during the Portuguese period to a 'split personality' after liberation to an identity under threat in the interim period between 1967–87. In post-colonial Goan society, especially after the Opinion Poll, there was a growing anxiety that the Goan identity and culture (the nostalgic images of Goan countryside and the *susegad* insulated village life) was in the process of erosion leading inexorably to its extinction in the not too distant future, if the downslide was not arrested in time. While writers like Olivinho Gomes (2002) argued that the Goan identity had been affirmed emphatically by the collective will of the Goan people in the Opinion Poll of 1967, it was a close call as just 54 per cent voted to retain Goa as a separate Union Territory. As a follow up to the victory in the Opinion Poll, those groups that wanted to carve a separate identity for Goa, including the Catholic Church, backed the Konkani movement.

The MGP, which dominated Goan politics for the first decade and half, received its major support from the Hindu areas. It vigorously promoted Marathi and the language of Maharashtrian expansionism and there was a fear that the expansionists would enter and occupy Goa through the back door. To counter this threat the Saraswat Brahmins along with the Catholic community, joined by many from the Bahujan Samaj (non-Brahmin Hindus) agitated for the language of Konkani. Sinha (2002, 170-1) holds that the Konkani language struggle, which culminated in the passing of the Official Language Act declaring Konkani as the official language of Goa on February

4, 1987, was a political movement, not a linguistic one with the agenda of ensuring a separate status for Goa.

C. Process of Modernisation and Issues Related to Development, Environment and Ecology: From 1961 onwards the state experienced rapid economic growth. With the departure of the Portuguese, massive public funding was earmarked for development projects and as a result industry, mining, tourism, agricultural productivity, mechanised fishing, banking, real estate, education, health care and business all started to develop and expand. All these new industries and public sector ventures required a lot of skilled workers and the period after liberation witnessed a huge influx of migrant workers into the state. The mining boom which began in the 1950s and got a further boost after 1961 also led to an inflow of workers, especially from the neighbouring states. The transportation network of roads, bridges and public transport developed after 1961 brought every part of the state within a few hours' bus journey. By 1985–86 every village in Goa had been connected by electricity and by all-weather roads. Goa's per capita income was Rs. 17,406 against the national average of Rs. 10,151 in 1999–2000 (Sinha 2002, 174). But all this progress came at a price. Tourism became the main industry in Goa, generating a lot of employment and foreign exchange, the tourism boom reflected in the growth from 450 hotel beds in 1961 to 30,617 beds in 2000, but there were a lot of unhealthy side effects (Statistical Handbook of Goa 2001).

The process of modernisation and development that transformed the state of Goa also brought in several negative side-effects such as a burgeoning migrant population, increased crime rate, unrestrained industrialisation and ecological destruction, drug culture, spiralling real estate prices, etc., all of which led to several NGOs spearheading struggles related to issues of sustainable development and ecology. The various movements against the ill-effects of the process of modernisation in Goa are related to the issue of post-coloniality and the threat of the outsider to the identity and aspirations of the Goans. Communities such as the fisher folk, tribals and lower castes that were submerged and denied access to resources in colonial Goa were at the forefront of many of the recent social struggles in Goa. Civil society movements are often struggles of particular sections of society that are denied access to natural, non-renewable resources such as land, forest and water. The struggle by the *Ramponkars* (traditional fishermen), whose means of livelihood were being impinged upon by the mechanised trawler owners, is an example of such a civil society movement where issues of livelihood and access to resources are intertwined with discourses on social status and cultural identities.

After 1961 the process of mechanisation of the fishing sector which had already began in other parts of India, spread to Goa. The Department of Fisheries offered several schemes aimed at developing infrastructure, providing financial assistance to the traditional fishermen to mechanise the country crafts, regulate fishing and enhance fish production (D'Cruz 2008, 177). The *Ramponkars*, who lived on the periphery of the Goan agrarian economy, and were mostly illiterate were reluctant in accepting mechanisation of their occupation and so the state government extended these schemes to the fishing companies and other investors from within and outside the state. With the blue revolution bringing in a large flotilla of trawlers and mechanised crafts, the fishing sector soon acquired the status of an 'industry' and soon the *Ramponkars* realised that they could not compete with the complex technology and the commercialisation of the fishing sector. So in collaboration with some citizens and activists who were agitating against Zuari Agro Chemicals Limited, they formed the Goenchea Ramponkaracho Ekvott (GRE, or the All Goa Fisher-people's Union) in December 1975.

While the main issue in this long drawn out *Ramponkar* struggle was the protection of their means of livelihood against rampant and reckless mechanisation of the fishing industry by the outsiders (non-fishermen) it was also a cry for recognising the existence of a community of 80,000 fishermen (G.R.E. *Souvenir*) that had been ignored and accorded peripheral status in 'Golden Goa'. It was not just a struggle between two communities, namely the traditional fishermen and the mechanised trawller owners, who were backed by the government, but it was an ecological battle to protect marine life and stop the rampant exploitation of marine resources for commercial purposes. Though it started as a local-level movement, it grew into a national movement with the All Goa Fisher-people's Union establishing links with fishermen in Karnataka, Maharashtra, Kerala, Tamil Nadu, Andhra Pradesh and Orissa. National-level organisations such as 'National Forum for Catamaran and Country Boat Fishermen

Rights and Marine Life' and the 'National Fisherman's Forum' (NFF) demanded a Central Marine Bill and this issue was debated in Parliament. The *Ramponkar* struggle, which was supported by the Catholic Church, yielded results with the passing of the Goa, Daman and Diu Marine Regulation Act (1980) that put a ban on monsoon fishing from June 1 till August 31 and also restrained trawling within 5 km from the shore. After this victory the battle moved to the legal realm with both parties filing court cases and the state government ignoring violations against the twin ban. Though the Supreme Court, on the basis of studies conducted by the National Institute of Oceanography and the report of the state government, passed an Order in 1994 that banned monsoon fishing and mechanised fishing within 5 km from the shore, the state government has been lax in implementing it and disputes between the traditional fishermen and trawler owners have continued.

I would like to discuss three issues that emerge from the fishermen's struggle, which will contribute towards a theoretical understanding and forming a typology of civil society movements in Goa. The first is the cultural identity of a subaltern group such as the fishermen community. The sub-culture of the fishermen comprise attributes such as being anti-modern, illiterate, not open to development, involved in an occupation that is polluting and low in social status. They occupied a low socio-economic status in colonial Goa, never part of the decision making process of Goa *Dourada* and looked down upon by the elites. Thus the *Ramponkar* struggle was to deconstruct the *Ramponkar* sub-culture of colonial Goa and to weave new discourses that empower and assert their higher status in post-colonial Goan society. The second issue, closely related to the first, is the manner in which the fishermen through their struggle re-invented their identity as 'Western Goan Catholics' which had been foisted by the pro-Portuguese Catholic elite of the old Goa *Dourada* image. The fishermen, by linking with and becoming part of the national fishermen movement, came to a new broader understanding of their collective 'Indian' identity. The fishermen's movement made these fishermen, most of whom had never gone beyond the shores of Goa, accept their Indian-ness and integrate in the national mainstream.

The third issue emerging from the fishermen movement is the realisation that there was both continuity and change in socio-cultural identities and hierarchies from colonial Goa to post-1961 Goa. The Portuguese rulers may have left Goan shores, old elites and dominant classes may have declined or disappeared but new elites and classes had risen. The nexus of dominant caste and upper class has usurped economic and political power and has replaced the Portuguese rulers, indulging in huge land grabs and amassing wealth at the cost of the subaltern groups such as *Kunbis, gaudde* (both tribal communities), *Harvis* (fisher folk), etc. The entry of migrants from different parts of India and the transformation of Goa into a bustling, cosmopolitan, urbanised centre has led to renegotiations and new combinations of cultural identities and socio-economic statuses. The biggest change in post-colonial Goa noticed in the *Ramponkar* struggle and other subsequent social movements was the emergence and formation of the educated middle class which supported and mobilised protests and struggles against various issues. This was seen in the agitation against the polluting Zuari Agro Chemical Company in 1975 when teachers, students, concerned citizens, activists and priests joined the victims of the pollution to successfully close the polluting unit. The impact of the *Ramponkar* struggle was profound since it was supported by educated middle class citizens such as Mathany Saldanha, the clergy of the Catholic Church and backed by sound legal advice and well-researched academic studies conducted by the National Institute of Oceanography and other research institutes. This has been the pattern found in most of the civil society movements in contemporary Goa such as Nylon 6,6, Meta strips, Regional Plan, Tribal movement and the SEZ agitations.

A brief analysis of the Nylon 6,6 and Meta Strips struggles reveals some important points for a better understanding of civil society movements in Goa. Both the movements were issue-based ecological movements. While the former struggle was against an industrial plant being put up by DuPont Corporation, America's largest chemical corporation, the latter agitation was against a factory being set up by a large corporate, Meta Strips Ltd. In both cases the state government was hand in glove with the polluting companies—the then CM, Pratapsingh Rane had rejected the objections of the Chief Town Planner who felt the proposed location of DuPont's Nylon 6,6 was hazardous for the future of the environment surrounding the site, while the Meta Strips factory was given pollution clearance by the state government without proper investigation. Both the agitations were successful in closing down the polluting units due to a combination of facilitating factors. The Nylon 6,6 agitation, a local issue concerning the villages of Kerim and Savoi-Verem in Ponda taluka, was transformed into an all-Goa issue with the formation of Ecoforum, a grand alliance of four of Goa's prominent environmental groups (Alvares 1999, 129). The impact was heightened since Ecoforum contacted international environmental organisations like Greenpeace and the issue was publicised in international media, thus giving an international dimension to a local struggle. In the case of Meta Strips, the active role of the Catholic Church increased the impact of the agitation. Sinha (2002, 132) describes the diocesan mouthpiece, the *Renovacao*, as the journal of the 'people's movement' against Meta Strips. In both cases there was violence leading to deaths. What is common to both the agitations and also to other subsequent environmental struggles is the growing awareness among the locals that politicians, a few elites and commercial interests should not decide without the consent of the local people what model of development is best suited for Goa's ecosystem. These movements expanded the identity of the average Goan to include the right to decide the optimum utilisation of the state resources.

Conclusion

When we look back at post-colonial Goan history and try to review and recover 50 years of Goan heritage and culture, there is a tendency to overlook civil society movements as an insignificant component of the mosaic of Goa 2011. But if we wish to capture frame by frame the rapid changes in post-colonial Goa then we need to study the origins of such movements, their sources and patterns of recruitment, ideological orientations, and organisational dynamics including leadership, their impact upon society and the process of institutionalisation. This paper has attempted to construct a socio-cultural theory of civil society movements in Goa. A theory of movements implies a theory of social structure and the social ferment in post-liberation Goa indicates people cannot be imprisoned in a fossilised social structure. With post-colonial Goa undergoing rapid changes under the influcncc of social processes such as modernisation, industrialisation, urbanisation and migration, civil society movements cannot be understood only through the prism of changes in the present social structure, but any study of social movements in Goa need to take into account the historicity of colonial rule, the attempts in post-colonial Goan society to deal with the fissures of the past, and the role and place of 'outsiders' and the best ecologically sustainable model of development in the future vision of Goan society. T.K. Oommen (1990, 13) views social movement and protest as a manifestation of the creativity of human beings and an effort to redefine or recapture the past, to restructure the present and reorient the future.

REFERENCES

Alvares, Claude. 1999. "Goa: The Politics of Environmental Abuse". In *The Transforming of Goa*, edited by Norman Dantas, 114–136. Mapusa, Goa: Other India Press.

Angley, Prabhakar. 1999. "A Culture Conceived and Misconceived". In *The Transforming of Goa*, edited by Norman Dantas, 5–10. Mapusa, Goa: Other India Press.

Apte, Bal V. 1999. "Of Konkan–Kashi and Goa's Golden Age". In *The Transforming of Goa*, edited by Norman Dantas, 11–16. Mapusa, Goa: Other India Press.

Cohen, Jean L. 1987. *Class and Civil Society: The Limits of Marxian Critical Theory*. Massachusetts: Univ of Massachusetts Press.

D'Cruz, Sharon. 2008. "One Sea...Three Contenders: The struggle between *Ramponkars*, Trawler Owners and the Government in Goa". In *Goa in the 20th Century: History & Culture*, edited by P. Malekandathil and Dias. Panaji, Goa: Institute Menezes Braganza.

Goenchea Ramponkarancho Ekvott. 1995. *20 Years Souvenir*. Cansaulim, Goa.

Gomes, Olivinho. 2002. "Goan Identity in Crisis!". *Goa Today*, August.

Heredia, Rudolph. 2011. "Democratizing Democracy: Civil Society and Social Capital". *VJTR* (September) 75 (9): 641–6.

Marshall, Gordon, ed. 1994. *Oxford Concise Dictionary of Sociology*. Oxford: OUP.

Newman, R.S. 1999. "The Struggle for a Goan Identity". In *The Transforming of Goa*, edited by Norman Dantas, 17–42. Mapusa, Goa: Other India Press.

Newman, R.S. 2001. *Of Umbrellas, Goddesses & Dreams: Essays on Goan Culture and Society*. Mapusa, Goa: Other India Press.

Oommen, T.K. 1990. *Protest and Change: Studies in Social Movements*. New Delhi: Sage Publications.

Sinha, Arun. 2002. *Goa Indica: A Critical Portrait of Postcolonial Goa*. New Delhi: Bibliophile South Asia & Promilla & Co.

Xavier, C.H. 2004. "Goa's confrontation with the past". *Goan Observer*, July 10. Accessed September 15, 2011. http://www.goanobserver.com.

CHAPTER 5

The Student Movement in Goa of the Early Eighties

An Insider's Story

SUSHILA SAWANT MENDES

Introduction

I owe the conceptualization of this paper to my journalist friend, Fredrick Noronha, of the Goa Research Network. He expressed the need to record the Student Movement in Goa in its proper historical setting and so this paper is a small step in that direction. The main aim of this paper is to place on record and analyse, as an insider, a movement which began in the late 1970s and continued till the 1980s, but which went much beyond the scope of what is generally perceived as a 'students' movement'. The writing of this paper coincided with the publication of the international bestseller by Fali S. Nariman, the former Solicitor General of India, *Before Memory Fades: An Autobiography* (Nariman 2010). This provided me with the required methodology to write a narrative such as this. His book had reminiscences, anecdotes and reflections on the events and people in his life. While Mr. Nariman has written an autobiography, this paper is an attempt to record the history of a movement before memory fades—of a group of young students whose main strength lay in the fact that they, in all sincerity, wanted to bring about a change for the betterment of society but yet refused, to the very end, to be part of any political party.

My Encounter with the Student Movement

I was a late entrant, as I came to Goa from St. Xavier's College, Mumbai, in June 1978, by which time the All Goa Students Union (AGSU) was riding on a halo of having successfully ended the 50 per cent bus agitation for students. From St. Xavier's to Carmel College in Nuvem was a cultural shock, as the novitiate kind of atmosphere in Carmel's was very different from the very liberal attitude of the Jesuits. It was, however, an excellent training ground for inculcating leadership qualities in an 18-year-old. The 'I can' factor was nurtured here, after being elected as the General Secretary of the Student's Council and bagging the coveted 'Orator of Carmel College' trophy. This positive attitude and belief in myself was reinforced when I was selected as an NCC Under Officer to represent Goa for a para-trooping programme, conducted by the Army Para Training School in Agra. The icing on the cake was the collection of many trophies at inter-college elocution competitions.

It was at one of these elocution competitions, wherein I bagged the shield for criticising the student movement as a violent one, that I had my first contact with student activists. It was the first face-to-face meet with Felicio Esteves, Desmond D'Costa, Mohandas Loliencar and Cleofato Almeida Coutinho (my husband since the past 23 years). They had all come together to change my way of thinking with their persuasive arguments (Personal interview with Mohandas Loliencar, Margao, 5-5-2010). This encounter was an important lesson in the technique of making an enemy a friend. This interaction was also a wake-up call for me, on the need to take a studied stand on social issues.

Formation of PSU and *Udent* Magazine

Regular meetings to plan strategies to strengthen the movement were common. To have clarity on the ideology required to take the movement forward, study circles were also frequently undertaken. Everything was transparent and the reassuring factor was that the group was not a puppet in the hands of politicians. The first major event was conference held in Ramnathi, Ponda, from July 9-12, 1981 organised by the then AGSU on the theme of the need of an ideology to guide the future of the students' movement in Goa. This was followed by a workshop on July 13 and 14 held under the banner of Sangarsh Natya Manch (a cultural group) which was initially guided by activists of the Aavhaan Natya Manch of Mumbai. The need for a strong and independent students' organisation was expressed at this conference. In keeping with this view, a new banner replaced the old. The Progressive Students Union (PSU) was formed as a breakaway group of the AGSU (*Udent* August 1981a, 9-10). *Udent,*[1] an organ of the PSU, began as a monthly student's newsletter/ magazine published regularly from August 1981 till October 1985.

The main reasons for this split were cited in the very first issue of *Udent* in August 1981 as the 'opportunist and unprincipled outlook' of a section of the old AGSU leadership, who were both using the union for personal gains and making it 'a tail of the ruling political parties'. The PSU introduced itself on *Udent* as "we are a growing group of students who have felt the need of showing concern for moral values, concern for freedom from poverty, hunger and employment, freedom to live a nice and decent life, a life without fear" (Ibid. b, 1-2). These words clearly show that the PSU was ready to take on issues which went beyond the scope of students' problems but extended to general 'social problems'.

Udent was the brainchild of an eight-member staff team consisting of Cleofato Almeida Coutinho, Edmund Antao, Manoj Kamat, Khagendra Hegde Desai, Julio D'Silva, Thalmann Perreira, Raju Naik, and Carlos Monteiro. These students represented most of the colleges from Panjim, Vasco and Margao (*Udent* September-October 1981a: 2). In June 1982, the first three members continued and the rest were replaced by the following new members: Jennifer Colaco, Sudhakar Rao, Babacier Gonsalves and myself (*Udent* June 1982a: 2). Prashant Naik and Lester Fernandes joined in 1983. Mohandas Loliencar was the permanent advertising in-charge from the first till the last issue.

As a member of the editorial team, it meant writing news reports, articles as well as travelling to Curchorem for the proof reading work. We were into investigative journalism, without any perks or salary.

---

1. The publisher was always Cleofta A. Coutinho but it was printed in different places.

The experience of visiting commercial sex workers in the slums of Baina, Vasco, to write an article, was an eye-opener as most of these workers were open to stopping this profession if the government provided them with a healthy option (*Udent* January 1984, 11). *Udent* exhorted the students of the need to realise that they have a special responsibility towards society: a responsibility 'to better the lot of the exploited'. It spoke of the need to fight against 'the oppressive structures that bind us' (*Udent* August 1981c: 2). A column titled 'Flashes from Goan History' encouraged students to write on individuals who inspired them. Accordingly, articles were written by students on Shennoi Goembab (Wagle 1981: 5), and Luis de Menezes Bragança (Miranda 1982: 5). 'Goans in the Movement,' was another column with articles on Evagrio Gorge (Martins 1981,9, 12), Mark Fernandes (*Udent* June 1982b: 8, 12) and other freedom fighters.

Involvement of PSU in Various Agitations

Goa, at this time, was rocked by the infamous marks scandal, wherein the marks of the niece of a politician were increased so as to ensure her a seat in the Goa Medical College. The AGSU had spearheaded this protest. Protests and police lathi-charges were a common occurrence of the movement. The success story of this agitation had built a strong base in favour of the credibility of the students' movement in Goa. The PSU later took up many cases, especially in the rural areas where students were without teachers for long periods. One such case was solved in the Canacona Higher Secondary School. The Union did not shirk from using methods like *gheraoing* (a mob encircling a person/s to demand immediate answers over an issue/s) the head of the institution and the closure of the institution for an indefinite period with the cooperation of the students. There were also day-to-day *morchas* (protest marches on the streets, over an issue accompanied with the shouting of slogans), takeover of the ADEI office of the Education Department and a *rasta roko* (blocking of the traffic, as a symbol of protest over an issue) of the National Highway No. 17 (NH 17). All these protests finally brought the Director of Education to Canacona, escorted by the Deputy Collector and Deputy Superintendent of Police for talks. The Physics and Konkani lecturers were appointed on a priority basis. This agitation highlighted the fact that the backward areas were being given step-motherly treatment by the government and that only an 'uncompromising militant struggle' could awaken the authorities (*Udent*, August 1981f, 6, 9). Another agitation was undertaken at Neturlim, Sanguem, as a toilet-cum-bathroom was converted into a classroom for students at the Government High School in the village. The school building was incomplete from 1977 till 1981. The government had not taken the contractor to task as he had political connections. The school students did not even have a laboratory. The villagers and the Sarpanch (the elected head of the village panchayat) joined the students in this struggle, with delegations meeting the Education Minister and the Director of Education. The agitation resulted in the school building being completed within a span of six months (*Udent* September-October 1981c, 9). The gratitude of the villagers was noticed when 30 years later in 2011 the villagers invited all the ex-members of the PSU to the village to commemorate their victory, which even after the passage of so many years had not yet been erased from their public memory.

Large scale deforestation was taking place with the nexus of contractors and politicians in the deep forests of Canacona. In order to investigate this in July 1981, a few student activists of the PSU visited the Kotigao village (25 km away from NH 17) in Canacona taluka. A report was published by the *Udent*. It exposed the lack of medical, educational and health facilities in the village. The only school was housed in a stable with cow dung flooring and a thatched roof without any walls. Illegal felling of trees was carried out after night fall. The local MLA had, in fact, built a new saw mill in the village after his election. The PSU exposed the illegal and indiscriminate deforestation and the lack of basic amenities in the lives of the villagers of Kotigao (*Udent* August 1981c, 2).

The PSU also helped in selling the donation coupons of the Lokvishwas Pratisthan, a registered Trust set up under the stewardship of Narayan Athawale, editor of the Marathi daily *Gomantak*. This trust was doing exemplary work in running a school (for speech and hearing persons). The government paid only lip service to the Trust; but did not help it with any grants when they needed it the most. *Udent* made an appeal to the student community to help the Trust (Ibid.d, 4).

An interstate racket in black-marketing of exercise books was exposed by the students in Margao. Two retail outlets were selling exercise books which belonged to the subsidised variety (as paper was supplied by the government at concessional rates) meant for sale at low prices in the neighbouring states of Maharashtra and Karnataka, whereas Goa did not have a subsidy scheme. The *modus operandi* was the pasting of the front and back covers of the note book with coloured paper in order to cover the government price (*Ibid.* e, 5).

The PSU also championed the cause for educational institutions to have elected councils of student representatives. Signature drives were conducted to persuade the managements to examine the issue from a fresh perspective. The St. Xavier's Higher Secondary School, Mapusa, was one such institution, it had 11 classes with a total strength of over 900 students but did not have an elected Students' Council from its inception till October 1981 (*Udent* September-October 1981b, 5). The representatives were always nominated. The PSU was frequently looked upon as an outsider by the school managements and accused of 'instigating the students' without actually studying each case on its merits. At present, of course, all Higher Secondary Schools in Goa have an elected Students' Council.

A major issue in the educational sphere was the case of the refusal of admission by Principal Tirodkar of the Parvatibai Chowgule College, Margao, to the General Secretary of the Students' Council, Edmund Antao. Edmund was a scholar throughout his career, having earned the second rank in Std. XII of the Goa State Board of Higher Secondary Examination. It was an issue of 'victimisation of student activists by the College authorities'. Edmund's nine-day hunger strike ended with his pre-dawn arrest by the police. Ms Sabina Martins started a fast unto death in the Margao Municipal Garden after this arrest. Edmund later broke his fast after a reassurance by the then Chief Minister Pratapsingh Rane. However this oral assurance was later rolled back by the government (*Udent* November 1982, 1, 4, 10).

Camps Organised by the Students' Movement

The PSU also organised 'Go to the village programmes' that involved fighting injustice in all the other sections of society as well. The ideological stand of the movement demanded that it moves on beyond

movement. This had a ripple effect in the rest of the country, especially in Mumbai, Chandrapur and Gadchiroli in Maharashtra. The Andhra Pradesh Radical Students' Union, the Radical Students' Union in Tamil Nadu and the Punjab Students' Union were a few organisations of those times. 'Naxalism was like mumps, measles or love, you had to get it at a certain age and then get over it' (*Ibid.*, 4).

The Vidyarthi Pragathi Sanghatana (VPS), Mumbai and its cultural wing the Aavhaan Natya Manch had very close contacts with the PSU, Goa. We attended their camps and conferences in Mumbai (one camp was held in Karjat) and similarly a large number of their activists attended our conferences in Goa. The Revolutionary Students' Organisation Coordination Committee (RSOCC) was formed, which was an attempt to bring together like-minded organisations from all over the country (Pamphlet August 1982). RSOCC had a meeting in Bombay on November 13-14, 1982. Goa and Punjab were the new members of this forum (*Udent* December 1982, 13). The Goan students showed solidarity with the students of Tamil Nadu by attending the Tamil Nadu Radical Students' Union's May Day celebration in Dharmapuri. A lot of importance was given to attending the study circles, where discussions were held on the need for a strong ideological foundation for the Union. Many a times, we had overnight sessions in faraway places. All the activities were secretly undertaken because of the fear of repression by the state police force. The PSU was an organisation based on gender equity and respect for women. All activities were strictly within the limits of moral and ethical propriety and absolutely safe for us women.

Encounters with Police and Prisons

In October 1981, Ambrosio Rodrigues, a worker of the Madras Rubber Factory (M.R.F.) was killed in a police firing at Costi, a few km from Sanvordem. The workers had gathered at the entrance of the Costi Mines to protest against Chowgule's decision of hiring 50 labourers from Belgaum to operate their Costi mines, when the local mine workers had struck work. This protest was led by the Co-ordination Committee of Trade Union in Goa (Interview with Adv. Mario Almedia, Margao, 4 April, 2010). A group of us went to Sanvordem and later, in a show of solidarity attended the funeral. Sanvordem saw the fire of the workers, who targeted government property by attacking the police station and burning a railway patrol office. The police fired tear gas shells. I still remember the fear writ large on our faces. The image that is still vivid of that incident is of Alito Sequeira (presently Associate Professor of Sociology, Goa University) wearing a *kurta* with a cloth bag, reassuring us that nothing would happen if we joined the *morcha* (a protest march). The Police had just shot a man in cold blood. That was the first time in my life, as a young girl of 18, that I had a firsthand experience of police brutality. I was petrified then that the next bullet could target one of us.

A few months later, at a protest meeting in Collem, against the high-handedness of a local policeman against a school teacher named Custodio Fernandes, a group of eight girls and about forty villagers were arrested for unlawful assembly. Since we preferred judicial to police custody, we spent a day at the Aguada prison. Adv. Anacleto Viegas represented the students like he always did, without charging any fees. He was, however, perplexed that none of our parents came to meet him, especially since we were all girls. On my release, when I confronted my mother with that question, her reply was very reassuring. She said she had full faith in me and was confident that it was for a social cause and not for the wrong reasons that I was in prison. I remember writing in my Confidential Report as a Gazetted Officer Grade I about this arrest, and again in the following year, when this case was withdrawn by the government. That case was the famous Desmond D'Costa *versus* The State.

Looking back, I find that all the members of the PSU were extremely committed individuals. None of us were career minded like the present generation is. The most positive fall out was that all of us studied as much as we could, so as to remain students of the Union for as long as possible. Some of us who started working as school teachers supported the full timers, by contributing a small amount of our even smaller salaries each month. Being fully involved activists, there was never enough time to study. Desmond D'Costa and Edmund Antao were gold medalists amongst us, despite their activities. Desmond, in particular, tutored many of the members, even late at night. Owing to his guidance, many village boys became graduates and are doing well in life.

The Union had a very strong ideological base. The members read a lot of literature like Shetty's booklet on *How Marx failed in Hindu India* (Shetty 1978). The booklet of the Civil and Democratic Rights Movement, Tamil Nadu, titled *New Democratic Revolution and Organization for Civil and Democratic Rights* (Manifesto 1985) was a much respected book of that period. *Mother* by Maxim Gorky was also a must read. Sandesh Prabhudessai's mother, Shobha and Mohandas Loliencar's mother, Premabai were often compared with the protagonist of this book. Both have since passed away, but to date (even after a period of 30 years) they are still fondly referred to by all of us as our *Aaee*.

The members were sometimes accused as being Marxist in orientation. Other than Marxism being often viewed by the Roman Catholic Church as anti-religion and anti-Christ, there seemed to be no problem with being labelled a Marxist. In the study circles we discussed ways and means to help the poor; we were convinced that the 'state machinery' was using the police to safeguard the interests of the capitalists as against the workers. If these were Marxist views we had no qualms in being called 'Marxists'. The movement had a very strong intellectual base; every action was taken after discussion and debate. If Marxism makes a person sensitive to the injustices and evils present in our society and if Marxism makes one 'question the wrongs,' then our society could do with a few more Marxists. Somewhere at the back of their mind, every PSU member, I am sure, suffers the pain of not fulfilling the tasks that we all dreamt about and had together set out to achieve.

This movement was successful because it fitted into a particular moment and space in Goa's history. The previous generation had shown the way. The Goan ethos had been moulded with stories of courage in the face of persecution by the Portuguese authorities. Each family in Goa had a role to play in the freedom struggle. Some were more actively involved (as prisoners in Portuguese prisons) than others, while many worked underground for fear of getting arrested. Our generation inherited this legacy. Some parents of our colleagues were not very sympathetic to the activities of the Union, while others such as Sandesh Prabhudessai's mother, and Mohandas Loliencar's mother, are both fondly remembered for the largess of their heart in cooking meals for all of us at short notice. It was basically fear and the protective shield that all parents have towards their children. It needed great courage for a parent to come to terms with the fact that his or her 'child was in prison', however worthy and noble the cause may be. Today, if my 21-year-old daughter was imprisoned I would definitely not respond in the same 'chilled out manner' in which my mother responded more than 30 years ago.

The Union had the backing of all right thinking individuals. Politicians knew that the members could not be bought for a price. The PSU had the societal backing that it deserved. Help came from strangers. Adv Dukhle from Quepem stood as security for those that were arrested after the Collem incident without knowing any one of the arrested. Adv Viegas fought all the legal cases without charging us a penny. The villagers of Ibrampur in Pernem welcomed us in their home during the village camps. The members respected each other for the principles that each was pickled in.

Conclusion

From the Students Union we graduated to the Civil Liberties Movement and the Navjavan Bharat Sabha (a youth organisation which mobilised workers to fight for their rights). Police brutalities were openly condemned. As a non-political organisation, we volunteered as witnesses to expose these brutalities—even when people in the streets, who were actual witnesses, chickened out of testifying at judicial inquires because of the fear of police reprisals. The courage came from the fact that if others were bold, so could we; especially for a just cause, we just toed the line. Today there is a reversal of faith. Corruption is almost justified because it is so rampant in the society of today. Nobody will deny that there is a strong need for a civil liberties movement in Goa today.

Many members continued their activism in forums of their choice. Sabina Martins went on to lead a woman's collective, Bailancho Saad, and is now very active in the Goa Bachao Abhiyan. Roland Martins found his calling in the 'Consumer movement'. Desmond D'Costa joined the judiciary. He was the most intelligent of us all, topping the university every year, and breaking every Bombay University record. Prashant Naik is still very active in the Konkani movement and worked as the President of the Konkani Bhasha Mandal. Sandesh Prabhudessai entered the field of the media, first the print media, as editor of the Konkani newspaper, *Sunaprant* and then television. Cleofato Almeida Coutinho resigned from the judiciary to practice law and has contributed positively to society as a member of the Goa Law Commission. Some like me became teachers in schools and colleges.

Dr. Bernadette Gomes gave up a well paid job as a lecturer in a college to do what she always wanted to do but never had the time to do–painting! Her creative talents have been ably proved with each of her exhibitions on Goan themes being 'a total sell-out,' but for our Burny commercial success has never been a criterion of excellence. I was re-appointed as Vice-Principal of my college for two tenures and later completed my Doctorate in the History of Goa. Prashanti Talpankar is an Associate Professor and a research scholar. She is also well known as a stage and cinema actress in Konkani dramas and films. Ratnamala Diukar has recently won a prize for her contribution to children's literature in Konkani. Mohandas Loliencar is a very successful business man. Edmund Antao surprised us all in choosing to be a very active and dedicated member of the Crusaders for Christ Movement.

Meeting like-minded individuals was the sweet fallout of the movement. A lot of the members felt more secure among our own; maybe that was a major criteria why most of us chose life partners within the organisation. Where else would one meet a person who had no objection to their spouse going to jail, if need be, in the future? The comradely feeling that the members of the Students Union once shared has still not waned. On August 1, 2011, our whole group, along with their families met to commemorate the 30th anniversary of the formation of the PSU.

All of us have retained our maternal surnames after marriage with the full support of our spouses. This organisation moulded a large number of individuals into honest and responsive citizens. Perhaps that's one reason why most were picked up in the job market and are doing reasonably well in their chosen vocations. Our association with the Union made us very strong in our fundamentals. All of us are fearlessly independent, and still not afraid of being imprisoned for a right cause. One may call it 'romanticism of a lost cause' or 'youthful foolhardiness', but it was an effort to fight against injustice, a commitment to the underdogs of society and a sincere attempt to bring about a change, which we termed as the, 'new democratic revolution'. The essence of that students' movement was the fact that it remained apolitical till the end. The lack of that attribute is perhaps why movements, more often than not, lose their credibility today.

REFERENCES

Author unknown. 1982. "Call to observe August 14, 1982 as Anti-Repression Day". Pamphlet, 14 August. Mumbai: The Revolutionary Student Organizations' Co-ordination Committee.

Loliencar, Mohandas. May 5, 2010. Personal interview. Margao.

Manifesto. 1985. *New Democratic Revolution and Organization for Civil and Democratic Rights.* Tamil Nadu: Organization for Civil and Democratic Rights.

Martins, Beethoven. 1981. "A camper writes...". *Udent*, November, I (IV): 12. Edited by Cleofato A. Coutinho. Margao: Kaveri Corporation Printers.

Martins, Roland. 1982. "Goans in the movement: Evagrio George". *Udent*, August, II (II): 9, 11. Margao: Navdeep Pvt Ltd.

Mendes, Sushila. 1982. "Pernem camp survey". *Udent*, December, II (V): 9, 10. Margao: Navdeep Pvt Ltd.

Miranda, Avertino. 1982. "Flashes from Goan History IV: Menezes Braganza–the Fiery Patriot". *Udent*, February, I (VI and VII): 5. Margao: Kaveri Corporation.

Miranda, Avertino, and Tina Xavier. 1982. "In defence of hutment dwellers". *Udent*, March, I (III): 5. Margao: Kaveri Corporation.

Nariman, Fali S. 2010. *Before memory fades: An Autobiography*. New Delhi: Hay House India.

Pinto Almeida, Mario. April 4, 2010. Personal interview. Margao.

Shetty, V.Y. Rajshekar. 1978. *How Marx failed in Hindu India*. Bangalore: Karnataka Rationalist Association.

Suraiya, Jug. 2005. "Looking for Naxals". In 'Jugular Vein', *Times of India*, February 20: 4.

Udent. 1981a. "Ramnathi and After". News report, August, I (I): 9-10. Margao: Kaveri Corporation.

Ibid. b. "Here we come." Editorial: 1–2.

Ibid. c. "Kotigao anatomy of a Goan village". News report: 2.

Ibid. d. "Help the physically handicapped": 4.

Ibid. e. "Students expose exercise-books racket". New briefs: 5.

Ibid. f. "Canacona Higher Secondary Students on warpath". News report: 6, 9.

Ibid. g. "Thane people's problem and the students". News report: 5.

Udent. 1981a. Editorial board. September-October, I (II and III). Margao: Kaveri Corporation.

Ibid. b. "Demand for Students Council in St. Xaviers' H.S.S". News roundup: 5.

Ibid. c. "Neturlim high school in a toilet". News roundup: 9.

Udent. 1982a. Editor and Staff Team. June, II (I): 2. Margao: Navdeep Pvt Ltd.

Ibid. b (Author unknown). "Goans in the Movement: Mark Fernandes": 8, 12. Margao: Navdeep Pvt. Ltd.

Udent. 1982. "Chief Minister betrays students". November, II (IV): 1, 4, 10. Margao: Navdeep Pvt Ltd.

Udent. 1982. "Punjab students' union joins RSOCC". News roundup, December, II (V): 13. Margao: C.A. Coutinho. Navdeep Pvt Ltd Printers.

Udent. 1984. "I sell my body… I have to...!". *Udent* special, January, III (V): 11. Sanvordem: U.K. Printers.[2]

Wagle, Vishnu. 1981. "Flashes from Goan History II: Shennoi Goembab". *Udent*, November, I (IV): 7. Margao: Kaveri Corporation.

1. This article was written by me. It was, however, published without my name.

Chapter 6

The Struggle against SEZs in Goa*

Savio Abreu

The struggle against Special Economic Zones (SEZs) in Goa is aptly expressed in the slogan *'Amkam SEZ naka, amkam PEZ zai'* (we do not want SEZ, we want PEZ, that is, People's Economic Zone; in Konkani *pez* also means rice water, which is normally drunk around mid-morning). This was the slogan of the people's movement against SEZs in Goa. The image of Goa projected by the media and the tourist industry is that of scantily clad foreigners sun bathing on the golden beaches, a large number of churches in magnificent Baroque style, numerous wayside crosses and, of course, locals who are easy going, laid back and fun loving. But in the recent past the state has grabbed the headlines for very different reasons. Goa became the first state to successfully fight against SEZs and force the government to reject all the 15 SEZs in Goa, even the three notified ones. This is a report of the successful struggle by various people's movements that has caught the imagination of the entire country and has served as a catalyst for similar people's movements against SEZs and other forms of land grab by the government and big private players in other parts of the country.

Genesis of the Struggle

Goa is the smallest state in India with respect to total area, with only 3,702 sq. km, and one of the smallest in terms of total population,

---

* This article first appeared in *Social Action*, July-Sept., 2008, Vol. 58, No. 3 and is reproduced with the permission of the Editor, *Social Action*.

which is only 13.5 lakh (according to the 2001 Census). In such a small state the Goa government has tried to bring in not just one or two but 18 SEZs promising to generate 3.76 lakh jobs, according to the government statement made in the Assembly. The first mention of SEZ was made in 2003 when the then Chief Minister, Manohar Parrikar told UNI, "We are very much serious to have the SEZ set up in Goa and the proposal is likely to come up for clearance before the cabinet shortly" (*Herald* May 19, 2003, 3). The idea was that if several export-oriented industries exist at one of the industrial zones such as Verna Industrial Estate, that zone could itself be converted into a SEZ within 12-18 months. And so Mr. Parrikar directed the Managing Director of the Goa Industrial Development Corporation (GIDC) to earmark land for food parks and biotech parks in the then newly acquired land in Verna at a meeting held on December 29, 2004 (*Goan Observer* Jan. 12-18, 2008, 4). In keeping with this plan the Goa government sent 16 applications for setting up SEZs in Goa to the Board of Approvals in 2006. In a short span of time huge tracts of land had been handed over to companies and more so without taking the local people into consideration. Since the Special Economic Zones Act of 2005 and the Special Economic Zones Rules, 2006, came into effect on February 10, 2006, seven SEZs were approved, of which three were notified. The notified SEZs in Goa are: Cipla's Meditab Specialities Pvt. Ltd., notified on April 10, 2007; K. Raheja Corporation, November 6, 2007; and Peninsula Pharma Research Centre, July 10, 2007. The list of the approved SEZs along with details of place, area and other requirements is given in Table 6.1.

Fraud in Land Allocation to SEZs

The information obtained by members of the SEZ Virodi Manch (SVM is a people's movement against SEZs, supported by various non-governmental organisations such as Council for Social Justice and Peace, Jagrut Goem and Goa Bachao Abhiyan) through RTI reveals that there has been no assessment study conducted by the State government to study the impact of these SEZs on the people living in the villages. In addition, no discussion was held in the Legislative Assembly on this issue. By analysing the information obtained through RTI from the (GIDC), and Directorate of Industries,

Table 6.1: List of approved SEZs in Goa

Name of the Developer	*Place*	*Area (lakh sq m)*	*Electricity required (MW per day)*	*Water required (lakh litres per day)*	*Employ-ment*	*Status*
Meditab Specialities Pvt. Ltd., Kundaim, Goa	Keri, Ponda	12.32	30	100	100,000	Notified SEZ
Peninsula Pharma Research Centre Pvt. Ltd.	Sanco ale	2.04	20	1.18	25,000	Notified SEZ
K. Raheja Corporation Pvt. Ltd., Mumbai	Verna	7.92	96	40.6	50,000	Notified SEZ
Paradigm Logistics & Distribution Pvt. Ltd., Mumbai	Verna	2.65	36	16.61	50,000	Approved SEZ
Inox Mercantile Company Pvt. Ltd., Mumbai	Verna	5.52	48	2.79	50,000	Approved SEZ
Planetview Mercantile Company Pvt. Ltd., Mumbai	Verna	1.32	13	0.73	25,000	Approved SEZ
Maxgrows Finlease Pvt. Ltd., New Delhi	Verna	2.04	01	0.5	5,000	Approved SEZ

Source: SEZ Virodi Manch (SVM); *SEZ ki Zameen Ghotala; Atharva,* 22-24.

the SVM found several fraudulent allocations of land to different companies who had sent their application to the government to put up a SEZ.

In the case of Peninsula Research Centre Pvt. Ltd. in Sancoale the, company was not even registered at the time of application, but "under formation". Secondly, the company applied for 2 lakh sq. m, while the GIDC granted it 2.04 lakh sq. m at the 286th Board Meeting held on March 28, 2006. Similarly, in the case of Planetview Mercantile Company Pvt. Ltd. in Verna, the company was not registered at the time of application. Interestingly, page 5 of the application says Gems and Jewellery SEZ but page 7 describes it as a Biotech Park. In the case of Cipla's Meditab Specialities Pvt. Ltd. in Keri, proforma GIDC application form was not submitted and so there are no details about projects to be manufactured, daily water and power requirements, etc., in the application submitted on April 3, 2006. Land measuring 12.32 lakh sq m was allotted to Meditab at the 286th Board Meeting held on March 28, 2006, even before receiving the application. This is without the mandatory seven-day notice to the Board of Directors and without time to study the project and its impact on the area.

In the case of K. Raheja Corporation Pvt. Ltd. in Verna,, the application was dated April 12, 2006, while the allotment was made on April 19, without proper time to study the project and without the required seven-day notice to the Board of Directors for the meeting. There is neither an inward stamp nor company seal on the application, both of which are required. Nearly 7.92 lakh sq. m land was allotted at the rate of Rs. 600 per sq. m, and additional land of 2.75 lakh sq m in the form of open spaces and internal roads was allotted initially free of cost and subsequently, at the 295th Board Meeting on March 9, 2007, at the rate of Rs. 100 per sq. m. While several companies in the Verna Industrial Estate are new companies with no experience at all, K. Raheja is purely a real estate developer. In the case of Reteline Exports Pvt. Ltd. in Quitol, Betul, several irregularities have been found. The government invoked an urgency clause to acquire land for Auxiliary Services for Food Park measuring 4.28 lakh sq. m under section 17, sub-sections 1 and 4. Of the acquired land, 2.5 lakh sq. m belong to a tribal çommunity in Goa called *gaudde.* This land has a huge plantation of coconut trees, cashew trees and other fruit-bearing trees. For the tribals the land is the only source of livelihood and it belongs to 40 families. The people of Betul passed a Gram Sabha Resolution on January 26, 2007, stating that no land should be acquired for the Auxiliary Services for Food Park and that the project should be scraped.

Irregularities in land allocation are also seen in the case of Inox Mercantile Company Pvt. Ltd. in Verna, where the area allotted is 5.52 lakh sq. m, which is in excess of the 4.85 lakh sq. m which the company had applied for. In fact, in the application made by this company, the area requested for earlier was 5.52 lakh sq. m, which was thereafter cancelled and decreased to 4.85 lakh sq. m. How did the Board officials come to know about the initial figure of 5.52 lakh sq. m and allot the same to Inox Company? Financial irregularities are also seen in the case of Paradigm Logistics and Distribution Pvt. Ltd. in Verna, which had paid Rs. 31,730,228 *vide* Receipt No. PNJ-51 dated 17/04/2006, even prior to the approval of the Board Meeting dated 19/04/2006. This raises serious questions about how the payment was made and received for allotment of plot even prior to the Board taking the decision of allotment.

Reasons for People's Opposition

From the above cases the following issues arise. The first is that allocation of land was done in a hurry and without following proper rules and regulations. These companies, mentioned above, have been specifically floated for the purpose of grabbing huge tracts of land under the guise of SEZ. The main issue concerning SEZs in Goa is that they seem to be nothing but big land scams. Very important questions were raised by the anti-SEZ movement, such as: On what basis did the GIDC and the Government of India accord approval to applications for SEZs in Goa? Was any detailed socio-economic study done to determine the most suitable location for these industries and their basic requirements? Was any Environment Impact Assessment conducted by the industries? Is there any Master Plan for the industrial development of Goa?

The GIDC, being a statutory body, has to advertise in the daily newspapers while disposing of any property belonging to it, and the property is required to be sold by auction or tender so that no loss is caused to the revenue of the state. The disposal of the land for SEZs in such a haphazard manner and at prices below the market value has adversely affected the revenue of the state. In addition, the said land was not acquired for SEZs nor has it been declared as SEZ area and no Resolution has been passed by the Board to change the purpose of acquisition. While the land was originally acquired solely for industrial purposes it has now been allotted for SEZs which will have a land use incorporating industrial, commercial as well as residential. The Board also resolved to waive the transfer fee, sub-lease fee, etc., to these companies, without even a request for the same from the applicants and without the matter being on the Agenda, thereby draining out the public exchequer and giving the impression that these private companies were doing a big favour to the economy of Goa by coming to Goa. These issues point to a fraud being played out on public revenue and the people of Goa by government officials in connivance with these companies, with politicians also involved (*Goan Observer*, 4-6).

Another important issue concerning SEZs in Goa was that of the strain on natural resources, especially water. As seen from Table 6.1, all the companies would require a large amount of water and electricity supply per day and a lot of manpower; the Companies would also carry on a substantial amount of construction activities. The approval for allotment of land to these companies has been given without the preparation of any Feasibility Report or, for that matter, without even taking into consideration the prevailing ground realities as regards water and electricity supply, or what impact the said construction activity would have on the environment. At an awareness programme organised by SEZ Watch and Jagrut Goem on September 27, 2007, the convenor of Jagrut Goem, Aravind Bhatikar, warned the people about the ramifications of SEZs on the state's water, land and other resources over the next five years, that is, till 2011 (*Herald* [Sept. 28, 2007], 4). These SEZs would lead to the depletion of the water tables and other environmental problems. As it is, people in Goa suffer from the problem of inadequate water supply and the deficit of water is estimated to be 215 MLD.

The SVM put an advertisement in the newspaper with the caption 'SEZ: Selling Goa and Goans' (*Herald* [Dec. 1, 2007] 7). In that and they put forth the reasons why Goans are opposing SEZs. The SEZ developers have stated in their applications that a workforce of around 3 lakh people would come to Goa along with their families. Our roads, water and power supply, garbage management facilities are already crumbling and will not be able to sustain around 8-10 lakh people who will come to Goa on account of SEZs. Since the laws of Goa do not apply to SEZs, it will be difficult for Goans to stop manufacturing processes from all over the world being undertaken in these SEZs, which might pollute our water, air and environment and destroy Goa for our future generations. SEZs were conceptualised for bigger states which have plenty of cheap labour and barren land. Goa has neither. SEZ is not suitable for Goa.

In that same advertisement, the SVM questioned the government argument that the SEZs would deliver a bonanza of jobs to the Goan youth. The central attraction of the SEZ scheme has been the facile assumption that handing over thousands of hectares of land cheaply to promoters of industry and relaxing the laws of the land, including those that relate to the welfare of the industrial workers, protection of the environment, taxation, etc., would automatically promote industrialisation and solve the nagging unemployment problem of the country overnight. The SVM questioned this assumption by asking: 'Despite the government's promises, have Goans got decent employment from industrial estates? Why are Goan villages filled with migrant workers? Why have Goans become a minority in their own land? The SVM cautioned the Goans to learn from their experiences in the past. We have lost our land to industrial estates, but our children still have to go out of Goa for jobs. SEZs will not be different' (*Herald* [December 1, 2007], 7). In a hard-hitting editorial in one of the local newspapers, Averthanus L. D'Souza refuted the position of the government and various business houses that SEZs would lead to creation of massive job opportunities (*Herald* [December 11, 2007], 6). In another article, 'Continuing SEZures' (*Herald* [December 24, 2007], 8), he brings out the arbitrary manner in which the land, natural resources and environment of Goa are getting decimated due to the *ad hoc* and completely unscientific basis on which the Government of Goa has been allocating land for various uses. He argues that though about 400,000 jobs are estimated to be created by the different SEZs, there is no indication of what kind of jobs would they be and what their educational and skill requirements would be. Local information indicates that about 90,000 persons are listed on the rolls of the Employment Exchange. According to Averthanus L. D'Souza, even if all these 90,000 people are absorbed in the SEZs they will still require around 3 lakh workers who will have to be imported from outside the state. By estimating on an average four dependents per person, Goa will have to cater to the needs of approximately 1,200,000 more persons who will take up residence in Goa (this would almost double Goa's population in the next five years). This will put an enormous strain on the infrastructure as these workers will have to be provided with houses, and all the basic amenities like water supply, electricity, garbage disposal, transportation, etc. Averthanus L. D'Souza predicted a complete breakdown of all basic infrastructure services within the next five years if the government goes forward with the programme of setting up the SEZs.

The Success of the Anti-SEZ Movement

While the people's struggle against SEZs in Goa gained momentum and grew in numbers and intensity only in the later part of 2007, opposition to the SEZs existed much before that. When information of the intention of the Government of India to approve SEZs in Goa was made known, even before the Goa government had received any SEZ proposals, in July 2005 the Council for Social Justice and Peace had organised a symposium in collaboration with other local bodies (Fernandes 2007). This symposium was a realistic balancesheet on SEZs in Goa and the government was forcefully cautioned against approving any SEZ in Goa. While there were a few scattered articles in the local dailies warning about the possible implications of SEZs in Goa right from 2005 when the SEZ policy was accepted by politicians in Goa, general awareness spread among the people only in 2007 when villagers and concerned citizens began agitating against the SEZs in various parts of Goa like Keri, Pernem, Sancoale, Loutolim, Verna and Quitol. This struggle of the villagers gained momentum when it got support from various NGOs like Council for Social Justice and Peace, Jagrut Goem, Swadesh and Goa Bachao Abhiyan, and they came together under the banner of SVM. Formed in mid-2007, the SVM is an apolitical issue-based movement which drew its strength from different people's movement at the grassroots level against SEZs across the state. Most of the members of SVM are from the middle class and that has been the strength of the movement. Some of the members painstakingly gathered a lot of information on the SEZ projects by filing hundreds of RTIs from early 2007; using that information they filed an FIR against the chairman and the directors of the GIDC Board on October 22, 2007. This complaint has not yet been registered by the Goa police. Details and proof of the alleged illegalities of the GIDC regarding the land scam in the prime industrial area of the Verna Plateau were given to the police in the FIR that had been filed.

The agitation against SEZ projects in Goa gained momentum in November and December 2007 through several awareness meetings in different parts of Goa which were attended by people in large numbers. One such solidarity meeting organised by the SVM at the historic Lohia Maidan in Margao on December 14, 2007, was attended by thousands of people. Well-known social activist Medha Patkar's letter expressing support to the people of Goa in their fight against SEZs was also read out in that meeting (*Herald* [Dec. 15, 2007], 1, 3). The anti-SEZ movement was also boosted by the support of political parties like the BJP, NCP (*Herald* [Nov. 13, 2007], 3), college youth under the banner Youth for Goa (*Herald* [Dec. 1, 2007], 3) and some politically backed groups like Goa's Movement against SEZs (GMAS) who put lot of pressure on the government to scrap all SEZs in Goa. The opportunism of the politicians to grab the limelight in this people's struggle is described by Ervell E. Menezes who says, "Meanwhile the politicians are all jumping on the anti-SEZ bandwagon because they only wait for a platform from which to derive mileage" (*Herald* [Dec. 14, 2007], 6). The differences between the political and apolitical organisations opposing the SEZs came to the fore in a public meeting held in Verna by 'Youth for Goa' (*Herald* [Dec. 21, 2007], 3). The position held by non-political organisations like SVM was that most of the politicians in Goa, irrespective of which party they belonged to, had vested interests and stood to benefit from the development of SEZs and so taking the support of politicians in the anti-SEZ struggle would damage the integrity of the struggle (*Goan Observer*, 4-6).

The snowballing of the anti-SEZ movement forced the Congress government to constitute a Cabinet sub-committee on November 14 to examine and arrive at a decision on SEZs (*Herald* [Nov. 16, 2007], 1; *Herald* [Nov. 15, 2007], 3). The growing opposition to SEZs in Goa also forced the Goa Chamber of Commerce and Industry (GCCI) to recommend to the government to set up a SEZ review committee wherein all the concerned parties/stakeholders be allowed to make a detailed presentation of their positions (*Herald* [Nov. 21, 2007], 4). The GCCI also urged the government to take appropriate steps following the outcome of the review committee.

The anti-SEZ agitation was supported by knowledgeable, challenging and thought-provoking articles, editorials and regular features in the local newspapers. The media gave a lot of publicity to the struggle and that kept the pressure on the Goa government. The active involvement of Goan intellectuals and the Goan middle class in the anti-SEZ movement was one of the main reasons for the success of the movement.

Finally, on December 31, 2007, the Goa government decided to scrap all the SEZs in their present form (*Herald* [Jan. 1, 2008], 1). This decision was reached at a meeting of the Cabinet Committee on Infrastructure after taking into consideration the 'White Paper on SEZ in Goa' (*Herald* [Dec. 30, 2007], 1) and the Task Force recommendations (*Herald* [Dec. 31, 2007], 1). December 31, 2007, will go down as a special day in the history of people's movements in Goa since people's power dared the political establishment and succeeded in ensuring that development is for the benefit of the people and not a few elites.

Many reasons can be attributed to the success of the anti-SEZ movement in Goa, such as, the role of the middle class intellectuals, the extensive use of RTI to get information and expose land frauds, the collaboration and working together of different NGOs, the linking of SEZ to the loss of Goan identity due to huge influx of migrant workers, the linking of SEZ to the control and use of natural resources like land, water and forests, etc. What needs to be highlighted is the strength and resilience of civil society seen in the spirited struggle and never-say-die approach of the villagers of the affected areas, who fearlessly stormed into police stations, into government offices, into the Chief Minister's office, and who were even prepared to take on the SEZ developers by physically stopping the development work on the SEZ sites. They were the real heroes of the anti-SEZ struggle. One of the fallouts of this movement is the increased general awareness and activism among the villagers of Goa against any form of land grab, especially against the big real estate developers.

The Struggle Continues

The decision of the Goa government on December 31, 2007, to scrap all the 15 SEZs does not mean that the anti-SEZ struggle is over. A very important follow-up is bringing the guilty to book. The then leader of the Opposition, Manohar Parrikar, and the alliance partners had also demanded investigations against those who have violated the process of land allocation to the SEZ projects, and also a White Paper on land allocated for SEZs (*Herald* [Jan. 4, 2008], 6; *Herald* [Jan. 16, 2008], 1). The SVM, which spearheaded the people's movement against SEZs, had demanded that the government order a CBI inquiry into the whole SEZ imbroglio and the illegal functioning of the GIDC regarding the land scam in Verna Plateau (*Herald* [Jan. 26, 2008], 12). To the demand of taking back land allocated for SEZs, the then Chief Minister Digambar Kamat had said, "I will cross the bridge when I come to it" (*Herald* [Jan. 12, 2008], 1), but later the GIDC in a board meeting on June 13, 2008, had decided to revoke the land allotted by it to seven companies for setting up SEZs in Goa (*The Times of India* [Jun. 14, 2008], 1). The GIDC also decided to refund the money paid by SEZ promoters to the corporation for the land, roughly around Rs 100 crore. The people's movement will have to pursue this matter and ensure that the guilty in the SEZ land scam are punished. Charles Fernandes, the convenor of SVM, said that while the decision of the government to take back land from the SEZ promoters is good, their battle is to see that those responsible for the fraud land allotments are brought to book and the land should be handed over to its original owners and not to the GIDC (*Herald* [Jun. 14, 2008], 1).

The matter of scrapping the three notified SEZs is still pending and the battle has now shifted to the legal arena. The State government realised it had no legal authority to denotify the three notified SEZs, which have already become legal entities, and so referred the matter to the Central Government. But after dilly-dallying on the issue for several months the Union Ministry of Commerce refused to denotify them (*Herald* [June 3, 2008], 1). According to them the developers of the three notified SEZs have already made investments and the issue of compensation of investments made and also refund of fiscal benefits would arise. Therefore, they decided that it would not be possible for the Central Government to withdraw the notifications declaring them as SEZs. The major challenge before the SVM and other anti-SEZ organisations is to be a watchdog and put pressure on the government to denotify the three notified SEZs. According to legal experts, if the government denotifies these zones they will probably have to compensate the developers (*Herald* [Feb. 29, 2008], 1). On the other hand, the SVM has directed the Goa government to flatly refuse to pay compensation to the SEZ promoters and, on the contrary, ask them to pay heavily for rampant hill cutting and other works carried out on the allotted land that have led to wells and springs drying up (*Herald* [March 5, 2008], 2). While three SEZ promoters—Cipla's Meditab, K. Raheja and Panchabhumi—are fighting a legal battle in the High Court against the Goa government, the villagers of Loutolim, Verna, etc., have filed three separate petitions before the High Court challenging the impropriety of the Goa government and the GIDC in allotting land to set up SEZs in Goa (*Herald* [May 2, 2008], 1). The petitioners have asked the High Court to issue a writ quashing the land allotments made to the SEZ developers. So the battle against the SEZ promoters is only half won and will have to be pursued to its logical end.

The anti-SEZ struggle in Goa was neither an anti-development movement nor was it against industries. The anti-SEZ stir has grown and broadened into a struggle for the control and proper utilisation of natural resources, especially land, and a general awareness and activism is visible in many parts of Goa, seen particularly in the stand taken by some Gram Sabhas against big real estate developers. But the challenge before civil society movements in Goa is to find alternatives to the development model that promotes big projects like SEZs. Otherwise the danger is that the government and big business interests will reintroduce the SEZs in other forms like food parks, IT parks, etc. Dr. Marian Pinheiro, in an editorial article 'SEZ: How many more?' suggested alternatives to SEZs such as inviting the world's best educational institutes and universities to set up shop in Goa so that Goa could become the world's Special Education Zone (*Herald* [Jan. 22, 2008], 6). He also proposes making Goa a Special Healthcare Zone and a Special Tourist Zone. Whatever the alternative models, the intellectuals in the SVM and other people's organisations need to come up with development models that are ecologically sustainable, people-friendly and take into consideration the socio-economic and cultural status of Goa, otherwise the widespread awareness and activism will only lead to general discontent and unrest.

REFERENCES

2003. "Government serious to have SEZ set up in Goa: CM". *Herald*, May 19: 3.

2007. "Jagrut Goem explains ramifications of SEZs". *Herald*, September 28: 4.

2007. "NCP too joins anti-SEZ chorus". *Herald*, November 13: 3.

2007. "GPCC to appoint panel to study SEZ issue". *Herald*, November 15: 3.

2007. "Govt panel to examine SEZ". *Herald*, November 16: 1.
2007. "GCCI proposes government set up SEZ review panel". *Herald*, November 21: 4.
2007. "All you wanted to know about SEZs". *Herald*, December 1: 7.
2007. "Students pledge to fight unitedly against SEZs". *Herald*, December 1: 3.
2007. "Noted activist Medha Patkar comes out against SEZs". *Herald*, December 15: 3.
2007. "War drums sound against SEZs". *Herald*, December 15: 1.
2007. *The Navhind Times*, December 15: 1, 16.
2007. "Differences among anti-SEZ groups comes to fore at Verna meeting". *Herald*, December 21: 3.
2007. "Govt unprepared to host SEZs, reveals report". *Herald*, December 30: 1.
2007. "Scrap SEZs, proposes Task Force". *Herald*, December 31: 1.
2008. "Govt decides to dump SEZs". *Herald*, January 1: 1.
2008. "SEZ Chors?" *Goan Observer*, January 12–18.
2008. "Take back land allotted for SEZs, Oppn tells govt". *Herald*, January 12: 1.
2008. "Now guns turned on SEZ 'plotters'". *Herald*, January 16: 1.
2008. *Atharva*, February 1, III (2).
2008. "Govt to use 1897 Act to denotify Goa SEZs?" *Herald*, February 29: 1.
2008. "CM warned over attempts to foist SEZs on Goa". *Herald*, March 5: 2.
2008. "SEZ: people move court over land". *Herald*, May 2: 1.
2008. "SEZ Thunders". *Herald*, June 3: 1.
2008. "Goa decides to revoke SEZ land allotment". *The Times of India*, June 14: 1.
2008. "Govt to take back land from 7 SEZs". *Herald*, June 14: 1.
BJP (Bharatiya Janata Party). *SEZ ki Zameen Ghotala*. A leaflet issued by the Goa wing of the BJP.
De Abreu, Caetano. 2007. "The Alchemy Under SEZ?" *Herald*, November 22: 6.
De Silva, Orville. 2007–08. "Goa: Sold for a Song". *Nityasangam*, December 2007–January 2008, II (10): 3, 5.
De Souza, Juino. 2008. "SEZs: Scoring a tactical win". *Herald*, January 4: 6.
D'Souza, L. Averthanus. 2007. "More SEZures". *Herald*, December 11: 6.
———. 2008. "Dissipative Governance-I". *Herald*, January 26: 12.
Fernandes, Maverick. 2007. "Council for Social Justice and Peace (CSJP)". *Renewal*, December 16–31, XXXVI (24): 22, 23.
Menezes, E. Ervell. 2007. "Road to glory". *Herald*, December 14: 6.
Pinheiro, Marian. 2008. "SEZ: How many more?" *Herald*, January 22: 6.

CHAPTER 7

Sons of the Mountains

The Gouly of Goa

BERNADETTE GOMES

Introduction

Communities have evolved within specific ecological niches. Nevertheless, each community gets its essential identity from the history and environment it finds itself in. Goa is no exception to this. Communities such as the 'Mitgaude', 'Agri', evolved around the salt-making areas, 'Reinder' around toddy-tapping in the plains and groves, and 'Kharvi' around fishing in the coasts. One particular community definitely shaped by its ecology and history is the 'Gouly' of Goa. This paper traces their evolution from a self-sufficient, nomadic, pastoral tribe to the most backward community in Goa, forced into settlement and robbed of its identity.

Methodology

According to a Census conducted by the Department of Social Welfare, in 2003, the present population of the Gouly is 7,583. They constitute 0.56 per cent of the population of Goa. They are distributed in 11 talukas, and live in 114 exclusive hamlets. For the purpose of this survey, 82 hamlets were selected randomly. Sample size of population was 6,801.

The survey consisted of two parts: (a) Collection of anthropological data; and (b) Collection of socio-economic data. The paper will locate the Gouly in the context of the ecology of the Sahayadris, bring out their self-image, and conclude with their present socio-economic status.

The Traditional Gouly Homeland

To understand the Gouly and their present predicament, we have to begin with their physical environment. The eastern half of Goa is hilly and nestles the foothills of the Western Ghats. While the western area has plains lined with sandy beaches, in the eastern half the Sahayadris rise into majestic, steep, breathtaking peaks. Sonsogad, Catlanchi Mauli, Wagheri, Dudhsagar, Karmalghat, Morpila, Saleli, Siddhnath are some of Goa's well known peaks. The ecologically rich environs of the Western Ghats have provided an ideal home for many tribes. The secluded elevated plateaus abound in a variety of grasses and have been an ideal place for pasturage. This is the traditional homeland of the Gouly of Goa.

Etymology

The name 'Gouly' is derived from the root '*gou*' which stands for cattle. The dwelling place is common for people and cattle and is called a *gouvol*. Gouly are the people who dwell with their cattle in a *gouvol*.

Who are the Gouly?

A lot of dust has been raised recently on the origin, racial and regional background of the Gouly. Who are these people? It is difficult to place them in a single racial stock. The members show significant Dravidian and Mediterranean racial traits. J.H. Hutton calls them as Proto-Asians. In Maharashtra they form a large group identified as *Dhangar*. Amongst them are several functional groups that have got specialised and entrenched in the village community as castes. In Goa they live as an independent tribe. They were never a part of the village community system and never lived in the villages along with other populations. An average Gouly is well built and medium to tall in height. They do not display exclusive proto-Austroloid traits (such as the Kunbi) or Mediterranean traits (such as the Toda). Fuchs (1973, 23) says that the aboriginal people are survivors from later prehistoric population groups and the Gouly are a semi-aboriginal tribe clinging to their animal breeding past.

Pastoral communities calling themselves Gavli, Gollas, Gollar, are found in Karnataka. They are entrenched as castes in the village communities. K.S. Singh (2005, 10-11) points out that in India, as compared to other parts of the world, tribes had some reciprocal contact with other communities. Such contacts often led to a tribe evolving as a functional group within the village community system. All tribes did not develop uniformly. Often, patronage given by local kings quickly transformed tribes into caste-like groups and got entrenched in the villages as functional groups. Thurston (1975, 133, 285, 382) has illustrated how Gollas Kurubas, and Irulas in south India were divided as village dwelling groups and forest dwelling groups. The village groups had taken on a caste character and the two did not even intermarry.

Gouly Language

All Gouly in Goa speak Konkani, but they state that their mother tongue is Dhangari, a fact which has led to them being branded as outsiders.

Colonial History and the Gouly

The insulation of the Goa Gouly must be viewed in the context of their ecological setting and the colonial history of Goa. The Portuguese conquered Tiswadi in 1510, then added Bardez and Salcette a few decades later. The other areas such as Antruz, Hembadbarcem, Canacona, Bicholim were under Adilshahi rule.

For nearly two centuries Goa was the area outlined by these three talukas. Accounts of early European travellers are very revealing. The 'Suma Oriental' of Tome Pires (1990) written between 1512 and 1515 has no mention of the Gouly amongst the people of Goa. Jan Huyghen van Linschoten (1988), the Dutch traveller in Goa, around 1598, makes no mention of the Gouly in the Old Conquests of Goa. Francois Pyrard de Laval (1990), a traveller to Goa in 1619, and

Abbe Carre (1990) in 1682 make no mention of the Gouly either. The first Portuguese mention of the name Gouly appears in the Relatorio (1865, 17) at the time of demarcating the areas of Sattari. They are mentioned as '*tribus*' (tribe). Lopes Mendes (1886, 239) writes about the Gouly as 'a pastoral people who live in the mountains of the New Conquests, they live as wanderers and are very wild'. Later Oliveira Mascarenhas (1898: 113) mentions a pastoral community called as Gouly. While this could be cited as one of the reasons why Gouly were missing in the popular accounts of travellers, folklore traditions establish a different reality.

Folklore encodes people's memories, and their relations with the peoples of the region. We get valuable insights into the existence of Gouly interrelations with the rest of the people. Folksongs enacted during the *denlo padvo* festival celebrated by non-Gouly cattle keepers in the plains, have references to Gouly:

Matarechea gharant ponos pikla
Chimti bhor tandleant Gouly lipla.

The *Ranmale*, which is a form of folk theatre, has *savangs* (enactments) referring to the Gouly:

Ami ranantle gouly
bendak bandli ankdi
khandar ghetli ghongodi
mateak bandli pagadi

Some of the *chourong* (folksongs) sung during the Shigmo festival mentions the Gouly. A *dulpod* sung at wedding receptions and parties has references to Gouly from the Ghats:

Ami Goulim,
dudvalim,
devun ailianv
Ghantavelim.

These few examples illustrate the antiquity of the Gouly in the Ghat region.

Insulation of the Gouly

There were two main reasons why the Gouly remained insulated from the rest of society:

* Being pastoral nomads, they preferred to remain within the confines of the elevated plateaus where fodder was available in plenty. They could also freely practice swidden agriculture (slash and burn farming), mainly millet. Reciprocal relations existed for obtaining commodities not available to them. Though they forged *jajmani*-like relations with the neighbouring tribes, Gouly never merged into a composite society; they never came to live as a sub-group in a larger social group.
* Certain colonial dictates added to the territorial exclusion. In 1885 a grazing tax of 50 paise per cattle head was introduced by the Portuguese (Boletim 1885 (No. 73), 290). The Gouly thus preferred to remain in the Ghats, and maintained selective contact with the rest of the communities.

Settlements

The Gouly were a semi-nomadic tribe until very recently. They moved as clans with their cattle and clan gods. The remnants of this way of life can still be seen from the settlement pattern today.

Table 7.1: Clans and Settlement Pattern

Sl. No.	*Taluka*	*Hamlet*	*Total No. of Houses*	*Clan Name*	*Clan Houses*
1	Sattari	Murmune	04	Kalo	04
		Bondir	18	Dhoiefodo	18
2	Ponda	Farmagudi	04	Zoro	04
		Kodar	04	Kholekar	04
		Bhutkhamb	12	Kholekar	11
3	Salcette	Paytemol	07	Shelko	06
4	Quepem	Padimol	13	Yemkar	13
		Karlamodi	11	Bavdano	10
5	Sanguem	Ambeamol	17	Rekdo Zoro	16
		Walkini Col III	07	Varak	06
6	Canacona	Sheli	09	Kholekar	09

Habitation

The dwelling unit is called a *gouvol*. It is a unique hut where people and animals dwell under the same roof. *Gou* stands for cattle, and *vol* stands for an enclosure. Gouly are the people who dwell with their cattle in a *gouvol*. A typical *gouvol* is an elongated rectangular structure. The rear portion is semi-circular. The front portion of the thatch slopes down towards the entrance, forming a crescent shaped arch. The walls are made with strips of cane, woven to form a matting. There is no front door to a *gouvol.*

The front portion of the hut acts as a stable and is reserved for the cattle. The inner portion forms the living area. The rear has a small compartment in which provisions are stored. This room also serves as a shrine to their clan deities.

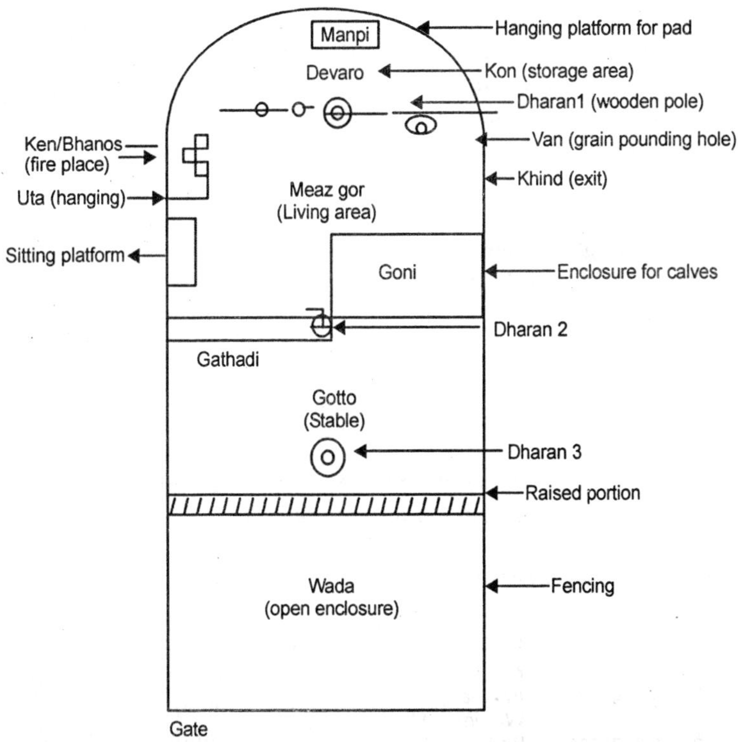

Fig. 7.1: Structure of Gouvol

Dress and Ornaments

The most ethnically significant item of clothing for the men is the *pagoti* (turban) worn on the head, and the *kamol* (blanket) thrown around the shoulder. They may wear loin cloth or a towel around their waist. The *rajkadi* or the earring made of aluminium or brass is the most important ornament for men. They wear a silver bangle called as the *kodem* and an armband called as the *bhavkuri.* The women wear a *sari* called as *chirkut/bonder*. Traditionally women had to wear the *sari* well above the knees. They wore an armband called *tollman* and married women wore a necklace called as *davul.* Very young girls draped a cloth around the waist called as *shepato.*

Social Organisation

The Gouly in Goa live as 27 exogamous clans (*kuls*). The clan name is used as a surname. Some clans have distinct lineage groups (*gharani*). Each clan has its own clan deity, often a female and a male deity. There are some clans which are totemic. They are named after a plant or animal which they treat as sacred. The following are some totemic clans:

* Shingado (antelope).
* Dhoeifodo (buffalo).
* Davno (artemisia pallens).
* Kharvat (ficus asperrima).

Occupation

The Gouly traditionally herded buffalo. They cultivated millet (*nachne*) on the slopes, in the form of *kumeri.*

Pregnancy and Childbirth

There were no special rituals or taboos to be observed during pregnancy. There is no custom of women going over to their maternal home for the birth of a child. Many Gouly women even today are well equipped to deliver a baby singlehandedly. Childbirth is accepted as a matter of fact. The elder women assisted whenever they could.

Gouly women do not observe a period of confinement. Many get back to their chores the next day. On the fifth day, Gouly observes *panchvi*. This is the day when they believe the Goddess comes to visit the child. The mother is ceremonially taken to the stream for a bath. The baby is named and the elders conduct genital worship of the newborn.

Rites of Passage

Every child has to have its head shaved (*zaval kadop*) at the age of one. The mother's brother had the special privilege of cutting the hair. A boy had to wear a turban (*pagoti*) on reaching puberty.

Marriage

Gouly traditionally practiced child marriages and group marriages. *Palneant lagn* is a term which indicated that the bride and the bridegroom were sometime still in the cradle when the betrothal took place. Polygamy was practiced in the past. Today, however, it is rare. Girls and boys had to be betrothed before reaching puberty. The bride could be handed over only after puberty. This was done ceremonially as *ghor bhorovni*. Besides puberty, a young girl's capability to bring home a small herd of cattle was an important qualification to consummate the marriage and shift residence to the conjugal home.

The simple marriage ceremony is preceded by a symbolic marriage ceremony for their respective totem tree. As there is no priesthood amongst the Gouly, the head of another clan performs the marriage rituals. The people raise an invocation to the High Goddess *Malchi Pander*. The elders make a public declaration of the marriage, and seek blessings of the clan deities.

The Gouly observe four types of marriages:

* *Lagn*: Is the usual marriage for both partners.
* *Kapdachem/dhakudponachem lagn*: Marriage between a widow and a widower.
* *Patachem lagn*: Second marriage for a man after the death of, or desertion by, the first wife.
* *Gottnar lagn*: Fourth marriage if the third wife deserted or died.

Kinship

Gouly treat their parents' siblings as their quasi-parents. Mother's sister's children and father's brother's children are quasi-brothers and sisters. No marriage is permitted between parallel cousins.

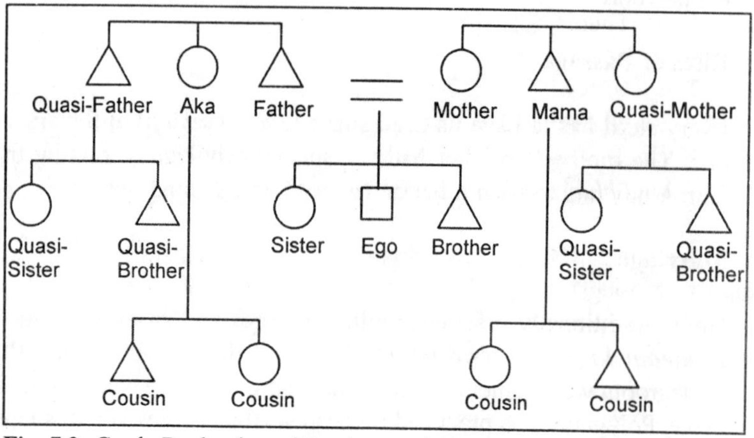

Fig. 7.2: Gouly Reckoning of Brothers and Sisters

A woman has the first privilege of asking her brother's daughter's hand in marriage for her son. Likewise, a man can ask for his sister's daughter's hand in marriage for his son, but such marriages are believed to turn out bad. They are, therefore, rare amongst the Gouly.

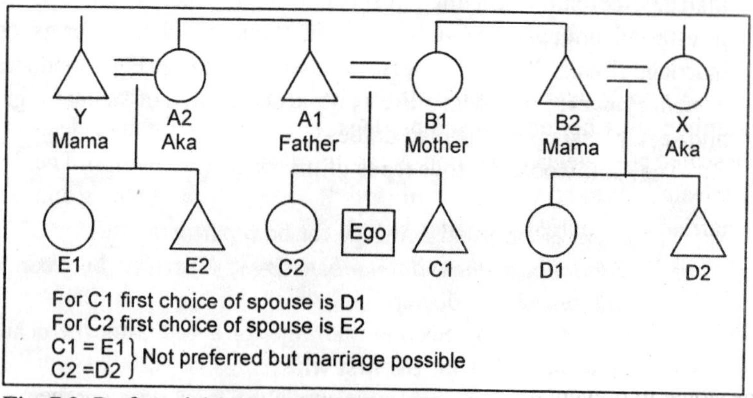

Fig. 7.3: Preferential Spouse from Kin Group

Kinship terminology often points to the nature of relations amongst members of the kin groups. The mother's brother and the father's sister's husband are addressed as *mama*. Likewise, the mother's brother's wife and the father's sister are addressed as *aka*. Kinship is also maintained through a classificatory system of brothers. Marriages are not permitted between the offsprings of those classified as brothers. There are four categories of brothers:

- *Sokko bhav* (blood brother).
- *Bapul bhav* (quasi-brother).
- *Haad bhav* (bone brother).
- *Dud bhav* (milk brother).

Thus bone, milk, and blood are used as idioms to identify kinship relations amongst the Gouly.

Family Structure and Inheritance Rules

The Gouly live as nuclear units. The structure and average size of the *gouvol* did not permit joint residence. The entire clan is functionally joint, behaving as a single homogenous family. The Gouly were traditionally nomadic, as such, they could not possess any immovable assets. The main property they inherited was in the form of cattle and metal implements.

Death and Burial

When a Gouly dies, she/he is first kept in a squatting position, with the back resting against the pole of the hut. The corpse is laid out on a bamboo stretcher and carried out legs first. Gouly bury their dead in a seated cross-legged position. Many have taken to cremation. The burial site is marked with a pile of stones. Boys who died young and unmarried were buried only after a symbolic marriage to the *rui* plant. Gouly males could go to the afterworld only as married men. On the third day after death, a ritual called *mati* is observed. Family members pour *panchamruta* (a mixture of milk, ghee, cow's urine, dung and honey) into the grave through three hollow stalks. Mud is pulled over the stones to prevent wild animals from digging out the grave. Another ritual called *pani* is observed on the 11th day. The dead person is offered food and water at noon. The same night, members of the clan observe a vigil. To keep awake, the elders narrate stories like *Basu Rajachi katha, Kondu rajachi katha*, etc. The spirit of the dead person is brought back to the clan in a symbolic way (*sodun hadop*) after three months. There is no *shradda* after one year.

Memorial Stones

At the time of the burial, a large shale or basalt stone is placed at one end of the burial area. It is always placed upright. This is called as a *visavo*, and represents the dead Gouly member.

Ancestor Worship

Ancestors, or *purwoz*, are all those who die a natural death, leaving behind an offspring. Age and manner of death are important criteria to classify types of spirits. During Dussera, all clan ancestors are served a ceremonial meal at the site of the memorial stones. They are also invoked at all celebrations, weddings, and before undertaking any important activity.

Religion

Gouly cosmogony begins with the fertility of the earth. The soil which gives birth to all plants, which in turn provides fodder to all cattle, is sacred. All of nature is the manifestation of the Goddess *Malchi Pander*, their chief goddess. She is aniconic. Till date there are no statues or temples dedicated to her. The buffalo is the most sacred animal. Gouly are nature worshippers. Being nomadic, they never built temples. They carry the symbols of their clan gods in the form of natural stones called as *tandle*. These are stored in a sacred cane basket, the *pud*. When the clan moved, the *pud too* moved with them. An area in the rear portion of the *gouvol* is reserved for placing the *pud*. Thus, each hut is at once a sacred and mundane space.

The people celebrate Dussera as their main festival. When a clan is in distress, they may make a vow to the goddess. In the following year the same clan invites the male members of the *mhal* to perform the thanksgiving dance, called *powo/gaja*. The women perform a dance called *vakun fugdi*. This is a dance form simulating the movements of buffaloes and is performed only amongst the Gouly.

Dussera celebrations take place over three days. The first night is *zagor*. The sacred platform *manpi*, which houses the basket with the sacred stones, is decorated with bamboo strips and five coconuts. The clan led by the elders prays to the goddess and their clan gods. The clan then keeps awake the whole night with folksongs and stories. The second day is *pati*. All the sacred baskets are brought out at a *maand*. The sacred stones (*tandle*) are exposed, and the clans pray together. This is one of the rare occasions when all clan god symbols are brought together and exposed. The third day is *kharga puja*. All implements used in daily life were placed at a temporary altar and invocations are made to the goddess *Malchi Pandeṛ* seeking her blessings for the following year.

The Gouly have two important totem trees: the fig tree (*rumod*) and the *kolam* tree (*anthcephalus cadamba*). Trees like *palas* (*butea monosperma*) and *rui* (*calatropis gigantia*) are considered to be sacred.

The Agarkhase

It is also called the *ayikhase*, the Gouly supreme general body meeting. Only male members can be a part of such meetings. No non-Gouly members can ever take part in an *agarkhase*. There is no hierarchy, but every *agarkhase* must have a moderator (*gaudki*). All community problems are sorted out and justice is meted to those who have erred. The *agarkhase* has the power to declare a social boycott on any family or individual. The most severe punishment is reserved for those causing the death of a buffalo.

Socio-economic Status

The Gouly today are no longer actively nomadic. The pressures of modernity have forced them into a settled lifestyle. For the Gouly, settlement has come along with a great sense of loss of identity. Theirs has been a riches-to-rags story, from a self-image of unchallenged sons of the mountains and plateaus to encroachers in their own land.

Some development indicators point to a very dismal state of the community. Given here are the findings of the study:

Education

* Total population surveyed: 6,801.
* Graduates (male): 25 (0.76%).
* Graduates (female): 10 (0.34%).
* Post-graduate (male): 1.
* Post-graduates (female): 2.
* 12th Std. (male): 73 (6%).
* 12th Std. (female): 27 (1.2%).
* SSC (male): 148 (5.35%).
* SSC (female): 61 (2.4%).

Employment

* Government servants: 89 (2.8 per cent).
  - Doctors: 4;
  - School teachers: 4; and
  - Hawaldar: 7.
* 'D' category employees: 74.
  - Private employment: 78;
  - Self-employed: 234 (3.67 per cent); and
  - Casual labourers: 2,005 (29.5 per cent).
* No regular income: 2,437 (42 per cent).

Basic Amenities

* No PWD water supply: 29 hamlets (35 per cent).
* No electricity: 11 hamlets (13 per cent).

Data Analysis

Out of the 82 hamlets surveyed, 41 had no motorable roads. There are five hamlets where the people have to wade through a stream to reach their homes. These streams swell during the monsoons and make it difficult for children to attend school.

The accessibility of transport depends on the distance of a hamlet from a main road:

* Walking distance 20-30 minutes – 16 hamlets.

* Walking distance 40-60 minutes – 10 hamlets.

The availability of health facilities too depends on transport. Almost all Gouly depend on primary health centres for services. Private health care is rare.

Post-Liberation Scenario

The Gouly of Goa are the least developed community today. Liberation came as a paradox, leading to loss of self-image and a change in identity from native to outsider. They still remain relatively isolated from the rest of the population. Like many tribal communities in modern states, as Vandana Shiva (1991) comments, the rights of indigenous people have not been fully recognised. Their distribution on elevated plateaus and hills has posed special challenges to their integration with the rest of Goan society. Nomadism and language have been additional factors that led to their economic alienation. Nearly 90 per cent have no immovable assets. In most land records they have been listed as encroachers and Dhangari, the spoken language of the Gouly, has never been recognised as one of the spoken languages in Goa.

Their folklore abounds in stories of immense natural wealth gifted to them by the goddess *Malchi Pander*. The *Bosurajachi katha* is a narrative of how several kings came to capture their mountains, but none could conquer the lands endowed to the Gouly. The elders speak of times when ironsmiths and silversmiths came trudging up the Ghats to sell their wares. They had enough wealth to buy what they did not produce and lived as a nation in their own right. The only intruder they say they feared was the occasional leopard. Being just over 7,500 people, they do not constitute a significant vote-bank. Political will, thus, has been weak in the face of meeting challenges of development for the community.

REFERENCES

Carre, Abbe. 1990. *The Travels of Abbe Carre In India and the Near East (1672–1674)*. Translated by Lady Fawsett. New Delhi: Asian Educational Services.

Fuchs, S. 1973. *The Aboriginal Tribes of India*. Delhi: Macmillan India Ltd.

Grierson, G.A. 2005. *Linguistic Survey of India*. Delhi: Low Price Publications.

Hutton, J.H. 1951. *Dhangar Caste in India*. Bombay.

Linschoten, Jan Huyghen van. 1988. The Voyage of John Huyghen van Linschoten to the East Indies. Vols 1, 2. (1598 English Translation). New Delhi; Asian Educational Services.

Mascarenhas, O. 1898. *Atravez dos Mares*. Lisboa: Recordacoes da India.

Mendes, A. Lopes. 1886. *A India Portugueza*. Lisboa: Imprensa Nacional.

Pires, T. 1990. *The Suma Oriental of Tome Pires (1512–1515)*. New Delhi: Asian Educational Services.

Pyrard de Laval, Francois. 1990. *The Voyages of Francois Pyrard de Laval (1619)*. Vol 2, Part 1 (London: The Hakluyt Society). New Delhi: Asian Educational Services.

Relatorio da Commisao Encarregada de Demarcar os Terrenos da Provincia de Sattary 1865. Lisboa: Imprensa Nacional.

Shiva, Vandana. 1991. *Biodiversity: Social and Ecological Perspectives*. Malaysia: World Rainforest Movement.

Singh, K.S. 2005. *The Scheduled Tribes, Vol II*. New Delhi: OUP.

Thurston, E. 1975. *Castes and tribes of Southern India, Vol IV (1919)*. Delhi: Cosmo Pub.

CHAPTER 8

The Music of the Catholic and Hindu Gaudde

Voicing the Unheard through Heritage

CLÁUDIA PEREIRA

I would like to thank Savio Abreu for organising a multi-disciplinary seminar on Goa and the privilege to present this paper. My main thrust is that the dances and songs of the Catholic Gaudde performed in specific religious rituals, formerly repressed during the Portuguese colonialism for not being Catholic and considered as heretic are now-a-days repositioned under the marketing of tourism as an authentic cultural form of Goa's heritage that resisted its colonial past. The Gaudde, an unprivileged social group, therefore, use the historical past in Goa to show their previous invisible resistance to the Portuguese governors, a lesser known aspect of colonialism in Goa. The Gaudde transformed the memory of their colonial resilience as Goan heritage, marketing it as pre-Portuguese. To this day, their Catholic *dharma* encompasses dances and music that are still similar to those of the Hindu Gaudde—the group they belonged to before they converted to Christianity—and so the words of their songs must be interpreted in the light of Hindu ritual logic, albeit the names of gods have been replaced by those of Christian saints, to whom they pray.

Now-a-days Gaudde comprise about 9 per cent of the total Goan population, of 1.344 million inhabitants (cf. Government of Goa 2005, Government of Goa 2009). The majority of the Gaudde are Hindu (57 per cent) and the rest are Christians (cf. Governemnt of Goa 2005, Government of Goa 2009). The original group has, over time, split into three different castes:

- The Hindu Gaudde, the original group, in Konkani called the Konkanne Gaudde because the term refers to an inhabitant of the Konkan area and hence to Hindu in general terms and pre-Portuguese.
- The Catholic Gaudde, a part of the Hindu Gaudde who converted to Catholicism when the Portuguese colonised Goa, from the 16th century onwards.
- Neo-Hindu Gaudde, a part of the previous Catholic Gaudde who performed the *Shuddi*, a Hindu purification ceremony, between 1926 and 1932, to become Hindu.

This paper is based on my one-year fieldwork among Catholic and Hindu Gaudde in a village in South Goa, between 2006 and 2007, and it is focused only on them, as it is difficult to generalise the rest of Gaudde in Goa due to their heterogeneity.

The religious rituals and music of the Gaudde were forbidden during the Portuguese colonial rule and regime, and Catholic Gaudde reacted to this interdiction by performing them in secrecy until the present. This process of maintaining their rituals and traditional music has become a means of invisible resistance to Portuguese colonialism, but it's also part of their contemporary ritual structure and collective memory (Axelrod 1996, 387-421). This is due to the local experience of Catholicism among the Gaudde and its relationship to Hinduism and the worship of territorial entities, resulting from the peculiar process of religious conversion in Goa. Although their rituals are still performed as per their religious calendar in the village, Gaudde started to present them to tourists. The Government of Goa attests to the Gaudde culture as one of the state's originals. Therefore, contemporary relevance of Gaudde's heritage arises for being considered pre-Portuguese, showing the resistance of a subaltern group of the previous Empire.

Descriptions of Goan culture have given pride of place to the cultural heritage of the elite, in which there is a visible Portuguese influence that is not present in the case of the Catholic Gaudde. Recall that the predominant image of Goa both in India and abroad is one of a strong emphasis on its Portuguese colonial inheritance, particularly in terms of architecture, music, dress and eating practices, along with the region's paradisiacal beaches and the trance music festivals, organised by hippies who have supposedly found a place where time stood still. However, now-a-days the Catholic Gaudde are asked to go to hotels, mansions, state events and Hindu temples to demonstrate the "authentic" culture of Goa, when their traditions played precisely the part of a passive means of resistance to the Portuguese colonial administration. The Gaudde are an alternative voice in the market of tourism of Goa and for that reason they have a significant cultural meaning in the heritage of the state of Goa, as well as in their own social status.

The Gaudde Pre-Portuguese "Authenticity" in the Folklorisation of Their Music

The Gaudde are known by their specific way of dressing and particularly by their music and dances, considered a synthesis of Catholic, Hindu and territorial practices that show a long-term negotiation between Portuguese and local culture. This shows us how their unprivileged status was imaginatively used as a tool to promote their cultural identity through heritage, reshaping their social image through tourism. Therefore, a process of heritagisation, in which the dances and songs of their rituals were presented and interpreted as heritage, used as a tool to raise their social status and consequently to promote the culture of a state of India, that is Goa (cf. Poria, 2010, 218-9).

The songs of Gaudde Catholics were only transmitted orally through several generations, since they were illiterate. For the first time, the lyrics of the songs of the Catholic Gaudde were transcribed during my field research, becoming documented. Besides, they were also translated into Portuguese for the first time in 2006, after centuries of colonial regime, unlike the lyrics of the songs of the Goan elite, as *mando,* which were translated into Portuguese throughout the 20th century. The analysis of the songs of the Catholic and Hindu Gaudde revealed they are identical, which indicates that its proximity was not interrupted with the conversion to Catholicism and Church prohibitions. So its plausible to say that the Catholic Gaudde kept their Hindu cultural heritage, reinventing it within the Christian religious practices and symbols, like the replacing of local gods with Christian saints.

The Catholic Gaudde also added some rhymes dealing with their colonial representations of the Portuguese, namely specific constructions of Portuguese directly related to their administration of Goa:

Intruz	*Intruz* (*translation*)
(son)	(son)
Avoi khushal zaun choi maka sort logoli	Oh my mother, I had the best luck of my life, I am happy
Prem futlo gue noxiban vocol Leboli	Apart from that bought a bag with money
Te bhair gheun eilo dudnvanchi Potoli	(This verse is implicitly referring to the dowry that the groom received).
Sogli khobor sangliar tum ojap zatoli	If I tell you be surprised to hear
Motte administração sorte motmotyali	**This kind of luck just happens to important and ruling people [Portuguese]**
(mother)	(mother)
Atam maka sang re chedya tuka kushi lagoli	My dear son, tell me how did you get this woman
	When you saw her, you felt happy
Sunek choin muji umet samki bhagoli	But how is she going to stay in a hut?
Pun amgue khopik ti kon bhashen ravtoli	We are poor
(future daughter-in-law, son's bride)	(future daughter-in-law, son's bride)
Te pasot zast na tumi dhostai korchi	Do not worry, you're my mother-in-law
Ho novro tum mãe, hanv sun tumgeli	He is my husband and now I am your daughter.
hi khop tumegeli maka nirmiloli	In this hut is my luck, my life
Mucode mizas na jeuchya nachin a Ambili	I do not feel bad about eating ragi. (*Ragi is flour porridge cooked in water. The Gaudde grow this grain and therefore, this food is associated with them, considered strong enough but unrefined.*)

In this excerpt from the song, sporadic luck is compared to permanent privileges enjoined by the 'Portuguese' or people linked to 'colonial rule' and attributed to the administrative staff. Such classificatory logic demonstrates the social distance the Gaudde felt from the Portuguese, and the nature of their relationship seems to be just bureaucratic.

The dances and songs of the Catholic Gaudde are offered to the spiritual entity that protects them in the area around their homes, the *vaddo* (Konkani word that means a territorial division similar to 'ward', but with local specificities). This spiritual entity is called *Gaon-Purush*, a spirit with a human shape whose name comes from the Konkani *Gaon,* village, and *Purush,* the first inhabitant of the village. The Hindu Gaudde, neighbours of Catholic Gaudde, also offer their similar songs and dances to the same spiritual entity, though separately.

These traditions are recreated contemporaneously with new aims. After Goa's annexation to India in 1961, a folklorisation process of their music slowly started, that is, they became an object of traditional performances to be consumed by tourists, being considered a form of "authentic" and local culture of Goa state, which is seen as 'Pre-Portuguese' heritage (Pereira, 2010). This repositioning of traditions as tourism attractions are a wider process of government-driven folklorisation that has taken place not only in Goa, but throughout India (Chatterji 2004, 3-4).

It is important to note that the local culture of the Gaudde (who have few capitalised resources) was transformed into a state heritage that represents Goa in national and international events, which is also a powerful symbolic and economic capital for the group. This dynamic reveals a world trend, in which backwardness and marginalisation are inverted and promoted to "culture" (Handler, 1988). The Gaudde as a social group are reshaped as "culture", under the argument of "authenticity" of its pre-Portuguese background.

This process could only take place in a post-colonial time, that is, after Goa was liberated from Portugal (cf. Loomba 2004, Shohat 1992). It was only in 1987 that the Gaudde, who hadn't learned how to speak Portuguese, saw Konkani recognised as an official language. Songs in Konkani acquired then a social meaning by participating in the legitimating of Goa's cultural and political identity. And Goa was officially declared as a state of India in the same year. The development of the tourism industry facilitated the establishment of folklore groups and traditional dances and music were objectified as genuine culture and a sign of the Gauddes' and Goa's authenticity.

The Gaudde music related to oral tradition fit in the characteristics of others of the same type. On the one hand, no one knows who composed them; on the other, they may assume different configurations depending on space, generational or historical context.

They also represent what the people have as the most "pure", therefore "authentic". But that's not all. The songs of the Gaudde can also be read in the light of all the general circumstances of the reflective processes of inventing a culture, studied in other parts of the world. First, the importance of the "sources" collected from the elderly for the construction of their folklore as happens with the Gaudde. Second, the importance of "individuals" who work as mediators between the social, cultural or political hierarchy, and the rural people. Among the Gaudde, the initiative came from a teacher in the mid 1970s and was continued by a woman who is still the current coordinator of the group (Pereira 2010).

Final Reflections

Gaudde music and dances have moved outside their cultural sphere. The dances were fixed, the lyrics of the songs repeated and standardised and the meaning objectified in a folklorisation process that offers Goa's traditional culture to the public. This has contributed to the conservation, restoration and reinvention of so-called traditional practices. The dances are still performed in their own religious rituals in a much longer and complex form and have not lost their original meaning (cf. Cohen 1988). Rather, reinforced by external confirmation, they attract young Catholic Gaudde to perform them. Among the Gaudde Hindu women of the village, the dances were not objectified and currently they have difficulty in memorising them, paying less attention to its performance during rituals.

The folklorisation of Gaudde dances, in which regional and cultural practices are institutionalised and transported to tourism, takes place in a world trend of local cultural claims fearing global homogenisation processes. The threat of the disappearance of cultural references into an assimilation by a transnational culture has led to some reactions of an increasing valorisation of local collective identities, along with a nostalgic feeling about the past (MacCannell, 1976). The folklorisation of Gaudde dances, marketing their colonial past, is one of these cases, common in developing countries (cf. Greenwood 1977). In Goa, this initiative came from the government and the Gaudde middle-class leaders, social actors with a particular interest in promoting an identity version. The government intended to promote an authentic culture in order to become a state of India, needing distinctive and unique features, like the Gaudde dances were considered. In the revitalising of their traditions, the Gaudde leaders found a way of both raising their own social status and being recognised as a Scheduled Tribe while gaining economic and social benefits.

These dynamic processes allow Goa's past to be protected, using history to legitimise their cohesion and collective memory (cf. Hobsbawn 1984, 12). This does not deny Gauddes' traditions' authenticity, it just means it needs to be contextualised since it was their only means to contest ruling classes and are now constructed through them (cf. Briggs 1996). After all, the past is constructed in the present, acquiring meanings that negotiate different social and political actors' interests and powers (Herzfeld 1991).

Heritagisation processes are no longer confined to the elite and dominant classes' culture. Today, India's heritage includes growing alternative versions, as in the Gaudde's case. Their process reveals the knowledge of a lesser known aspect of Portuguese colonialism, which does not coincide with the representations of the settlers: their influence in groups that were not the elite, but culturally and socially distant from the colonial administration and the relevance of their past to their present lives. Now-a-days, in the village, the castes that were close to the Portuguese administrators are still, after nearly 50 years, valued and respected as, for example, speaking 'Portuguese', indicating that their former proximity to the colonial rulers was and still is a sign of status. But these castes refer to the Gaudde as 'tribal', a category consolidated through Portuguese and post-annexation literature, which translated the Gaudde as the first inhabitants of Goa. The revitalisation of the Gaudde's rituals and practices reinforced this tribal classification, contributing to the group's recognition as a Scheduled Tribe and raising of their social and economic conditions.

Performances of the Gaudde, devalued by other caste groups in Goa, are now-a-days understood as art, aesthetics and communication simultaneously. Sometimes they perform side by side with performances of Portuguese music. Thus, the musical heritage integrated the Gaudde in a meaningful Goan society; they finally have a voice as their arts and performances gained symbolic significance in the reconfiguration of their post-colonial identity.

REFERENCES

Axelrod, Paul, and Michelle A. Fuerch. 1996. "Flight of the deities: Hindu resistance in Portuguese Goa". *Modern Asian Studies*, XXX (2): 387–421.

Briggs, Charles. 1996. "The politics of discursive authority in research on the 'Invention of Tradition'". *Cultural Anthropology*, 11 (4): 435–69.

Chatterji, R. 2004. "Performative Genres as Boundary Markers". *Indian Folklife*, 3 (4), s.n. 17: 8–10.

Cohen, E. 1988. "Authenticity and commoditization in tourism". *Annals of Tourism Research*, 15: 371–386.

Government of Goa. 2005. *Survey report on the Scheduled Tribes of Goa (Gawda, Kunbi, Velip)*. Pangim: Directorate of Social Welfare.

Government of Goa, Directorate of Planning, Statistics & Evaluation. 2009. *Economic Survey of Goa 2007–2008*. Pangim. Accessed February 3, 2009. http://goagovt.nic.in/documents/e-survey0708/e-survey-2007-08.htm.

Greenwood, D.J. 1977. "Culture by the pound: an anthropological perspective on tourism as cultural commoditization". In *Hosts and Guests*, edited by V.L. Smith, 129–139. Philadelphia: University of Pennsylvania Press.

Handler, Richard. 1988. *Nationalism and the politics of culture in Quebec*. Madison: The University of Wisconsin Press.

Herzfeld, M. 1991. *A place in history: social and monumental time in a Cretan Town*. Princeton: Princeton University Press

Hobsbawn, Eric. 1984. "Introdução: a invenção das tradições". In *A invenção das tradições*, edited by Eric Hobsbawn and Terence Ranger, 9–24. Rio de Janeiro: Paz e Terra.

Loomba, Ania. 2004 (1998). *Colonialism/Postcolonialism*. London and New York: Routledge.

MacCannell, D. 1976. *The Tourist: a new theory of the leisure class*. London: Macmillan.

Pereira, Cláudia. 2010. "As danças e as canções dos Gaudde católicos de Goa. O testemunho da resistência invisível ao colonialismo português através da sua tradição oral, agora folclorizada". *Revista Camões. A cena e as vozes – 500 anos desde o Auto da Índia*, edited by Rosa Perez and Miguel Brito. N. 20: 86–103.

Poria, Y. 2010. The story behind the picture: preferences for the visual display at heritage sites. In *Culture, heritage and representation. Perspectives on visuality and the past*, edited by E. Waterton and S. Watson, 217–228. Surrey and Burlington: Ashgate Publishing.

Shohat, Ella. 1992. "Notes on the 'Post-Colonial'". *Social Text*, N. 31/32, Third World and Post-Colonial Issues, 99–113.

Chapter 9

Konknni: A Language at the Crossroads

Pratapananda Naik

"The English have no respect for their language, and will not teach their children to speak it... It is impossible for an Englishman to open his mouth, without making some other Englishman despise him."

– Preface to Pygmalion (1912), by George Bernard Shaw

Konknni: A Politicised Language?

In the history of humankind, languages, dialects and scripts are used not only for communication but also for domination, manipulation and suppression of weaker groups. This is true also for Konknni. Its scripts and dialects are today at a crossroads. The politics of language concerns policies and decisions about official and standard languages, language planning, language academies and educational language policies. A politicised language is neither the preserve of a profession nor the office of the state; it is a resource open to all, allowing one to consider and to use language for persuasion and control.

Konknni: The Early Phase

The Portuguese conquered the Tiswadi area of present-day Goa in 1510 from Sultan Adilshah of Bijapur. Till the arrival of the Portuguese, we have no historical proof to say that Konknni was used as a written language. The Jesuit and Franciscan missionaries were the first ones to write Konknni in Roman script to help spread

Christianity. The first printing press in India was brought to St. Paul College, in present-day Old Goa by Jesuit missionaries in 1556. Between 1556 and 1561, they printed *Doutrina Christam* (Doctrine of Christianity) in Konknni in Roman script. During the pre-liberation period (before 1961) in Goa, the Hindu community and the Catholic masses, used Konknni for oral communication. The Hindu community used Marathi for primary education, for popular religion, accounts, written communication theatre and other spheres of their lives. The Catholic elite used Portuguese at home and for education. They used Konknni to converse with the Hindus and the common folk of the Catholic community who did not know Portuguese language.

Portuguese language was considered the language of the cultured people. The Catholic elites looked down upon Konknni as a language of the servants and socio-economically backward common people. Konknni in Roman script was used for popular religious practices and for mass media. Konknni written in Devanagari script hardly existed during this period. It had practically no influence over the members of the Hindu community. Marathi enjoyed the privileged position among the Hindu community. Due to this, the Hindu community identified Marathi as their intellectual and cultural language. However, there was no animosity or rivalry among the users of these three languages, namely Konknni, Marathi and Portuguese. These three languages coexisted with unity and harmony.

After 1965, due to the teaching of the Second Vatican Council, the Catholic Church all over the world replaced Latin by local languages in the religious domain all over the world. Due to this the Church in Goa too actively promoted religious services in Konknni. The Church contributed to standardise Konknni in Roman script, which had its roots in the 16th century. This dialect may be called Bardeshi.

After the liberation of Goa, Konknni language suffered a number of setbacks. This happened partly due to lack of vision and leadership on the part of the minority community and partly due to the manipulative tactics used by self-proclaimed protectors of Konknni. After the liberation of Goa the elite Catholic community switched over to English while retaining the Portuguese language.

The Great Divide

After the liberation of Goa, Catholic schools introduced Konknni in Devanagari script as a third language in their schools. The proponents of Devanagari succeeded in convincing a few leaders of the Catholic community that Devanagari script was the 'natural script' of Konknni and was related to our nationalism and patriotism! The majority of the students who studied Devanagari Konknni were from the Catholic community. They were familiar with the Roman script and Bardeshi dialect due to religious literature and mass media. But Bardeshi dialect was not taught in schools. A different dialect called Antruzi was thrust upon them in the name of Konknni and nationalism. According to late Mr. Ulhas Buyanv, one of the stalwarts of Opinion Poll in Goa and a veteran Konknni singer, 'a Konknni dialect of 3 per cent Hindu Saraswats was forced upon 30 per cent Catholic community'. Students of the Catholic community who had opted for Konknni had no real option. They were not familiar with Marathi. Besides, they never identified with Marathi as their language. Between Marathi and Konknni they were forced to take Konknni in Devanagari script. Students learnt Konknni not out of conviction or love of Konknni but out of sheer compulsion. Therefore, they never took interest in keeping up the language they learnt. Once they finished their education they gave up reading and writing Konknni in Devanagari script! This situation created a strong feeling of dislike towards Konknni in Devanagari script among the Catholic community. In Goa, from Standard V onwards, the medium of instruction is English and so school managements discourage their students from speaking Konknni or any other vernacular language in the school premises. Hence students use English as their everyday language of conversation both inside and outside the school premises. The dialect and script which Catholic students were not familiar with was taught in schools. Due to this they developed a dislike of their own mother tongue and, instead of using it for oral communication, they preferred to use English in all domains of their lives!

If the textbooks had included the Konknni dialect of the majority community and Bardeshi dialect of the Catholic community, this unhealthy tension could have been avoided and a healthy blending of the two dialects would have helped to promote a new standard dialect of Konknni in Goa. Dialects and scripts are emotional issues. In a democracy one group cannot impose its preferences on the others. Language is far more important than its scripts. Unfortunately, among a section of Konknnis (Konknni speakers), Konknni language was identified with the Devanagari script and with a particular dialect called Antruzi!

The Stance of the Proponents

When New Delhi gave recognition to Konknni there was no mention of its script in the minutes. Excerpts from the meeting of the General Council of the Sahitya Akademi held on February 26, 1975 concluded that since Konkani fulfilled the criteria formulated by the Akademi for recognition of a language, it was recognised as an independent modern literary language of India. On November 21, 1981, the Advisory Board of Konknni, which consisted of a majority of Devanagari proponents, recommended that Devanagari should be the script for Konknni. Since then Sahitya Akademi has accepted Devanagari script as the official script of Konknni. Konknni speakers, writers and leaders of various scripts were not consulted for such a major decision. There was no public debate to come to a consensus on this important issue of the script. The entire process was a clandestine exercise of a few. Subsequently, whenever the question of script was raised, the proponents of Devanagari script silenced the voice of their opponents by vociferously proclaiming that the Sahitya Akademi has recognized Konknni only in Devanagari script!

Consequently, Sahitya Akademi awards were given exclusively to books written in Devanagari script. This tradition continues to date. It is an open secret among Konknni writers that these awards are distributed among the supporters and well-wishers of Devanagari script. This manipulation reached its climax during the selection of a Konknni book for the Sahitya Akademi award for 2005. Three jury members recommended a book; two jury members were the publishers of the very same book, which was selected for the award! The Sahitya Akademi's recognition to Konknni first sowed the seed of division among the supporters of Konknni and supporters of Marathi. Second, it created a rift between supporters of Devanagari script and the supporters of the other two major scripts of Konknni, namely, Roman and Kannada scripts. This gap is widening day-by-day. Prior to the recognition, these three groups lived and worked together with dignity. A popular language of the people does not need the recognition of an external organisation. The Sahitya Akademi's recognition did more harm than good to the unity and harmony of Konknni and Konknnis!

The Impasse

The Sahitya Akademi could solve this impasse by giving annual awards in turn to books published in Devanagari, Roman and Kannada scripts. This is possible if the Advisory Board of the Sahitya Akademi resolves the script issue by mutual understanding. In 2010, the representatives of Konknnis using Roman and Devanagari scripts approached the Sahitya Akademi and requested it to consider their demand. But the Sahitya Akademi refused to accept their request.

In 1985 the Goa government founded the Goa Konkani Akademi (GKA), whose chief objective was to bring about speedy development of Konknni language, literature and culture and also to promote cultural unity of the state through Konknni language and literature. The GKA started actually functioning from 1986; it was filled with proponents of Devanagari and they interpreted Konknni as Konknni written in Devanagari script.

Till 2005 the GKA hardly did anything to fulfil its primary objective. In 2005 due to the demands of Roman script supporters, the Goa government ordered the GKA to publish and to give financial assistance to books written in Roman script. Roman script readers and writers who preserved, promoted Konknni and fought for it to become the Official Language of Goa have become second-class citizens in Goa itself! Anyone who supports or demands equal status to Konknni in the Official Language Act, 1987 is considered a 'fundamentalist', 'promoter of disunity' and so on by the proponents of Devanagari.

At present, in the name of promoting local languages and culture, the Goa government gives lakhs of rupees to the GKA, Marathi Akademi, Kala Akademi and Art and Culture Directorate. Is there a need for the government to spend such an enormous amount of taxpayers' hard-earned money for language and culture? The government's involvement through its departments or autonomous institutions to promote local languages and culture has further divided the local people. Each group envies the other group. It is high time that the concerned citizens question the government about the relevance and the need for such an exorbitant expenditure on language and culture. Any language or culture is maintained, developed and promoted with the active support of its native speakers. When the government takes the initiative to promote a language or culture, it gradually kills the zeal of native speakers and in turn harms the progress of that language. Besides, manipulation, corruption, nepotism and degradation of the society are bound to enter and get rooted even in the field of art and culture. A written language or a particular culture cannot be kept alive merely by government's financiai support.

When Konknni was included in the 8th Schedule of the Constitution of India on August 20, 1992, there was no mention of its official script. According to the 71st Amendment to the Constitution in the Eighth Schedule to the Constitution, the then existing entry no. 7 was to be re-numbered as entry no. 8, and before entry 8 as so re-numbered, the entry "7. Konkani" was to be inserted. From this one could conclude that the official script of Konknni for all Konknnis is not officially decided or accepted by the people.

On February 4, 1987, the Goa Legislative Assembly passed the Official Language Bill. In the Official Language Act, under definitions 2c it is stated that 'Konkani language' means Konkani language in Devanagari script. Who included the definition of Konknni in the Official Language Act and what was the need to include such a definition? The majority of the Konknni supporters were then totally unaware of this addition or the implication of such a definition. According to Tomazinho Cardozo, the ex-Speaker of the Goa Legislative Assembly and ex-President of the Dalgado Konknni Akademi, this was the biggest fraud or conspiracy of the 20th century as far as Konknni was concerned.

The main objective of the State Language is to give preference to native speakers for government jobs. The Official Language Act of Goa is biased towards one section of the Goan community. Konknni is not a compulsory subject in the education system of Goa. In other states the State Language is compulsory in education. In Goa, for government jobs, the knowledge of Konknni (in Devanagari script) is essential and the knowledge of Marathi is desirable. With this policy those who know Konknni in Devanagari script and Marathi are given preference for jobs. Due to this, the present Language Act does not promote unity and harmony among natives in Goa. Instead it has created disunity, mistrust and division in Goa. Prior to the Official Language Act, the situation in Goa was much more cordial and friendly. It was falsely presumed that Konknni in Devanagari script would promote unity in Goa. But the reality is that the Hindu community has not fully accepted Konknni in Devanagari script in most of the spheres. It continues to use Marathi for religious services, education, mass media and cultural domains. In Goa neither the Hindu community nor the Catholic community has fully accepted Konknni in Devanagari script for all the domains of their life. It is nobody's baby, yet this unwanted baby is artificially kept alive through generous grants of the government. Konknni in Devanagari script alone cannot become a true bond of unity among Goans. This writer's experience for the last 35 years has shown that in Goa, Konknni for oral communication and English for written communication will definitely unite all Goans irrespective of their caste, creed and region. Therefore, for government jobs the knowledge of oral Konknni alone should be sufficient. Language fanaticism does not promote a language; rather it creates hatred towards it and its speakers.

The Language Scenario in Schools

In 1990 the Bombay High Court ordered the managements of private schools to pay the government pay scale to their primary teachers. These primary schools were of English medium. Instead of challenging this verdict in the Supreme Court, the managements approached the local government for assistance. For the reasons best known to the government, it decided to give grants only to those schools which use Konknni, Marathi or any other recognised Indian languages as the medium of instruction. The Catholic community leaders, especially the priests and nuns, were asked to run their schools in Konknni medium to avail the grants. This major decision created innumerable problems for parents to educate their children in Konknni medium. Besides, it further increased their dislike for Konknni in Devanagari script. Those who were financially better off preferred to send their children to English medium primary schools. Those who belonged to the Hindu community continued to send their children to either Marathi or English medium schools. Those who cannot afford English education continue to send their children to Konknni medium schools. English medium primary schools have become a common practice in our country. Hence let the parents decide the medium of instruction of their children. In a democracy they have a right to choose the medium of instruction.

From September 30, 2008, Catholics have been in the forefront of Konknni education in Goa, managing 128 Konknni medium primary schools. Hindu managements administer only six Konknni medium primary schools and 48 Marathi medium schools. The Goa government manages 67 Konknni medium schools and promotes 888 Marathi medium primary schools. Why do the supporters of Devanagari not put pressure on the government and Hindu managements to start Konknni medium schools? In March 2011 the primary education scenario in Goa began to change due to the Right to Education (RTE) 2009 Act of the Central Government. The RTE recommends that, as far as possible, primary education be in the mother tongue up to Standard VIII. In Goa, in practically all schools from Standard V onwards, the medium of instruction is English. The parents and the management were disturbed by this new policy. Most parents demanded that Goa government should not change the existing system. The parents of students who are studying in minority schools went one step further and demanded that the government extend grants to English medium primary schools and to allow switch over of Konknni or Marathi medium schools to English medium. Supporters of Marathi and Devanagari script for Konknni resisted this move under the banner Bharatiya Bhasa Suraksha Manch (BBSM). The BBSM dragged the matter to the High Court. The High Court verdict is awaited.

The Directorate of Education has submitted to the Court the following data. For the academic year 2011–12, in Goa from Standards I to IV, 66,543 have enrolled in government and aided private schools, out of which 29,557 (46.31 per cent) parents have opted for English medium; 31,759 for Marathi (49.76 per cent); 2,502 for Konknni (3.92 per cent); 223 for Hindi (0.33 per cent) and 13 for Telugu (0.01 per cent). Data related to Urdu medium and the existing unaided private English medium schools is not available.

According to data for academic year 2008–09, Marathi medium primary schools (Standards I to IV) have the highest number of students, namely 40,151. Konknni has only 32,358 students. The vast majority of Devanagari supporters send their children and grandchildren to English or Marathi medium primary schools! Though Konknni is the State Language of Goa, in the entire State there is not a single Konknni medium middle school or high school–while Marathi, Urdu and Kannada medium high schools are found in Goa. Though Konknni is the official language of Goa, it is not a compulsory language in schools! In Maharashtra one cannot complete Standard X without studying Marathi, and without studying Kannada in Karnataka. Only in Goa can one complete his/her entire education without learning Konknni! Besides, one can live and die in Goa with dignity without speaking Konknni! In Goa the regional identity 'Goan' is far more important than the linguistic identity 'Konknni'. Therefore, we come across many natives who call themselves Goans and are ashamed to identify with Konknni or give the excuse that they do not know Konknni or take pride in not knowing Konknni!

The number of Standard X students who opt for Konknni as the third language has not crossed 45 per cent of the total number of students who appear for the examination. In March 2011, nearly 16,747 students appeared for the Standard X examination; Out of these 6,479 (38.69 per cent) students opted for Konknni and 7,182 (42.89 per cent) students for Marathi. The number of Standard XII students who opted for Konknni as the second language has not crossed 35 per cent. According to reliable sources, the majority of these students are Catholics. As on September 30, 2008, out of 129 Christian management high schools 128 schools offer Konknni as a third language. Most of the government high schools in North Goa District do not offer Konknni. Fifty per cent of schools run by the Hindu community do not offer Konknni as a third language. Devanagari supporters close their eyes to this naked reality.

Irrespective of what the medium of instruction is, the proponents of Devanagari script should have demanded that the government make Konknni a compulsory subject in schools. So far they have not done so. The reason is because Marathi, as per the Official Language Act, 1987, has been safeguarded in educational, social and cultural fields. Therefore, Konknni cannot be made the compulsory language in Goa for education. Fighting against granting official status to Konknni in Roman script and cursing the impact of English in Goa will not help the cause of Konknni in Devanagari script. Rather, it will lead to the natural death of the Konknni written in Devanagari, the so-called 'natural script' of Konknni.

In Karnataka, Konknni has been included in the school curriculum from the 2007-08 academic year in Kannada script. For the 2010-11 academic year, 54 schools are teaching Konknni in Kannada script as a subject from Standard VI. These schools belong to Catholic management. Though there is an option to teach Konknni in Devanagari script, not a single school offers this option within the school curriculum. The Karnataka government has recognised Kannada script and Devanagari script as the official scripts for Konknni in Karnataka. In this context, what prevents the Goa government from recognising the Roman and Devanagari scripts as the official scripts of Konknni in Goa?

It has been proclaimed by the supporters of Devanagari that hundreds of students have opted for Konknni at BA and MA level and they still continue to do so. When we analyse the composition of these Konknni students, a majority of them are girls. They opt for Konknni to get a degree till they settle down in life. To get a paper degree, Konknni is the easiest subject. Boys do not opt for Konknni. They know very well that there are no job opportunities for Konknni in Goa except in the teaching field. Most of these students of Konknni literature and even their teachers do not read any other Konknni material beyond their prescribed textbooks! The contribution of Konknni teachers to Konknni language and literature is a bare minimum.

The Kerala government has approved of teaching of Konknni in Devanagari script in Kerala, but in reality Konknni is taught as a subject only in one school. In Kerala not a single full-fledged Konknni periodical is published. In reality, Konknnis in Kerala exist, but Konknni continues to be mainly the spoken language among a small section of people of Konknni origin. Konknni is hardly used for written purpose in Kerala.

Konknni Language in Media, Literature and Culture

In Goa literate Hindus know the Devanagari script. Yet the vast majority of them prefer to read and write Marathi and not Konknni. Ten Marathi dailies are sold in Goa; the single Konknni daily in Goa has very poor circulation after 24 years of its existence! In Goa, besides this daily, there are only three Konknni periodicals in Devanagari script. The Roman script has 13 periodicals. Besides these, there are 82 Parish Bulletins which are published in Roman script. Catholics who read Konknni prefer to read it in Roman script. Day-by-day the use of Roman script for Konknni is gradually increasing among the Hindu community due to the efforts of Dalgado Konknni Akademi and Tiatr Academy. Since liberation, Konknni in Devanagari script has not united the entire Hindu community. It is highly Marathicised and Sanskritised. Yet, the Hindu community has not accepted it! Why has the majority of the Hindu community, which speaks Konknni, rejected Konknni written in Devanagari script? One of the answers is it uses the Konknni dialect of Saraswats. The common Hindu community, known as Bahujan Samaj, does not want the domination of Saraswats and Catholics. During the Portuguese rule the Saraswats and the elite Catholics who learnt Portuguese language profited by the government high posts. Therefore, the Bahujan Samaj prefers to identify with Marathi which they learnt in schools, which is common to both Bahujan Samaj and Saraswats. Besides, the Hindu community continues to use Marathi for their religious, cultural, social and other fields in life. Konknni in Devanagari script has failed to unite the majority and minority communities of Goa. Prior to Goa's liberation, written Konknni meant Konknni in Roman script. Spoken Konknni alone is the uniting factor in Goa. Konknni in Devanagari script has been kept alive mainly due to State and Central governments grants. In education it exists because of the support of the Catholic community. If the government stops or if the Roman script is given official status, will Konknni in Devanagari script survive? This is a serious topic for discussion and reflection.

The Church has supported and preserved Konknni in Roman script. As on August 26, 2008, 60,000 copies of the entire *Bible* in Konknni; 232,000 copies of *New Testament* and over 3 lakh of *Gayonancho Jhelo* (hymnal); 100,000 catechism books for students and 6,000 teachers' handbooks are printed in Konknni in Roman script. The Church uses Konknni in Roman script for the religious purpose. Archbishop's official circulars and pastoral letters are written and published in Konknni.

In the market, Konknni CDs, VCDs and DVDs of kantaram (songs), tiatrs, mandos, dulpods, dekhnnis, devotional hymns and films are found in great numbers. The text and lyrics for these is written in Roman script and produced mainly by the Catholic community. Hindus still continue to use Marathi CDs for religious socio-cultural domains. Tiatr is the most popular form of entertainment and commercially successful stage performances. At least 40 tiatr troupes perform thousands of shows in Goa and elsewhere. Tiatr is the most successful entertainment industry. Tiatrs are written exclusively in the Roman script. Though it is claimed that many Konknni *nattoks* (plays) are gaining popularity, they are limited to competitions and free shows. Konknni *nattoks* have not attained commercial status. On All India Radio kantaram, mandos, dulpods, dekhnnis and Konknni film songs are still popular. Konknni in Roman script is the heart and soul of Konknni. Therefore, Lorna, Chris Perry, M. Boyer, Jacinto Vaz, Robin Vaz, C. Alvares, H. Britton, Alfred Rose, Rita Rose, Antonette Mendes, Remo Fernandes, Wilmix Mazarello, Sharon Mazarello, Anthony San, Young Chico and other singers are popular in Goa irrespective of religion and caste.

The claim that there are over 50 lakh Konknnis is far from the truth. According to the Census of India 2001, in India there are 2,489,015 speakers whose mother tongue is Konknni. In Census data under Konknni entry Kudbi/Kudumbi, Malwani and others are included. This data includes 2,420,140 Konknni; 10,192 Kudubi/ Kudumbi; 46,851 Malwani; and 11,832 other speakers whose mother tongue is another language. According to Census 2001 the total population of Goa is 1,347,668, of which only 769,888 (57.13 per cent) persons have declared that their mother tongue is Konknni. According to Census 2001 in Goa, 8,190 have declared English as their mother tongue. This number is not realistic. There must be many more whose mother tongue is English, according to the definition of mother tongue given by Census 2001. Census 2001 defines mother tongue as follows: "Mother tongue is the language spoken in childhood by the person's mother to the person." If we take this definition literally, then the Konknni population in Goa is far below the recorded data of 769,888, because in a good number of Catholic families mothers speak to their children in English. Such households might have wrongly given their mother tongue as Konknni instead of

English. Similarly, those who have declared their mother tongue as Marathi have given the wrong information because most of them speak Konknni in their homes.

The Script Imbroglio

For other major languages of India, the majority speakers of a particular language are found in a particular State, for example, Marathi in Maharashtra, Kannada in Karnataka and so on. Though Konknni is the State Language of Goa only 30.93 per cent of total Konknni population is found in Goa! Konknnis are spread mainly in the States of Gujarat, Maharashtra, Goa, Karnataka and Kerala. They use different dialects and scripts. Konknni is written mainly in three scripts, that is, Roman, Devanagari and Kannada. Konknnis require Konknni only to maintain their cultural identity. In this context, Konknni does not help as a medium of instruction, as a common media for communication or to earn one's livelihood. So far Konknni has survived because it is a vibrant spoken language. The "one script, one dialect, one community" principle has not succeeded so far to unite Konknnis and it will not succeed in the future. If we force this "unity in uniformity" principle Konknnis will survive but Konknni will perish. The protagonists of this principle implicitly believe that Aryans, Brahmins, Sanskrit and Devanagari script are inseparable elements of the common umbilical cord and they are 'holy/pure/standard/best/high' for all!

An analysis of Alok Rai's book *Hindi Nationalism* (2001) will help us to understand the situation of Konknni in Goa better. This book looks at the politics of language in India through a study of the history of one language—Hindi. It traces the tragic metamorphosis of this language over the last century, from a creative, dynamic, popular language to a dead, Sanskritised, dePersianised language manufactured by a self-serving upper caste North Indian elite, nurturing hegemonic ambitions. From being a symbol of collective imagination it becomes a signifier of narrow sectarianism and regional chauvinism. The book shows how this transformation of the language was tied up with the politics of communalism and regionalism. Rai seeks to save Hindi from the politics of Hindi nationalism. If Hindi has to realise its inner potential and become a national language of communication, argues Rai, then it has to emancipate itself from its own repressed history, and dissociate itself from its deformed other—the Sanskritised Hindi of the pundits. It can only do this through a critical return to its troubled past. Konknni has many lessons to learn from *Hindi Nationalism.* Konknni will survive and flourish if we accept the principle of "unity in diversity" of Konknni dialects, scripts and cultures.

Supporters of Roman script have so far not opposed Konknni in Devanagari script. Then why is the Devanagari lobby opposed to the inclusion of Roman script in the Official Language Act? Why was the definition of Konknni in the Official Language Act given as "Konkani means Konkani written in Devanagari script"? In 1987 when Marathi was included in the Official Language Act, the Devanagari supporters did not oppose it. Why? The logic is simple. If the Roman script is given its due place, the use of Konknni in Devanagari script will be reduced and eventually it might die a natural death. According to Ancy Paladka, a Konknni poet from Mumbai, "For the survival of Konknni in Goa, Roman and Nagari scripts must be recognised as official and equal in the Language Act. If Marathi too becomes the official language of Goa the blame has to be borne by Nagari lobby only. For its own survival and honour Nagari lobby should immediately take necessary steps to rectify its past sin and join hands with Roman script supporters to obtain the official status to Roman script in the Language Act" (Ancy 2008, 73).

Since the inception of Goa Konknni Akademi, not a single Roman script writer or supporter has been appointed as its President. Kala Academy stopped giving awards to Konknni books written in Roman script from 1987 onwards. So far not a single book published in Roman script has been given the Sahitya Akademi award. Why is the Devanagari lobby silent about this injustice? They used Devanagari as a tool to suppress and oppress the minority community to perpetuate their supremacy in the field of language and literature and to grab awards, positions, jobs, power and government funds.

Marathi is used in Goa exclusively by the Hindu community for written communication, religious and cultural areas. If Marathi has a place in the Official Language Act, and Konknni in Devanagari script which the majority of Goans do not want has secured a place in it, then the Roman script (which is the most popular script) has a right to be in the Official Language Act. The question is not the script but the dialects in use. Devanagari script is heavily dominated by the Antruzi dialect of Saraswats of Ponda region, while the Roman script promoted by the Catholics use Bardeshi dialect of North Goa. Both these Konknni dialects vary at the phonetic, lexical, morphological, syntactic and semantic domains. Since Konknni is the language of identity both these groups want to maintain their identity through their own different scripts and dialects. In this sense in Goa the Konknni language, its scripts and dialects are at a crossroads. It is 'language politics' for identity (linguistic, cultural, social, psychological), power, prestige and economical control. The good of Goa and Goans is far more important than mere language, dialect or script controversy.

Language, scripts and dialects have become emotional and cultural dimensions of people here in Goa. Logic and facts are pushed to the backseat. The vast majority of Catholics think that Marathi is the language of Maharashtra and of Hindus. Devanagari script is imposed on them. Local Hindus do speak Konknni but identify with Marathi as the language of religion and culture. The Roman script is considered as foreign and Devanagari as the 'natural' script. This misconception prevails because language and script is associated with a particular religion. Locals, while speaking Konknni, use their own dialects. Nobody speaks Devanagari Konknni or Romi Konknni. Such Konknni does not exist. Yet, in popular writing and speeches these terms are often used and create further confusion. Devanagari and Roman scripts are used to write Konknni in Goa. Due to the effort of the Church, a particular dialect of Konknni (Bardeshi) in Roman script is fairly standardised. A similar process is also continuing in Devanagari script due to the education process. However, both Christian and Hindu communities have not totally identified with written Konknni in any script. The language suffers due to this.

In the Official Language Act, 1987, if the definition of Konknni was avoided, then both thc scripts would have flourished side by side. Here the Devanagari proponents put the fear in the mind of the leaders of the Catholic community that if they demanded the Roman script then Marathi would become the official language. Without becoming the official language, Marathi gets practically all the privileges which Konknni in Devanagari script enjoys in the Official

Language Act. In this 'language politics', Roman script was kept out of the Official Language Act. Devanagari protagonists accuse Roman script supporters of having awakened after many years and demanding a share in grants and awards. One could counteract this argument by saying, "What is wrong in democracy to demand equal share in grants, honours and awards?" In recent years, due to the constant pressure of supporters of Roman script, the present State government has started to give grants to Dalgado Konknni Akademi, a non-governmental organisation which was established in 1988 to preserve and promote Konknni in Roman script. Besides, the state government established its own autonomous institution, Tiatr Academy, to promote tiatr, the popular form of Konknni theatre. The government also gives some financial help for cultural functions organised by the supporters of Roman script.

The supporters of Roman script want not just monetary benefits; they want equal citizenship rights for their dialect and script. They do not ask for charity but for equality and justice. Because Article 29 of the Constitution of India says, "Protection of interests of minorities—(1) Any section of the citizens residing in the territory of India or any part thereof having a distinct language, script or culture of its own shall have the right to conserve the same." Article 347 reads "Special provision relating to language spoken by a section of the population of a state. On a demand being made in that behalf the President may, if he is satisfied that a substantial proportion of the population of a state desire the use of any language spoken by them to be recognized by that state, direct that such language shall also be officially recognized throughout that state or any part thereof for such purpose as he may specify." In democracy, there will not be peace and unity as long as injustice prevails and one group wants to dominate others and suppress their voice.

Proposed Solution

A few prominent people who are working for Konknni wanted to put an end to the manipulation of a fistful of people who were working under the narrow principle of "unity in uniformity". Under the leadership of Mandd Sobhann, various Konknni organisations from all over the world came together on August 20, 2011, in Kalangann,

Mangalore, and formed the Jagotik Konknni Songhotton (JKS, Global Konkani Organisation) to promote and work for Konknni with wider and in-depth vision. The objectives of JKS are to represent Konknni people and issues globally, to enrich and preserve Konknni for posterity, and to ensure the transmission of Konknni heritage perennially. The principles of JKS are: respecting every variety; seeking unity in diversity; and promoting a common identity.

Those who care for Konknni should be open to the ground reality and not be led by mere theoretical idealism or language/script chauvinism. In a democracy, mutual respect, understanding and unity in multiplicity and other values must guide any action. In Goa, Roman and Devanagari scripts are used to read and write Konknni. These two scripts represent two different standard dialects of Konknni. They could be compared to two wheels of a cart. For the survival of Konknni in Goa they are really essential. There cannot be true equality and harmony among the users of these two groups without justice. Justice will be given by amending the Official Language Act of 1987 to include Konknni written in Roman script side by side with Konknni written in Devanagari script. Let these two groups live in Goa with dignity as equal citizens, maintaining their identity and liberty. Konknni without the Roman script and the Bardeshi dialect will lose its separate identity and simplicity. According to a Hasidic saying, "The culture of the heart is greater than the culture of the mind." Konknni is primarily a language of the heart.

REFERENCES

Almeida, Matthew. 2005. "Evolution and Modification of the Roman script used for Konkani". *SÔD TSKK Konknni Research Bulletin*, 9: 158–186.

———. 2006. "Konknni versus Scripts". *SÔD TSKK Konknni Research Bulletin*, 10: 71–74.

Cardozo, Tomazinho. 2008. "Of Language, Script and Panic". *SÔD TSKK Konknni Research Bulletin*, 13: 34–37.

———. 2008. "Solving the Language Imbroglio". *SÔD TSKK Konknni Research Bulletin*, 13: 67–69.

D'Souza, Ancy. 2008. "Konknni Devanagari Supporters should act immediately". *SÔD TSKK Konknni Research Bulletin*, 13: 72–73.

Fernandes, Jason K. 2006. "Scripting Controversy: Debating the War of the Konknnis". *SÔD TSKK Konknni Research Bulletin*, 10: 39–48.

Gonsalves, Godfrey. 2006. "Roman Script for Konknni a Must: Now or Never". *SÔD TSKK Konknni Research Bulletin*, 10: 27–30.

Lopes, Nelson. 2006. "Roman script the soul of Konknni". *SÔD TSKK Konknni Research Bulletin*, 10: 15–19.

Mazarello, Wilmix Wilson. 2008. "Denying a Script is a Human right Violation". *SÔD TSKK Konknni Research Bulletin*, 13: 56–58.

Naik, Pratapananda. 2007. "A short history of Konknni in Goa in the Roman Script from 1556". *SÔD TSKK Konknni Research Bulletin*, 11: 58–69.

———. 2007. "Facts related to Konknni Language as Updated on 24 February 2007". *SÔD TSKK Konknni Research Bulletin*, 11: 91–102.

———. 2008. "Glimpses of Konknni in Roman Script". *SÔD TSKK Konknni Research Bulletin*, 13: 70–71.

———. 2008. "Konknni and its Scripts at the Crossroads". *Herald*, September 5, p 9.

Rai, Alok. 2001. *Hindi Nationalism*. London: Sangam Books Limited.

Chapter 10

The Return to Indianness

Goan Nationalism in the 1920s

Sandra Ataíde Lobo[1]

From the time of its commencement in British-India, the development of the Indian nationalist movement was watched with great interest by Goan elites. It was, however during the initial decades of the 20th century that this observation began to mould the perspectives of these elites and have a significant impact on local (that is Goan) political and cultural thought. During these years, the local critique of the colonial Portuguese administration, a critique whose articulation was a permanent feature in the 19th century Goa, took on added dimensions—as a result of the observation by the Goan elite of the nationalist movement that was growing in the neighbouring colonial territories of British India.

As a result of the engagement with the nationalist mobilisation in British India, the Goan critique directed against the colonial administration was also accompanied by a self-critique directed by the Catholic elite against themselves. Its object was their civic inertia, and their marked inclination towards frittering their energies in 'internal' dissensions rather than furthering the cause of 'local interests' *vis-à-vis* the 'foreign' power. The model for emulation on which this critique was based was the comportment of their Indian 'brothers' in all fields of social and political action. On the political front, the demand for Indian autonomy that was being mounted by the Indian nationalists, found parallel with a similar discussion that was being conducted in Portugal; a debate that was largely moved by

It was, however, only after the First World War, when the fight for British Indian independence gained a new strength, that there was a marked shift in the position of Goan intellectuals who had been sympathetic to the nationalist movement in the neighbouring colonial territory. This shift involved a movement from merely sympathy for similar attempts, into being a nationalist intervention where these Goan nationalists stressed a single Indian national identity, this identity being actively affirmed as transcending circumstantial colonial divisions.[8] The signs of this transformation were initially dispersed, and it was only in the middle of the twenties that it became obvious that these interventions were in fact symptomatic of a systematic development of a political movement for Goan liberation from colonial power.

One of the more significant of the Goan nationalists who articulated this position was Tristão de Bragança Cunha (1891-1958).[9] A member of the Third International, Bragança Cunha left Goa for France in 1914, with the objective of gaining a degree in Electrical Engineering. In Paris, he collaborated with a range of leftist periodicals, like the newspaper of Henri Barbusse's movement *Clarté*, and Louis Weiss' *L'Europe nouvelle*. Both of these newspapers were linked with the internationalist, and post-war pacifists' movements. In these periodicals he wrote in favour of the Indian movement, being responsible, for example, for informing the French public of the Jallianwala Bagh massacre in 1919 (Bragança 1992, 9). His brother, Francisco de Francisco de Bragança Cunha (1887-1954) left India in 1908 to study in London and subsequently in Paris, where he gained a Licenciate in Letters and then went on to lecture at the Sorbonne. Like Tristão, he collaborated actively with the French press, and being a friend of Sylvain Levy[10], interacted in the same environment of anti-imperialist neo-Orientalism, that was in its turn the result of the confluence of streams ranging from the spiritual, cultural, political and academic. In 1923 he collaborated as a translator for Rabindranath Tagore. Tagore was engaged at this point in time, in a journey across Europe seeking to educate the public and drum up support for the Indian nationalist cause. For his services, the elder de Bragança Cunha obtained an invitation from the poet to teach at Shantiniketan.

In the same period, António Aleixo Santana Rodrigues (1887-1966), who had been involved in the Goan Republican press since his youth, left for Lisbon to study medicine. In September 1921, in face of the persistence of the Portuguese press in equating the nationalist movement with Bolshevism, and their ridiculing of the Indian leaders, Santana Rodrigues granted two interviews to the Lisbon newspaper *Imprensa da Manhã*. In these interviews, Santana Rodrigues clarified the Gandhian position, recalled the ancient glories of Indian civilization, presented a critique of the British dominion, and referred also to the nationalist objectives of the constitution of a future Indian federal democracy. The importance attributed to these interviews is reflected in the fact of their translation into English, and their publication in the form of a bilingual flyer that was aimed to convey to the British Indians the Goan interests in the victory of the Indian movement (Rodrigues 1923). Later, Santana Rodrigues published a series of articles in the newspaper *Dia* dedicated to countering the negative Orientalist myths regarding Indian civilization, and Indian nature, as well as to highlighting the role of Indian intellectuals in the creation of a new humanism that was being drawn from the Orient as well as the Occident. These articles were eventually collected into, and published as, a book that was enthusiastically received in the circles of metropolitan and Goan intellectuals (Rodrigues 1926).

In 1921, this intellectual initiated in the newspaper *Bharat*, a series of articles dedicated to the theme of autonomy. In these articles, Santana Rodrigues affirmed that "the sentiment of autonomy is a persistent tradition of the Indian people" ("Autonomia" 1921. *Bharat* March 21). Condemning the disastrous effects of the Portuguese model of centralisation of governmental power, he proposed the resumption of the traditions of self-governance, namely the empowerment of the Comunidades of the Goan villages, as the only manner in which the "country could return to its antique splendor" ("Pela Índia: as razões da sua autonomia" 1921. *Bharat*, April 7). Finally, he denounced the "mise-en-scene" of the new autonomy law that had recently been promulgated, denouncing in particular the inequality that it subjected the Hindu population to, whom he described as "by chance the only inheritors of the Indian tradition and the instinct for autonomy" ("Pela Índia: a sua autonomia" 1921. *Bharat*, April 14). In July, Santana Rodrigues returned to the theme of autonomy to defend a federal model for the Portuguese Empire, agreeing to an arrangement that proposed substantial autonomy to the colonies and proportional representation for the electorate ("A representação parlamentar da Índia". 1921. *Bharat*, July 14 and 21).

Much of what Santana Rodrigues affirmed in his essays was not new to the discourse of the Catholic autonomist. What was new however, was the insistence on the integration of Hindus in the citizenship equation; and above all, the affirmation that constitutional equality in the Republic impacted on the practical inequality in its practice. In question was the unequal treatment that had been meted out to the populations of the territories of the New Conquests, the territories where the Hindu population dominated.[11] In this aspect, Santana Rodrigues went much further than did António Floriano de Noronha (1873-1931) in his celebrated monograph *Os hindús e a república portuguesa* (Noronha 1922). In this monograph Noronha, a magistrate, traced a gloomy history of the condition of the Hindus under Portuguese dominion, while at the same time defending the redeeming character of the Republican regime that has committed itself to a laicized state.

It was not by chance that Santana Rodrigues chose *Bharat*, a weekly publication published from Quepém, and directed by a Hindu, to make similar affirmations. This bilingual journal published in Marathi and Portuguese, was founded in 1912 in Panjim, and directed until his death, by the pharmacist, advocate and journalist Hegdó Dessai (? –1949). It turned out to be one of the most important and long-lasting Hindu publication with a section written in Portuguese. Between February 1914 and May 1915, Dessai suspended the newspaper in the sequence of Couceiro da Costa's attempt to limit its freedom of expression ("Bharat". *O Ultramar*, February 9, 1914). When he resumed the project he took the newspaper from his original location to the New Conquests. Again he suspended the newspaper between 1916 and 1920 due to financial problems. From this time, the newspaper grew in terms of radicalising its points of view, and in opening itself to collaboration with the intellectuals of the Catholic Left. It was because this journal was the first place of confluence between Hindu and Catholic nationalism, that I chose *Bharat* to trace the evolution of this movement.

Enthusiastically contesting the idea that Goa was essentially a Catholic 'country', in the subsequent years Hegdó Dessai fought for the affirmation of Hindu citizenship ("Goa é um paiz essencialmente catolico?".1920. *Bharat*, April 8). In this spirit, in June 1920, the newspaper supported the proposal of Bascora Sar Dessai (1889–1979) for the creation of a Hindu Provincial Congress "in the manner that one sees in the case of the Indian National Congress". The attempt was to consolidate the Hindu population so as to enable the demand for "their social, moral and economic well-being (...) [seeking] to put the Hindu on par with his Catholic brother" ("Congresso Hindu".1920. *Bharat*, June 10). This idea evoked strong apprehensions from Luís de Menezes Bragança (1878-1938), the cousin and brother-in-law of the Bragança Cunha brothers. By virtue of his consistent defense of secular and democratic values, Menezes Bragança was a much respected personality within the Hindu community. At this time the director of the newspaper *O Debate*, Menezes Bragança could not understand why, in a secular republican State, the Hindus should feel the need to attempt an identitarian-political association of this kind, especially since such a step would only intensify the communal tensions that already vitiated Goan society.

In a series of successive articles, the *Bharat*, and particularly Bascora Sar Dessai, engaged in a polemical debate with the republican Menezes Bragança trying to demonstrate that "if the Republic did treat Hindus as equals to Catholics, politically it did nothing, however, to ensure that we may, equally, benefit from Republican Equality. And what the Republic could not do, will be done by the Hindu class movement, initiated much before the implantation of the [Republican] regime" ("Movimento Hindu". 1920, *Bharat*, September 2).

Sar Dessai defended that the specificity of the problems of the Hindus justified an internal debate prior to a dialogue with the Catholics, which could and should take place in the common Provincial Congress that had been organized since 1916 (SAR DESSAI 1920. "Em pratos limpos". *Bharat*, October 7).

Additionally, and in continuation of its response to Menezes Bragança, the newspaper clarified the concept of Tilakism that it has been using by pointing to the influence that the Maharashtrian politician Bal Gangadhar Tilak exercised over the Goan Hindu community through the writings in his journal *Kesari*. The *Bharat* credited Tilak and *Kesari* with ridding the Goan Hindu community of "the political stagnation in which they vegetated and instilled in them a civic sense that the Indo-Portuguese press—it is unpleasant to say so, but even worse to hide it—had not been able to create in them"("Tilakismo". 1920. *Bharat*, September 2). It was as a result of this role that Tilak played as a rouser of their consciences, Bascora Sar Dessai pointed out, that the Goan Hindus hailed him as the apostle of the religion of the motherland, "the culmination of civic and moral virtues" (Sar Dessai 1920. "Em pratos limpos… Tilak e o Tilakismo". *Bharat*, October 21). Sar Dessai also recalled the indifference with which the Catholic elite still treated the claims of their "Hindu brothers". Referring to the new and regressive law that granted autonomy to the territory and restricted the right to vote in local elections to only those with a command over written Portuguese, he pointed out how the barrier of language was used to restrict their rights, since this law effectively excluded a good part of the Hindu citizens who were proficient only in written Marathi ("Tilak e o tilakismo". 1920. *Bharat*, November 4).[12] This article made it clear that the Tilakism of the Goan Hindus signified the incorporation of the civic activism and patriotism, positions that had defined the British Indian leader who was the first nationalist leader to defend the need of the Indian nationalist movement to abandon its hitherto elitist position.

Sometime later, agitated by the growing general indifference surrounding the meetings of the Provincial Congress, and inspired by the examples of Tilak and Gandhi, ("Gandhismo". 1920. *Bharat*, October 12), *Bharat* initiated a campaign in favour of a new link between the Goan elites and the masses, charging the elites as culpable for the lack of civic spirit in the population ("Verdades amargas". 1921. *Bharat*, January 6 and 18).

Towards the end of January 1921, this campaign resulted in the creation of the political party named the Pragatica Sangh (Sanga). The Sangh was envisioned not only to "contest elections" but above all to "create in the masses through oral propaganda effected by volunteers at the service of its directorate, a self-motivated urge towards what is called the civic conscience" ("O nosso movimento". 1921. *Bharat*, February 10).

The newspaper progressively developed a relationship to the movement in neighbouring British India. In April 1922, the newspaper gave prominent space to reporting the visit to Goa of N.C. Kelkar

(Narasiha Cintāmana Keḷakara), the new principal editor of *Kesari*. In addition to reproducing Kelkar's address at the Saraswat Braman Samaj in Margão, where other Indian nationalists also held forth, the editor concluded his report by repeating the central argument of Kelkar's address: "India is one and indivisible should be the slogan of all the movements concerned with the prosperity of India and the happiness of her inhabitants. And we believe that no one would wish us harm for this, for no one condemns a just aspiration, a legitimate desire, and one that at the end of it all, is natural" ("O Sr. N. G. [sic] Kelker. India is one and indivisible". 1922. *Bharat*, April 6).

The following years were replete with ever growing examples of this connection with Indian nationalism and its instructive influence on the political developments in Portuguese India. This process resulted in a multiplication of the polemic exchanged with the Catholic press and contemporary Hindus, bringing with it a spate of confrontations with the colonial power expressed in law suits where *Bharat* was charged with abusing the freedom of speech.

In 1923, this would result in outrage and polemic within the heart of the Hindu community, when Hegdó Dessai took a position against the commemoration of the Centenary of Vasco da Gama in 1924. Dessai argued his position saying: "We are Hindus and Indians. This is to say: we are not the Portuguese of Portugal, nor the converted Portuguese of India, we consider ourselves just as Hindus and Portucalised [aportuguesados] Indians by the power of Destiny. (...) This circumstance, nevertheless, does not prohibit us from being friends and admirers of the good Portuguese of Portugal and of India (...) Why, therefore is there so much noise [chinfrim] in response to our protest against the celebration of the centenary of a bad Portuguese?" ("Much ado..." 1923. *Bharat*, April 5).

The article 'Centuries later', for its evaluation of Portuguese colonization—"In sum, we are morally, economically, intellectually and physically devastated"—earned the newspaper another law suit ("Séculos depois". 1924. *Bharat*, December 18).

In July of the same year, *Bharat* published an article of a group of Catholic and Hindu students that intervened, contrary to the position of Pereira Batalha's newspaper Província, in a polemical debate around the theme of independence within the context of Republican egalitarianism. In this text, the youths argued that to want "an independent India did not offend the Portuguese Republic, on the contrary it proved that the Indians were so worthy of the republican ideal that in spite of the fact of their being dominated, they had the conviction of civic ideals and sufficient belief in their principles to loudly proclaim their aspiration to live now, or later, or in the remote future free and independent" (Um Grupo De Académicos. 1924. 'Agora nós', *Bharat*, July 10).

Demonstrating the emergence of a new political atmosphere in Goa were the statements of the chemical engineer Fernando de Costa (1906-?) at the 6th Provincial Congress, in March 1924. Fernando da Costa seems to have greatly agitated the proceedings of Provincial Congress, having been particularly booed in the session discussing administrative and financial autonomy. A report on the discussions held at the Congress indicated that Costa stated "that it is for the fourth time, if we are not mistaken, that he is a member of the Third International and declares himself a partisan of [demands for] an expanded autonomy, with members and a council composed purely of Indians, following the example of Canada; he wants instruction in the vernacular language; a Sanskrit school; and that schools teach above all, Indian History, especially of Portuguese India, because this history being better understood, will directly influence the character of the child (These considerations provoked much hilarity and were frequently interrupted with boos by the assembly). The President observed that Mr. Costa was out of order, the point that he raised being outside the scope of discussion. He therefore, requested from the members, permission to avoid putting his proposals to the vote (Approvals from the assembly)" (Cunha 1928, 198-9).

Later, Fernando da Costa would recall the session at a dinner party in Lisbon on December 25, 1925 ("Uma festa de união e paz". 1926. *Bharat*, February 4). It is through his address at this dinner that we are able to reconstruct the course of his intellectual trajectory. In this address he pointed out that when he was a student leaving for the metropolis, "I considered myself Portuguese, but with a fervent regionalism. Arriving in Lisbon this regionalism transformed itself into nationalism. I discussed with my compatriots, my colleagues, almost all being by then 'Portuguese'".[13]

From Lisbon, he left to Germany where he gained his Licentiate and was a part of the Third International. At this point, disagreeing with the ideology of Gandhian non-violence, he joined the International Communist Party; this party "being the only group that wants to, and can aid us in the exercise of war and provide armaments". In the Goan case, Fernando da Costa considered that the first step to take ought to be the demand for progressive autonomy. Suffering only deceptions (to use his own words) after his arrival to Goa, he returned to the metropolis the following year.

The dinner party where Fernando da Costa made this address was not simply a meeting among friends to celebrate Christmas. It was in fact a meeting of nationalists, almost all, if not all, being scions of well-known families from among the Goan Catholic elite, most of who were in Lisbon as students. The objective of the dinner was to discuss the founding of an 'Indian National Party'. Amongst others who spoke at this meeting, were Zacarias Antão, Benedito Fulgêncio Brito, Aires Gracias, Druston Rodrigues and Cunha Gomes. Fernando da Costa recollected that the idea had emerged some days before, at a dinner offered to the 'patricíos'[14] from British India who were studying at Oxford and were visiting Portugal.

From this meeting emerged a telegram of solidarity to the Indian students, and a motion, that affirmed that given that there "exist in Goa, various parties committed to the nationalist ideal, and believing the constitution of an 'Indian National Party' necessary and urgent, we appeal to the patriotism of our citizens to unite forgetting our religious differences and castes, cooperating in the resurgence and progress of our Hindu Homeland."

Between these two meetings, the promoters of this initiative had sent messages to the student groups in Coimbra and Porto. Having received patriotic messages from these groups, the promoters immediately sent the motion to the principal Goan newspapers, appending a list of names of all students associated with nationalist ideas. On February 4, 1926, *Bharat* dedicated a special issue to this event. The tenor of the text was received with some amount of shock, causing a surge of demands from a number of families to their children to distance themselves from this initiative.

As was to be expected, a text that set out as an objective the construction of a future Hindu Homeland had to deal with a good amount of resistance from large segments of the Catholic community, even though it was later clarified that in this case 'Hindu' was being used to signify Indian. On the other hand, over the following months, as the protests from those involved made obvious, there had been a certain amount of over enthusiasm on the part of the promoters of the initiative in adding the list of the students from Coimbra and Porto. Among these students, however, there were also some who did not hide their nationalist convictions, as was the case of Adeodato Barreto, leader of the students in Coimbra. As a result of this initiative, the leaders of the movement found themselves obliged to present multiple explanations, proffering these explanations particularly in *Bharat* and *A Índia Portuguesa*. This latter newspaper, under the direction of Padre António Gregório da Costa, would in latter times turn into one of the important supporters of the democratic Republican and Marxist opposition to the then recently installed Portuguese dictatorship.[15]

From among the proponents of this initiative in Lisbon, it would be Fernando da Costa, António Furtado, Telo Mascarenhas, António Noronha, and Druston Rodrigues, who, either under their own name, or Hindu pseudonyms, attempted to clarify the ideological quadrant within which they operated, and explain that they were not trying to create an anti-Catholic movement, but were attempting to integrate, or transcend the religious question. The principal message of this movement was synthesized by Druston Rodrigues: "What is it that we are attempting? (…) The complete independence of all of India, untied from all imperial connections and free of all foreign supervision; the establishment of a Republic of the United States of India, where Goa would be a federal state. Thus, what is at stake is not the emancipation of a people apt for self-government. We hope to achieve this yes, but more particularly we see their political liberty" ("Pela Pátria". 1926. *Bharat*, April 15).

A reading of these different texts allow us to see that the movement encompassed a Gandhian wing, as well as a branch of activists who were close to the more radical positions associated with the group that gathered around Jawaharlal Nehru. In an attempt to demonstrate to his fellow Goan citizens that this was not a movement of eccentrics, the Gandhian Druston Rodrigues published a series of interviews with Portuguese personalities: Eduardo Frias, Reinaldo Ferreira, Rocha Martins, Ferreira de Castro, Campos Lima, Mário Domingues, who, despite the diversity of their political positions, shared in common a sympathy for the Indian cause and the Goan initiative ("Sempre é tempo". 1926. *Bharat*, April 15; "Um inquérito". *idem*, May 6; "O nosso inquérito". *idem*, May 20, June 1)[16]. In September, Fernando da Costa brought to the newspaper a contribution of substantial weight; the recollections of the historically significant intellectual and republican politician Sebastião de Magalhães Lima of the lectures Costa had given at the Free University of Lisbon. In these recollections Magalhães Lima affirmed that the conference that Fernando da Costa dedicated to Gandhi, over which he had presided on June 30 of that year ("Em defesa da Índia". 1926. *Bharat*, July 29), had "the effect of being a veritable resurrection (...) It was a veritable flight of idealism" (quote by Costa 1926, "O nosso ideal". *Bharat*, September 9).

By this time, Druston Rodrigues had parted ways with the "party", but not with militant nationalism. He was shocked by the two articles of Fernando de Costa who, in an intolerant reaction to the criticism that the movement was suffering, categorized the Goans into "the nationalists, the fearful, the fanatics and the rogues" ("PNI". 1926. *Bharat*, April 8); and even insulted Menezes Bragança ("Ainda a moção". 1926. *Bharat*, April 13), a figure who was much respected in nationalist circuits.

It was into this convulsive environment that Tristão de Bragança Cunha arrived in Goa in July that year. Soon after his arrival he granted some interviews to the newspaper *A Índia Portuguesa*, elaborating on the international political moment ("Politica europeia: uma entrevista". 1926, August 28; "Política asiatico-europeia: 2ª entrevista". November 9). Towards the end of November he began associating with this weekly, dedicating his first articles to the theme of Indian nationalism and offering therein a Marxist reading of the movement ("O Nacionalismo indiano". 1926. *A Índia Portuguesa*, November 27, December 14). After this, and in the following years, T.B. Cunha collaborated regularly with periodicals associated with the opposition to the Estado Novo, such as *Bharat* and *Pracasha*. This latter newspaper was founded in 1928 by Venctexa Sar Dessai to spread awareness about the shuddhi movement, and relied on the aid of Menezes Bragança who soon became its principal editor.

What this chronology of events suggests, and the testament of the daughter of Luís de Menezes Bragança (Bragança 1992) confirms, is that this series of interventions, both in Goa and the metropolis, were coordinated and served to introduce the Pro-Indian Nationalistic thematic in Goan public debate. Later on, in 1928, the movement took a symbolic step forward with the creation of a Goan section of the Indian National Congress. The pertinence of this gesture, as is well known, was not evident to the British India national movement at the time. Nevertheless, what the interventions in the press, namely in *Bharat*, confirm for us, is that while this action united different political sensibilities of Goan nationalism, it was with difficulty that they could manage to keep these actions coordinated.

The papers that survived of the vast intellectual estate of Adeodato Barreto (1905-1937) elucidate clearly the crossroads in which the metropolitan movement found itself in its relation with the Goan elites to which they also belonged.[17] Among his manuscripts we encounter extensive fragments of letters that he wrote in 1927 to his colleagues in Lisbon. In these letters, the young intellectual, who presented himself as being of the "School of Gandhi", traced what he considered necessary for a nationalist strategy, recording that the movement depended on the support of the Goans to the cause. To his mind, capturing these sympathies was going to be impossible with the presence of incendiary declarations that sought "a sowing of the seeds of hatred and vengeance". Adeodato Barreto had in mind an article written by Telo Mascarenhas where the student labelled the Portuguese conquerors "pirates and tyrants that we should disdain and forget as the only form of vengeance for our ancestors"(Mascarenhas 1926, "A morte dos ídolos" *Bharat*, November 4).

The road pointed out by Adeodato Barreto was the pedagogy of nationalism, a method to "teach the Goans to love India". Within this framework, he considered it fundamental to join indoctrination with creativity, placing his hopes on the creation of a literature that would insinuate nationalism into the public spirit "even if it was contrary to their will". In other words, Adeodato Barreto articulated a route that would stress a cultural intervention with political roots, a route that, being less prone to polemic, could in time prove much more efficacious. In time, the idea would be converted into the project *Índia Nova*, an academic newspaper published in Coimbra, which was able to gather Goan nationalists not only from the Coimbra academy (which by that time had been enlarged by the presence of several Goan students, such as Telo Mascarenhas, who moved from the capital) but also from the Oporto and the Lisbon academic groups.

The activity of the proposed party in the metropole, converted into the Hindu Nationalist Centre, would diminish in the subsequent years. However, the nationalists continued to intervene in the Goan and metropolitan press in defence of the Indian cause. The above cited figures joined forced with other intellectuals, like the much-forgotten Carlos da Cruz (1907-1958), another collaborator of *Bharat*, who, first in Daman, and then in Bombay, engaged in intense political activity.[18] Most significantly, the list of intellectuals who converted to the cause grew after the enactment of the Acto Colonial.

Some of these young intellectuals, like António Furtado, Telo Mascarenhas and T.B. Cunha would end up playing a critical role in the movement for the integration of Goa into the Indian Union. At the moment of its birth, that was the moment of the start of the decades-long Portuguese dictatorship, the activity of the Goan nationalist, both in the metropole, and in Goa, interlaced itself with opposition at the Estado Novo, as well as opposition to the other anti-democratic movements that assaulted the world at the time.

This was a position that Menezes Bragança had already pointed out in his pamphlet titled *À margem duma ideia* (1927) concerning the creation of the Instituto Indiano de Coimbra, under the leadership of Adeodato Barreto. In this pamphlet, Menezes Bragança, alerted the young students to the critical turn that the country and the world was to take in a fundamental conflict of ideologies that required them to take clear political positions and be militant about their causes. At risk were "the principle of liberty, and the emancipation of the people. It is the ideal of democracy, the destroyer of acquisitive imperialisms, of dictatorships murderers of the people's claims, especially in the colonies, where they seek to restore the regime of subjection and subalternism".[19] By different routes, most of these intellectuals demonstrated that they internalized these notions significantly, dedicating a substantial part of their lives to interventions in the public cause.

The example of Adeodato Barreto would make a fine case in point of the commitment and agenda of these intellectuals. Barreto would intervene consistently from 1926, until his death in 1937, in the metropolitan press, and from time to time in the Goan press, not only in defence of the Indian nationalist point of view but equally on the values of democracy, of social solidarity, and of human fraternity. Engaging himself in lively polemical debates with some of the principal figures of the reactionary movement "Integralismo Lusitano" such as António Ferro, João Ameal and Alfredo Pimenta; Barreto defended these principles of political-philosophy, in newspapers such as *Voz da Justiça*, *Liberdade*, *O Povo*, *Seara Nova*, and *Círculo*. He defended these ideals not merely in the polemical debates but practically, offered free lessons to the mine-workers in Alentejo. For their part, as evidence of their gratitude for his solidarity, these workers gathered all their savings to ensure Barreto's treatment of the disease that would be responsible for ending his life.

Accompanying the development of this movement allows us to see the manner in which the Goa question could come to be transformed through the cultural and political actions of a significant minority of Goan intellectuals, both Catholic as well as Hindu, many years prior to the independence of India. These intellectuals would be joined in the subsequent years by others, thanks to the decisive role that these intellectuals played in augmenting a favourable opinion towards a future integration of Goa in the Indian federation, to the psychological rupture that was effected among the Goan elite thanks to the introduction of the Acto Colonial, and to the hardening of the position of the dictatorship and the kind of colonialist discourse that it permitted.

It would be correct to affirm that after the First World War there were two currents of thought in Goan public opinion as regards the future of the territory. The autonomist current had a politically relevant tradition since the beginning of the 20th century, and its more radical branch argued for dissolution of the colonial relationship and the inauguration of a federal solution for future relations with Portugal and her overseas territories. This current, composed of a variety of different sensibilities, was predominantly Catholic and it considered the continuation of a relationship with Portugal as necessary for the definition of Goan identity, and to continue the relationship with Western culture and Catholicism that had commenced *via* Portugal as a route. The feeling that this segment of the population entertained in relationship to a Portuguese identity was, however, fairly fluid, given that while on the one hand they demanded the equality due to citizens of Portugal, and partook in the sentiment of 'Portugalidade', at the same time, they did not hesitate to warn of a loss in these feelings of affection to Portugal in the events when local aspirations were not met.[20]

The second current that has been discussed in this article, proposed to the Goan public that they join issue with the struggle for Indian independence. This position alerted the Portuguese public opinion and the colonial authorities to the necessity to be alive to the possibility that such future of an integration of the territory to an independent India was seen by many as a natural course of events. This current saw Goa's future as one of the states of a future federative State of India. In addition to this general proposition, it was a position that emerged out of the self-critique by the Goan elite. This critique affirmed the need to move beyond the communal dissensions that marked the public sphere, if they were to resolve the differences between the two communities. Additionally, it introduced the themes of social reform, influenced by socialist and libertarian thought. Realizing the importance of forming a public opinion on the matters related to the exercise of the citizenship ensured an appeal to groups outside of the traditional sphere of the elites who mattered.

With respect to this nationalist current that was pro-Indian, the chronology of texts discussed in this article demonstrates that contrary to the nationalist narrative that consecrates T.B. Cunha as the pioneer of the Indian nationalist sentiment in Goa, the public sphere was already inclined in this direction and marked by a diversity of positions in the debate. Cunha was but one of the final, though important elements that held this position. Finally, the interventions of these intellectuals, both in Goa, and especially in the metropole,[21] was central to the opening of the debate in Portugal as regards the movement for Indian independence, contributing decisively to the formation of a current of public opinion in Portugal, especially among the left intellectuals, favourable to the Indian cause. Until these interventions, public opinion had been dominated by perspectives offered by the pro-British news agencies.

Through this intervention, these intellectuals integrated into the general debate around the problems of colonialism, the issue of the rights of people to self-determination, of the profile of states resulting from the battles for liberation, and of the future relationship

collaborated as a correspondent in Paris–to promise soon after it was initiated, the future collaboration of the well-known orientalist ("Sylvain Lévy". 1911. *O Debate*, June 5). The tone of this article, published on the occasion of the release of the *Melanges*, which paid tribute to Sylvain Lévy's 25 years as a teacher, suggests that Bragança Cunha was its author and that he was probably one of Lévy's students.

11. The laws, No. 1005 of August 7, 1920 and No. 1022 of August 20, 1920 instituted new rules for the civil and financial administration of the colonies. In conformance with these laws two councils, the *Conselho Executivo* (the Executive Council) and *Concelho Legislativo* (Legislative Council) were constituted substituting the previously existing *Conselho de Governo.* It was only the second council that would have elected representatives. The Decree 7030 of October 16, 1920 indicated the number of elected representative in each colony. In accordance with this decree, the *Concelho Legislativo* of the State of India was to have 11 elected representatives: 1 representative for the Concelho of Ilhas, 1 for Bardês, 1 for the combined territories of Mormugão and Salcete, 1 for the Concelhos of the New Conquests, 1 for the district of Daman, 1 for the Diu, 1 for the Comunidades, 1 for the commercial and industrial associations, 1 for the farmers' associations and landlords, 1 for the other class associations, and 1 for the 90 largest taxpayers.
12. The discussion is in reference to base 46 of the law that set up the rules for the future Autonomy Laws of each colony (dec. 7008/ 9.10.1920). In Goa this article would originate a long polemic regarding its applicability to the natives of Estado da Índia (see Rau 1926). It is to be noted that apart from the year of 1918, during which it was imposed a law of universal suffrage to all Portuguese citizens (law of 11.3.1918), since the law of 3.7.1913, the right to vote for general elections was restricted to the citizens who read and write in Portuguese, which means that it excluded most Hindu literate citizens. This was a clear step back in face of previous electoral legislation. Since 1878, when for the first time that capacity was introduced as one of the criteria to be a voter, any citizen that could read and write was considered regardless of the language of this literacy (PRESIDÊNCIA DO CONSELHO DE MINISTROS 1998).
13. A similar path is described by Telo Mascarenhas in his memories: "The wonderful knowledge about India that we gained awoke in us nationalistic feelings" (Mascarenhas 1976, 60). It is interesting to compare this trajectory from ideas to sentiments, with the one described by Aluisio Soares, who was living in British India at the time of these events. Aluisio Soares describes his wakening to Indian-ness as linked

to the events of Jallianwala Bagh and the climate of terror which subsequently was installed through the Empire: "On reading about these terrible events, my soul was filled with horror and indignation. (...) The point I am making is that for the first time I felt deeply involved in what was happening in India. The people who had been murdered and humiliated were no longer strangers to me. They became my flesh, blood of my blood. From a Goan I evolved into an Indian, even though owing to a historical accident I continued to be an alien" (Soares 1971, 1, 93-4).

14. "Patrícios" (originally from the same homeland, Pátria) was, and still is, a common way of Portuguese speaking Goans to refer to other Goans. The expression is hardly used by metropolitan Portuguese, which makes it very "Goan". In this case they were not referring particularly to Goans, but to Indians in general.
15. A position that would be maintained until Father Gregório da Costa was obliged by the Patriarch, in term under pressure from the civil authorities, to give up his direction of the newspaper ("Fusão deprimente" 1933. *O Anglo-Lusitano*, March 4).
16. The persons referred to were journalists, writers, and politicians who occupied a variety of positions in the political spectrum, ranging from republicans to anarcho-syndicalists.
17. I thank Kalidas Barreto for access to the papers of his father. I would also like to draw attention to the fact that I was dealing with a number of fragments of copies of his correspondence. This fact made it difficult to prepare a formal bibliography for the documentation. As such, based on its relevance I opted to include some informal citations.
18. In Bombay he arrived to lead the influential *O Anglo-Lusitano* and was eventually obliged to cease this activity by the British authorities, thanks to the pressure applied by Portuguese diplomacy (Faleiro 2010; *Source Material for a History of the freedom movement in India* 1978).
19. Bragança, 1927, 14–quoted in *Índia Nova*, July 3, 1928. In the sequence of this statement, Menezes Bragança alerted: "I do have to call the attention to the consequences of this medievalism, to the numerous devotes that this doctrine has in this land, whom, with an astounding unconsciousness, are giving it large publicity, missing the fact that they are smelting the chains of servitude. "Voluntary slaves, said Tacitus, make more tyrants than tyrants make slaves".
20. Critical moments that promoted these threatening postures were the Massacre of September 21, 1891; the events of 1895-97; and the implantation of the Republic in 1910.
21 By virtue of its proximity to British-India, Goa had easier access to alternative fonts of information, early on having formed a large body

of opinion sympathetic to the fight on the other side of the colonial border.

REFERENCES

Manuscripts

Adeodato Barreto's personal archive

Periodicals

[The dates correspond to the years I've consulted of the periodicals quoted in the text.]

Anglo-Lusitano (O), 1886–98, 1933. Bombaim.
Debate (O), 1911–21. Pangim.
Bharat, 1912–33. Pangim, Quepém.
Índia Nova, 1928–29. Coimbra, Lisboa.
Índia Portuguesa (A), 1895–98, 1909–33. Several locations.
Luz do Oriente, 1907–20. Pondá.
O Ultramar, 1889–98, 1910–30, 1933. Margão.

Legislation

[Texts of the mentioned "organic decrees" are available at: http://www.fd.unl.pt/ConteudosAreasDetalhe.asp?ID=45&Titulo=Biblioteca%20 Digital&Area=Biblioteca Digital]

"Decreto nº 7008" 1920. *Diário da República,* I Série. nº 202, October 9.
"Decreto nº 7030" 1920. *Diário da República,* I Série. nº 208, October 16.
"Lei nº 1005" 1920. *Diário da República, I Série.*, nº 151, August 7.
"Lei nº 1022" 1920. *Diário da República, I Série.* nº 161, August 20.
PRESIDÊNCIA DO CONSELHO DE MINISTROS.1998. *Legislação eleitoral portuguesa: 1820-1926,* org. e introd. Pedro Tavares de Almeida. Lisboa: INCM.

Monographs and Articles

Bragança, Bertha Menezes de. 1992. *Landmarks in my time*. Margão: Author's edition.
Bragança, Luís de Menezes. 1927. *À Margem duma ideia.* Nova Goa: Tip. Bragança & Cª.

Costa, Aleixo Manuel da. 1997. *Dicionário de literatura goesa,* Lisboa: Centro Cultural de Macau: Fundação Oriente, 3 v.

Couto, Maria Aurora. 2004. *Goa: A daughter's story*. Nova Delhi, Penguin Books.

Cunha, António Maria da. 1928. *Congresso Provincial da Índia Portuguesa: subsídios para a sua história*. V. 3, Nova Goa: Casa Luso-Francesa – Editora.

Faleiro, Valmiki. 2010. "The Little Known Patriot". *Herald,* August 25. http://issuu.com/herald-goa/docs/25_aug

Lobo, Sandra. 2009. "Índia Nova: nacionalismo e cosmopolitismo num jornal académico". *Cultura: revista de história e teoria das ideias* 26: 231–258.

Mascarenhas, Telo. 1976. *When the mango-trees blossomed: Quasi-memoirs*. Bombaim: Orient Longman.

Miranda, Lúcio de. 1940. *Adeodato Barreto* (ensaio biográfico e crítico). Bastorá: Tip. Rangel.

Noronha, António de. 1922. "Os hindús e a república portuguesa" *Índia Portuguesa: memórias escritas a convite do Governo-Geral da Índia Portuguesa*. Nova Goa: Imprensa Nacional, 2: (209)-368.

Rau, Siurama Bolvonta. 1926. *Notas à margem do Projecto do Código de Usos e Costumes de Goa (elaborado pelo sr. Doutor António Bernardo de Bragança Pereira)*. Bastorá: Tip. Rangel.

Rodrigues, Aleixo Santana. 1926. *A Índia contemporânea: com prefácio do Prof. Azevedo Neves*. Lisboa: J. Rodrigues & Cª.

Rodrigues, Santana. 1923. *The Indian national movement*. Lisboa: N. G. R.

Soares, Aloysius. 1971. *Down the corridors of time (recollections and reflexions). V. 1. 1891–1948*. Bombaim: Author's edition.

Source Material for a History of the freedom movement in India. V. VIII, part. 1: Goa Freedom Struggle vis-a-vis Maharashtra (1946–1960). 1978. ed. Maharashtra State Gazetteer. http://www.maharashtra.gov.in/english/gazetteer/Source_material_files/Source_material.htm

Chapter 11

The Post-1961 Press in Goa

Its Politics and Processes

Frederick Noronha

Impressive and gutsy piece by Raman Kirpal. He has done more in this one article than the Goan media has managed in totality in the 50 years since decolonisation. —*Reader's Comment* (First Post: 2011)

Introduction

Of all the changes taking place in post-1961 Goa, the media has changed quite significantly, if imperceptibly. Unfortunately there have been very few studies or seminars on this theme, with a few exceptions such as the Quepem seminar on the media (Government College, 1993), *In Black and White* (Noronha 2008c), Xavier Centre for Historical Research (XCHR) seminar discussions (XCHR 1987), few Goa Union of Journalists (GUJ) publications (GUJ 1991), etc. Criticism on Goa's media came out in the open in a big way perhaps only in the 1980s, and even more recently now.

On a personal note, one could say that this trend has paralleled the author's own career in the media over the same period. The student ferment of the late 1970s and early 1980s probably sparked off this trend. Many journalists who entered the media as idealistic students, fresh out of college and with a desire to 'change the world;, went through a mixed sense of frustration with the existing media and impatience over why change was not happening over such a long period. Today, many of that generation of campaigners and activists hold responsible positions in the media. Has the situation changed significantly? Let us investigate.

In the early 1980s, the walls of Panjim, and perhaps more so in places like Margao, were splattered with a summary and blunt critique of the media. Slogans were written against the existing newspapers, criticising them for hounding certain politicians of that period (Faleiro 2008b). Probably, it was this sentiment that led to the launching of 'alternate' papers like the *Herald* (former *O Heraldo*), in a new English-language avatar in 1983.

The past five decades can be somewhat simplistically, but perhaps which is useful for the purpose of analysis, divided into several distinct phases. The boundary markers might not be as sharp as made out to be in the discussion below, but all the same these divisions could help in understanding the situation.

The 1960s

The 1960s saw the demise of the Portuguese papers, and the growth and consolidation of new newspapers in the then-rising languages of the times. Strange though it may seem, but for understandable reasons, which are elaborated below, Konkani was not the popular language of the newspaper readers or the publishers' choice. Instead, it was English–if one goes by circulation, advertiser interest and influence wielded–and Marathi, especially in terms of growing circulation, encouragement to new writers (Mandrekar n.d.), and coverage given to smaller areas too. A small but noticeable development was the attempt to build the *Goa Monitor* newspaper, an initiative of politician Erasmo de Sequeira, son of prominent Opposition leader Jack de Sequeira.

Even at the risk of racing ahead of our story, it might be added here though that *O Heraldo*, founded around the turn of the 19th–20th century, continued in operation as a Portuguese daily till 1983. Then, it shifted from being a shoddily-printed tabloid with a shrinking circulation (estimated at 500 copies daily) to a broadsheet possessing at that time (Noronha 2008a), one of the most sophisticated typesetting and one of the best printing systems across the country. In those days, it used to call itself "the only Portuguese daily to be printed in Asia" (a claim that has been contested by some who point to the situation in Macau). It managed subsequently through various strategies to rebrand itself and currently claims to be the largest English language newspaper in Goa (*Herald* 2013).

The 1970s and 1980s

Coming back to our attempt to build a rough timeline. The 1970s were marked by the consolidation of the new dailies that had been set up in the earlier decade such as *The Navhind Times* in the English language segment and the *Dainik Gomantak*, in Marathi. There were attempts to build alternatives to these publications, some born out of competition and financial goals and others apparently from a realisation of the crucial need for competition within the newspaper market (Faleiro 2008a). None of these were successful or managed to sustain themselves.

It was only in the 1980s that competition among the daily newspapers entered the market in any real sense. The *Herald* started (Noronha 2008a) on an inconspicuous and, if one may take the liberty of saying so, inauspicious note, since the paper got the dateline printed wrong (with the date and day of the week not matching) below its masthead on the launch of its English language daily.

With regard to Marathi dailies, the *Tarun Bharat,* a daily from Belgaum known for its involvement in the border controversy there, set up its base in Panjim and Margao and later witnessed phenomenal growth. It brought in some degree of the politics of polarisation to its news pages, accompanied by an intense level of local news coverage. In terms of circulation figures it managed to sideline the Marathi *Gomantak* daily. In 1987, the *Gomantak Times,* an English language daily from the Gomantak group then owned by the Chowgule industrial house, made its presence felt, even though it lagged behind *The Navhind Times* and *Herald* dailies in terms of circulation.

Media in the 1990s

In the 1990s, the scenario changed further. Outside the world of print, the not-so-new but recently privatised technology of FM radio emerged on the scene changing the entertainment and music scene in Goa, before fading out temporarily to emerge a few years later.

Expectations that FM radio could be a source for local news, however, did not materialise for diverse reasons, particularly because of the federal government's policy of being cautious about private radio players broadcasting news (Noronha 2000).

The 1990s and the first decade of this century witnessed the growing clout of outstation newspapers, particularly in Marathi, in the Goa market. Other notable events in the 1990s include the birth of the weekly *The Goan Observer,* the demise of some smaller publications such as the weekly *Goan Post* (owned by the politician-businessman Surendra Furtado) and the growth of a number of free-sheeters (newspapers circulated without price, and dependent on advertising for their economics). Many of these have subsequently been closed, except the *Vasco Watch*, an initiative of a retired Navy Officer Cmdr Narayanan (Braganza 2008).

Media in the 21st Century

Since 2000 onwards the media in Goa have witnessed new trends. In 2003, on the occasion of the 20th anniversary of the shift of *O Heraldo* to being an English-language daily, its founder-editor, Rajan Narayan, quit the publication and launched his own weekly, *The Goan Observer*, amidst some contention about who and what was responsible for this change. In 2008, *the Times of India*, the largest English-language newspaper in the country, launched a Goa edition that dramatically increased the salaries of journalists, at least for some time. Wage hikes, not always voluntarily implemented, occurred in some other newspapers too due to fear of losing staff. This, however, resulted in a drastic rewriting of the media rules within the state. We shall discuss this issue in detail later on.

An overview of the media in Goa today would be incomplete without mentioning other forms of media besides mainstream newspapers such as magazines, radio, advertising, mobile phones, the Internet and all its many options. A flurry of magazines, mostly of the glossy type, and aimed at the advertising market and the upmarket readers in the state, are being produced in Goa currently. These include publications such as *Viva Goa*, *My Goa*, *Planet Goa* and *Target Goa*. Together with these magazines, the recent years have witnessed the launch of a number of cable or satellite TV outlets.

'Goa Newsline', launched by former *Gomantak* journalist Waman Prabhu was the first one to start. Subsequently, bigger players entered this market, launching local TV channels such as 'Goa 365', 'HCN' (affiliated to the *Herald* network and owned by the family of Raul Fernandes), and 'Prudent' (linked to the industrialist family of Timblos, with major interests in mining and luxury hotels).

The fluctuating fortunes of Konkani magazines and largely unsuccessful attempts at starting Konkani newspapers are issues that are widely acknowledged but unaddressed so far. In recent years, the revival of the Romi Konkani script has seen attempts to boost publications.

The 1960s is a crucial decade to understand media changes in Goa. This decade saw the most changes occurring on the media scene, but very little has been written about it. Till 1961, the newspapers were censored as the government did not allow freedom of press. After that, the first newspapers censored were "altogether a different experience", as suggested by Ave Cleto Afonso, a journalist in the 1960s who later moved into academia. In 1961, all the major papers such as *Heraldo*, *O Herald* (the predecessor to today's English language *Herald*) and the evening daily *Diario de Noite* in Panjim, and *A Vida* and *Diario de Goa* in Margao were in Portuguese. At that time, the Marathi press did not have any daily publication and this situation continued for sometime after 1961. This data is based on a personal discussion with Mr. Afonso (Afonso 2011). While *Heraldo* closed down immediately after its editor had some differences with the new administration, *O Heraldo* continued. *Diario de Noite* continued for a couple of years more while *A Vida* continued till May 1967, just after the Opinion Poll.

The demise of the Portuguese newspapers is one of the under-studied aspects of post-1961 Goa. While the falling circulation could have accounted for this demise, it could also have been due to lack of government advertising that aggravated the situation in some cases. Another reason could be because the Portuguese-speakers were sometimes mischievously identified as being 'pro-Portuguese' (Ibid.).

"The Portuguese newspapers after Liberation along with their staff had the handicap of having to prove their nationalist credentials almost at every point of time," says Afonso, one of the younger journalists in the 1960s (Ibid.). But some publications from the

Portuguese times also fell to the wayside simply because they couldn't keep up with the times.

Some of the issues that emerged from a closer scrutiny of media in post-1961 Goa are as follows:

A. The Levers of Power

The issue of who controls the media is a crucial one. In recent years, the media has changed in its character, a trend which some critics have failed to notice. The US-based anthropologist Dr. Robert S. Newman commented: "Goa's first post-colonial Chief Minister Dayanand Bandodkar and his fellow industrialists attempted to shape public opinion through their newspapers–there are almost no independent paper in Goa–and through tertiary educational institutions which they themselves had established. The Chowgules, for example, launched the newspapers *Gomantak* and *Uzvadd....*" (Newman 1984). He went on to describe links between the "big families" (businessmen, traditional landowners and those he describes as war profiteers) and tertiary educational institutions in the State.

In an earlier essay I have argued: "In Goa, the daily newspapers' editorial stances on various protest movements would tend to reveal a largely unfriendly attitude towards such actions. It is not perhaps coincidental that individuals and groups involved in protest issues in Goa have often felt that they have received an unfair deal from the media" (Noronha, 1999 b)." This comment is based on editorials on the subject of protest and the media response to it in Goa over a three-decade period, from the early 1960s to the 1990s.

But quietly, over time, and sometimes hardly noticed, the situation has drastically changed. Mining houses are linked with only a minority of newspapers read in Goa today. We see that The Gomantak Group, which includes both the Marathi *Gomantak* and English-language *Gomantak Times,* has been sold by the Chowgules to the Pawars of Maharashtra. The Dempos, which run the *Navhind Times* and *Navprabha,* have sharply reduced their stake in mining recently. Major newpapers like the *Lokmat* in Marathi and the *Times of India* have launched operations in Goa in the later part of the last decade, changing the very character of newspaper ownership here. However, it would be true to say that some mining houses have taken on an enhanced direct or indirect role in the cable and satellite TV arena in Goa even as the sector's involvement in print fell sharply.

Likewise, the relationship between publications and their readers have also changed in some ways, though one could debate how significant the changes are. From the 1960s till the early 1980s, a monopoly-type situation prevailed amidst the media here, resulting in publications adopting a dismissive stance towards their readers' concerns, knowing that local readers had little to choose from by way of alternatives. Since the competition has grown sharply, the arrogance of the past has given way to an approach of almost pandering to the reader.

But the growing clout of the advertiser in local newspapers cover the costs of newspapers and prices had remained static, or fallen in real terms over the past years, but the reader has been given short shrift in ways that make a vital difference.

B. The Politics of News

Another noticeable change that has happened in recent years is the growth of party politics, which has been increasingly influencing the running of some newspapers. In the past, newspapers have had their biases and favoured particular constituencies but this was done on the basis of either community, caste or language groups rather than on political lines. While some did favour the ruling party, or even adopted a policy to support whichever party was in power, now we find a direct involvement of politicians and parties with media institutions following, in a way, trends which have been there in the past in South Indian states such as Andhra Pradesh, Tamil Nadu and Kerala. The *Gova Doot* has close connections with a political party which has played a dominant role in Goa—both in Opposition and ruling, the BJP—and one can often see a direct convergence in issues and concerns raised by the party and the paper. Critical scholars like P. Sainath have pointed to the growing links of newspapers in Maharashtra with prominent politicians.

C. The Language Issue

One of the ironies of post-1961 Goa is the fact that the language divide in the Union Territory (later State) has played itself out in strange and unusual ways. Konkani is claimed to be spoken by "95 per cent" of the people (The Goa, Daman and Diu Official Language Act, 1987), yet only a very tiny segment of the population choose to receive their news in that language. The major chunk of Goa's readership is almost equally divided between English and Marathi. This is all the more noticeable as, in the wake of the political changes of 1961, the Portuguese language was replaced by English virtually overnight. Though causing problems to those who had studied in Portuguese, the transition to English was speedily accepted both by the new bureaucracy here and more significantly by the Anglophone section of Goa's expatriate population (mostly Catholic).

The politics of script and dialect, and issues of democratisation and hegemony, have only recently been hotly debated in Goa (Noronha 1999a). These issues, while not of direct relevance to the scope of this paper, are a major concern to our newspapers as they grope with the fluid language situation that could have crucial implications for the future.

D. The Need for Alternatives, Smaller Voices

Since the 1970s, there has been a growing concern about the need for diversity in Goa's media (Faleiro 2008a) (refer to Paul John's paper). Today, technology and changing economics have made it possible for alternative news flows and news control even at the regional level. However, more of such type of news needs to be compiled and capitalised on.

There has been an impressive growth in the role of cyberspace (Gomes 2001; (Noronha 2011). Likewise, even the Konkani stage has been able to maintain its vibrancy (Fernandes 2010) and perhaps growth, though there are no conclusive studies on this aspect in the face of television and growing media competition. Even conservative political organisations like the Shiv Sena adopted various ways of using the traditional media, such as even the blackboard hung on a village barber's wall, to spread their message.

Challenghes Facing Goan Media Today

Before concluding, it makes sense to evaluate briefly some of the challenges facing the media in today's Goa, after five decades of relative self-rule here. After growing in influence in post-colonial times, in tandem with an expansion of the media itself (due to financial, market and other reasons) and also due to the growth in literacy and the local middle class, the media faces new challenges today. Going by one's own perception, its credibility is not as high as it once was. This is not without reason, given the role sections of the media have played in a context of speedy expansion.

At the same time, large sections of the population are still untouched in their daily lives by the media. The politics-and-sports staple that most papers have offered seems to exclude large sections of potential female readership and youth (outside of sports). Advertiser interest predominates in the media, leading the reader to feel neglected or even sidetracked. The role of the advertiser in dominating our daily news media is apparent with every passing day, as cover-prices stay artificially low and large sections of the news-pages, including the front page, gets taken over to sell a commercial message. At one level, this might seem like an ideal win-win situation, in keeping prices low, helping newspapers build their revenues, and giving the advertisers access to an audience. But, for anyone involved with the process, it becomes clear that advertisers and readers make for strange bed-fellows, often with conflicting interests.

For a generation that grew up alongside the New World Information and Communication Order (NWICO) debate (Wikipedia 2004)—about the need to make global media representation more equitable—one is also struck by the media disparities within Goa itself. Debates about news-flows, which areas of Goa get covered, and who decides what makes news about Goa—regionally, nationally and internationally, as seen in the 2008 Scarlett Keeling case (Noronha 2008b)—are of crucial importance. Goa's news organisations hardly do justice in their coverage of most areas outside of Panjim. Leave aside more remote villages—even populous towns such as Vasco, Mapusa, Margao, Bicholim, Sanvordem or Canacona seldom get the coverage they deserve. Unless there is some naptha-pipeline disaster or a communal riot in one or the other area, coverage is restricted to the occasional accident and police blotter-stories, or the activities of local elites.

The language gap between Marathi, English and Konkani papers is another issue that needs to be addressed. Because audiences of one language might not read another, this leads to a situation where sectarianism, if not blatant communalism, can also be promoted unchecked. In 2009, for instance, the Goa government was faulted for releasing advertisements paid for by the state to newspapers with a controversial record on this front (Zee News 2009). This, by no means, is a comprehensive list of the challenges facing the media in Goa.

Other Trends in Goan Media

The last five decades also show other trends that need to be taken note of. Diversity among languages has grown in Goa, together with the entry of the big press from other parts of the country. In times when technology and economics makes it feasible to start new editions in different geographical areas, media diversity in Goa could get challenged by such new trends.

Trends have varied over this period. Das (Das 1980, 249), speaking of the reality in those times, suggests that mining houses were connected to prominent politicians, and besides presumably helping the ruling party in their elections financially "certainly helped through their media of newspapers". In 2006, Haksar *et al.* (Haksar, *et al.*, 2006) mention cases of hate speech and communalism spread through the press.

Radio has played an important role in Goa, even before 1961, when the overseas transmitters of the local station were known far and wide, in parts of Africa, in Asia and the rest of India too. Even till the 1970s, radio continued to play an important role here. Subsequent competition, technology challenges and maybe even an ultra-conservative approach in controlling radio have all contributed in making it less relevant as anything other than an entertainment medium. The growth of local regional news-based television operations are an interesting phenomenon and need closer scrutiny.

One needs to appreciate the economic challenges and pressures on the press and the manner in which they hinder a sustainable growth of the media. But, issues like media corruption cannot be blamed simply on a scarcity of economic resources. Online blogs (Penpricks 2007–8) which debate this issue often give a hint of such concerns.

Noronha, Frederick, ed. 2008c. *In Black and White: Insiders' Stories about the Press in Goa*. Goa: Goa,1556 and Broadway.

_______. 2011. "Encountering Cyberspace". In *Inside/out: New Writing from Goa*, edited by Helene Derkin Menezes and Jose Lourenço. Goa: Goa,1556 and GoaWriters.

Penpricks. 2007–8. Mostly anonymous. Accessed September 28, 2011. http://penpricks.blogspot.com.

The Goa, Daman and Diu Official Language Act. 1987. Act 5 of 1987. 'Statement of Objects and Reasons'.

Wikipedia. "Media in Goa". Accessed September 27, 2011. http://en.wikipedia.org/wiki/Media_in_Goa.

Wikipedia. 2004. "New World Information and Communication Order". Accessed March 24, 2013. http://en.wikipedia.org/wiki/New_World_Information_and_Communication_Order.

Xavier Centre of Historical Research. 1987. Seminar on "The Press and Goan History". March 28–29. Unpublished.

Zee News. 2009. "Goa govt was advertising in Sanatan Sansthan paper". Accessed March 24, 2013. http://zeenews.india.com/news/states/goa-govt-was-advertising-in-sanatan-sansthan-paper_574739.html.

Chapter 12

Tenancy Reforms in Goa since Liberation: 1961–1987

Remy Dias

Introduction

Land is basic to the life of people; its value cannot be underestimated. Land has also often been a major criterion for social prestige. Throughout history, the people who mattered owned land, and those who owned land mattered (others, often the majority, were kept in an inferior or subordinate position). Land has also been the basis of political power (Elkins 1975). It has also been held under many different tenure situations around the world, as in Goa too, reflecting in part the different reasons why it was owned as also varied cultural histories.

Goa was liberated on December 19, 1961, after being under Portuguese colonial domination for four and-a-half centuries. Decolonisation, a very significant political change, afforded the opportunity to undertake far-reaching land reforms that transferred property rights to the poor in Goa. Leaders—both at the central and state level—desired rapid economic development of the newly liberated territory. Tenancy reforms were undertaken in the post-colonial period to improve the asset base of the underprivileged sections of the society. This was viewed as a central strategy to relieve endemic poverty. The Government of Goa set up, in February 1963, the Land Reforms Commission (LRC) under the Chairmanship of A.L. Dias (ICS), to make a general survey of the then existing system of land tenures and land revenue administration in Goa. With the Goa Legislative Assembly passing the Agricultural Tenancy Act in 1964, tenancy reforms were introduced to reduce poverty and accelerate economic growth.[1]

The paper discusses the tenancy reforms implemented by the Maharashtrawadi Gomantak Party (MGP) and Congress-led governments when Goa was a Union Territory till 1987. Implementation of reforms was undoubtedly not smooth and had repercussions for the landed gentry. However, beginning with these reforms Goa witnessed reduction in poverty and there was a spurt of development activities in the post-liberation period. Government-led tenancy reforms were imbued with some effort to attain equity, social justice and dignity for a large section of the people, making liberation and freedom meaningful in the real sense of the term. Indeed, Goa has the largest body of tenancy reform legislation;[2] however, the efficacy of these legislations has been debated. The real impact on the conditions of the poor is muted by the unenthusiastic implementation of proposed changes (Besley and Burgess 1998/2000, 389-430).

Scope and Need for Tenancy Reforms

Immediately following India's independence, a conscious process of nation building considered the problems of land with a pressing urgency.[3] The national objective of poverty abolition envisaged simultaneous progress on two fronts: high agricultural productivity and equitable distribution. Accordingly, reforms were visualised as an important pillar of a strong and prosperous country. However, as stated earlier, tenancy reform is a difficult economic and political undertaking, for it involves realignment of economic and political power.[4]

Why were reforms essential? Finding effective means to relieve poverty is a defining mission for development economics. The rural poor are among the poorest in any country and giving them any assets promotes equity. This is very much desirable and many scholars have argued that a more equitable distribution of wealth can promote efficiency: when the poor have more assets they are able to get more credit and better insurance which, in turn, helps them invest more effectively. Consequently, offspring of beneficiaries of a reform may have better health and more education, and this may make them more productive. They may also be better able to start small businesses of their own by pledging land for availing loans. Arguing from a political economy perspective also favours redistribution. It is argued that when the poor have too little stake in the economy, they are liable to impose inefficient taxes on the rest of the economy (taxes here is a metaphor for crime, riots and, in extreme cases, civil wars) (Banerjee 1999, 1-38).

Following liberation in 1961, the government introduced in Goa both institutional and technological reforms simultaneously and concurrently, to bring about a change in the agricultural sector. However, more than providing security of tenure to tenants through legislation, other comprehensive and extensive reforms were not implemented in Goa.[5]

Liberation, Interim Administration and Agriculture

The agricultural sector in Goa at liberation had lots of problems and agrarian relations were very complicated.[6] The interim administration (1961–63), set up following Operation Vijay, did not undertake any substantial reforms for fear of antagonising the powerful landed gentry. Only limited attempts, though, were made to mitigate the sufferings of tenants. For instance, the rent payable by tenants was fixed at public auction of agricultural lands belonging to Comunidades, Mazanias (trusts managing temple property) and *bhatkars* (land-owners) and was based on the prevailing market price of paddy. It so happened that in February-March 1962, the market price of paddy declined considerably. Tenants were in a grave economic crisis as they had to pay higher rent which would leave them with little surplus for sustenance. In order to give some immediate relief, the interim administration reduced 20 per cent rent payable by tenants to Comunidades. This appreciable measure seems to have not been extended then to tenants under other tenure systems.[7]

Ground level realities were still worse, with tenants having to pay high rents which often exceeded a just and equitable ceiling. The interim administration gave some relief to tenants of Comunidade and Mazania lands by stipulating, in September 1962, that rents were not to exceed 50 per cent of the average annual produce.[8] This benefit was extended to tenants of private owned lands (*bhatkars*) in October 1962.[9] There was constant violation of this provision by Comunidades, Mazania and *bhatkars* forcing government to repeatedly issue orders for strict compliance.[10] Often, landowners and tenants could hardly agree on the rent payable and the matter had to be referred to the taluka administrator for adjudication.[11]

Security of tenure was not guaranteed by the erstwhile Portuguese regime and tenants were often evicted by the landowners. In 1961 alone about 3,500 tenants were dispossessed of the lands that they cultivated earlier. The interim administration took some effective measures to prevent eviction of tenants. Economic security of the cultivators was seen as absolute necessity to promote socialism.[12] Taking into consideration the weak financial position of tenant-cultivators, the government also allowed tenants to harvest *rabi* crops in 1962 on payment of just half the annual rent.[13] There was, however, no effective gain for tenant cultivators or any real loss to Comunidades and others. In order to protect the interest of the cultivators the government also stipulated that Comunidades were not to sell land without its permission.[14] The interim administration realised that the agrarian problem was too complicated but did not want to antagonise the powerful landed sections of society. So, it was thought prudent to allow the democratically elected government to effectively tackle agrarian issues.

Land Reforms Commission: Recommendations

On December 20, 1961, the Indian Parliament passed the Constitution Amendment Act, integrating Goa with India. The interim administration set in motion a two-tiered pattern of elections to Panchayats and Municipalities, and, an elected Legislative Assembly with Council of Ministers as the executive to administer the newly liberated territories. Goa was also to be represented in the Indian parliament by two elected members (Fernandes 1997, 1; Couto 2002, 25-26).[15] Elections based on universal adult franchise were held for the first time in September 1962 to 149 Panchayats in Goa (Couto 2002, 28). More than half of the total electorate of about 2 lakh exercised their vote and in many polling booths women outnumbered men. The electoral rolls were, therefore, tried and tested, for the first Legislative Assembly elections held on December 9, 1963 (Couto 2002, 28).[16]

Dayanand Bandodkar became the first Chief Minister (CM) of the MGP-led government following elections to the first Legislative Assembly of Goa in 1963. Bandodkar was Goa's CM for almost a decade, from December 20, 1963, till August 12, 1973. The success that MGP achieved was due to a variety of factors but the foremost was the ability of the party to articulate the interests of the Bahujan Samaj (Fernandes 1997, 1-8).[17] In order to make life tolerable and liberation meaningful to the toiling masses, the MGP introduced tenancy reforms in Goa and implemented them with a religious zeal. One of the first steps of the MGP government was the setting up of the Land Reforms Commission (LRC) with the stated objective of making recommendations regarding: security of tenure to tenants; levy of fair rent; regulating management and administration of Comunidades; prevention of indiscriminate resumption of land by *bhatkars*; prevention of fragmentation and consolidation of holdings; and land survey and maintenance of record of land rights.

The LRC was elitist in composition and its members, not being fully aware of the realities in the agrarian sector, recommended implementation of limited reforms.[18] The LRC's approach was 'dictated by the need for caution and gradualism in attaining the objectives laid down by the Planning Commission (of India)'. In making various recommendations, the LRC kept in mind conflicting interests of stakeholders in the agrarian sector and suggested a programme of reform which, if properly implemented, was 'to bring security and appreciable relief to the tillers, afford an opportunity to the Comunidades to play a constructive role in the agricultural economy of Goa and help in attaining the main objective of increased agricultural production.' This was indeed a laudable goal set by the LRC for the state; implementation, though, left much to be desired.

Tenancy Reforms after Liberation

Elections were held on December 9, 1963, to the first Legislative Assembly of Goa. This was the first ever full-fledged democratic exercise after four and-a-half centuries of colonial rule and witnessed an unprecedented 75 per cent voting. In an astonishing result, the MGP emerged as the single largest party with 14 seats (two short of majority), the UGP won 12 seats, the Praja Socialist Party won two, Congress got a single seat and one seat was won by an independent.[19] The MGP passed the Agricultural Tenancy Act in 1964 which came into force from February 8, 1965. The implementation of the Act was not smooth, though over the years Goa has managed to achieve desired results in providing security of tenure to the tenants.

All those who had been lawfully cultivating land belonging to others from July 1, 1962, onwards were considered as tenants. Even Comunidades were considered as owners of the respective lands which they controlled and the cultivators were considered as tenants. Significantly, sub-tenant cultivators were accepted as tenants, while the intermediary tenants lost all rights to land, bringing to an end the malpractice of sub-tenancy which was in existence in Goa before liberation.[20] Where land was held by two or more tenants jointly, but cultivated by even one of them, all were considered as tenants. In instances when there was a doubt about the tenancy of any land, the mamlatdar (officer in executive charge of a taluka) was empowered to hold an enquiry and decide accordingly. The mamlatdar had to, most interestingly, base his enquiry on the premise that 'any statement regarding existence of tenancy in the record of rights prepared in accordance with the provisions of Agricultural Tenancy Act, is true'.

A very noteworthy provision was related to a bar on eviction of tenants and restoration of possession. With this ended the pernicious practice of auctioning agricultural lands to cultivators at regular intervals. Auctioning of agricultural lands had been introduced by the Portuguese in 1735 and had continued till 1961; it had been responsible for rampant poverty among the rural masses in the pre-liberation period. With the coming into force of the Agricultural Tenancy Act, no tenancy of any land could be terminated and no person holding land as a tenant could be evicted except under certain circumstances. Thus, those who were evicted from July 1, 1962, were made eligible for restoration of their lands.

Even those tenants who were evicted during the period of chaos and seemingly unstable period from December 19, 1961, to July 1, 1962, were entitled for restoration of their lands. Such tenants who had been evicted during the intervening period had to apply to the mamlatdar and prove that the eviction was *mala fide* and was intended to defeat the purposes of the Agricultural Tenancy Act, 1964. The restoration of tenancy land was, however, done only after payment of arrears of rent, if any, by tenants.

Efforts were also made to give much required security of tenure to tenants. Any tenant in possession of any land or dwelling house and who apprehended that he might be dispossessed could apply to the mamlatdar for an order safeguarding his right to possession. Thereafter, mamlatdars held enquiry and, after being satisfied that the tenant was entitled to continue in possession, passed appropriate orders directing the *bhatkars* to not disturb the former's possession.

However, tenancy could be terminated by the tenant by surrender of his right to the *bhatkars*. Under certain circumstances, the latter also could terminate tenancy. Where the tenant surrendered his tenancy of any land to *bhatkars* then such surrender had to be only in writing to the mamlatdar. The mamlatdar had to be satisfied that surrender of land by tenants was voluntary and done in good faith. Such cases of voluntary surrender of tenancy were not uncommon in Goa.

Bhatkars could terminate tenancy if the tenant failed to pay the rent for any period on time or did any activity which was destructive or permanently injurious to the land. The *bhatkars* could also terminate tenancy if the tenant failed to cultivate the land personally or if he subdivided, sub-let or assigned any interest in land to others. The tenant could also not use the land for purposes other than agriculture. Agriculture included horticulture and cultivating food crops, grass or garden produce but not allied pursuits. Allied pursuits not included as agricultural activity included rearing or maintaining plough bulls, breeding of livestock, dairy farming, poultry farming, grazing on grounds reserved for the purpose and such other pursuits connected with agriculture.

To terminate tenancy the *bhatkars* had to give a 90-day notice to the tenants intimating his decision to terminate the tenancy and stating clearly the reason for such termination. The tenant could remedy the breach within the 90-days. If a similar breach occurred a second time then the tenant was liable to pay, by way of penalty, a sum equal to 50 per cent of the rent payable to the *bhatkars*. For the tenancy to be terminated the *bhatkar* had to apply to the mamlatdar after the expiry of the 90-day period. The mamlatdar could accord permission or submit the case to the government for necessary and appropriate decision.

Often, *bhatkars* filed applications with mamlatdars for terminating tenancy due to non-payment of rent. In such instances mamlatdars gave a 30-day notice to the defaulting tenant to pay. Those tenants who paid the arrears of rent within the period did not lose their lands. Often tenants could not pay rent due to crop failure. Depending on the seriousness of the matter the tenants were either allowed not to pay the rent or pay it within a year. Non-payment of rent even after the grace period was over often led to termination of tenancy.

In some instances land was mortgaged by *bhatkars* by way of usufructory mortgage to tenants. The tenancy of such land was kept in abeyance during the period the mortgage subsisted. After the expiry of the mortgage period it was decreed to be lawful for the tenant to continue to hold the land on the same terms and conditions on which it was held before the mortgage was created.

By way of amendment to the Agricultural Tenancy Act in 1966, tenants were given the right of first purchase. Those *bhatkars* who wanted to sell their tenanted lands had to give a 90-day notice for selling the land to the tenant indicating the price. Tenants could agree to the terms or appeal to the collector if the purchase price was too high. If the tenant was not ready to purchase at a price determined by the district collector in accordance with the principles laid down in the Land Acquisition Act, 1894, then the *bhatkar* was free to sell land to others. However, what is significant is that even if the *bhatkar* sold his land to a third party, the tenants continued as tenants under the new owner on the same terms and conditions as before.

The rights of tenants were also declared as heritable. Where a tenant died the *bhatkar* was deemed to have continued the tenancy if such tenant was a member of a joint family, to the surviving member or members of the said family. And if such tenant was not a member of a joint family then the tenancy was deemed to have continued to his heir or heirs on the same terms and conditions on which such tenant was holding it at the time of his death. The surviving members or the heirs were also entitled to partition and subdivision of the land leased subject to the conditions that each heir held his share as a separate tenant and the rent payable in respect of the land leased was apportioned among the shares according to share allotted to them. To prevent excessive fragmentation of land it was, however, provided that no partition or subdivision shall be permissible if the share allotted to any heir or any co-partner together with any other land already held by him was less than one-third hectare of *morod* land and one-fourth hectare of *khazan* or *kher* land.[21]

It was made lawful for a tenant to mortgage or create a charge on his interest in the land in favour of the government or cooperative society in consideration of a loan advanced to him.[22] During the mortgage period, neither the tenant could surrender the land to the *bhatkar* nor could the latter resume the land for personal cultivation. With this the land held by tenants was also not liable to be attached, seized or sold in execution of a decree or order of a civil court.

The GDD Agricultural Tenancy Act, 1976, provided that every tenant be deemed to have purchased from his *bhatkar* the land held by him as a tenant on the tiller's day and without any encumbrances.[23] The tiller's day is the date on which the GDD Agricultural Tenancy (Fifth Amendment) Act, 1976, was introduced in the Goa Assembly, that is, October 8, 1976. Even those tenants who had been evicted before the tiller's day could make application for such purchase. Such evicted tenants were deemed to have purchased the land on the day the final order allowing the application was passed.

Those tenants who were not in possession of the land on the tillers' day and which the *bhatkar* had not put to agricultural use could apply to the mamlatdar for purchase. The mamlatdar could either *suo motto* or on the application of the tenant hold an enquiry and direct that such land shall be taken from the possession of the *bhatkar* and restore it to the tenant. The purchase price payable by a tenant to the *bhatkar* in relation to the land which was deemed to have been purchased by the tenant was as given in the table shown here. The tenant had the option to deposit the purchase price either as a lump sum or in 10 equal annual instalments.[24] Land purchased by a tenant to tiller's day cannot be transferred by sale, gift, exchange, mortgage, lease or assignment without the previous sanction of the mamlatdar. However, no sanction was required if the tenant wanted to mortgage in favour of the government or a cooperative society for the purpose of a loan for effecting any improvement of such land.

Table 12.1: Purchase Price for Various Categories of Agricultural Land

Category of land	*Purchase price per hectare (in Rs.)*
Agricultural lands with cash crop cultivation:	
(a) Coconut trees	4,000
(b) Areca nut trees	3,000
(c) Mango trees	2,500
(d) Cashew trees	1,600
Paddy fields:	
(a) Kher	4,000
(b) Khazan	3,600
(c) Morod	1,600
Wet land with sugarcane cultivation	2,500

Another important measure which gave relief to the actual cultivators was regarding fixation of maximum chargeable rent. It was stipulated by the Agricultural Tenancy Act, 1964, that the rent payable by a tenant to the *bhatkar* in respect of any land shall not exceed one-sixth of the gross produce of such land. The rent payable was to be revised every five years by the government. The rent payable was, however, reduced when there were crop failures due to floods or any other cause beyond the control of the tenants. It is a fact that a large number of tenants have stopped paying rents to the *bhatkars* from the late 1970s.

Moreover, the liability to pay land revenue to the government was made the responsibility of the *bhatkars*. However, in *khazan* and *kher* lands tenants were made responsible for carrying out maintenance works, repair of dykes and embankments, bunds or ridges of tanks or rivers or other sources of irrigation. The responsibility of carrying out works of a recurring nature designed to conserve water such as the closure of apertures of the sides or wall of a tank such as *khan* or popularly known by any other name, was to be either of the tenant or the *bhatkar* according to the custom, usage or practice in vogue in respective villages. This could have been avoided as the high cost of maintenance works has been responsible for tenants abandoning cultivation of agricultural lands in recent years.

Relief was given to tenants as it was made unlawful for any *bhatkar* to levy any unauthorised rates, tax, fee, cess or other charge for service of any description or denomination whatsoever from any tenant in respect of any land held by him as a tenant other than the rent lawfully due in respect of such land. Whenever by reason of any natural calamity or like circumstances the payment of the whole land revenue payable to the government in respect of any land was suspended or remitted in accordance with such principles as may be provided for in this behalf the *bhatkar* was to suspend or remit, as the case may be, the payment to him of the rent of such land by his tenant. If land revenue is partially suspended or remitted, the *bhatkar* was to similarly suspend or remit the rent payable by tenants of such land in the same proportion. If no land revenue was payable to the government then no rent was payable to the *bhatkar* by the tenant.

Tenants also enjoy other rights too. For instance, in agricultural land leased to a tenant not covered by cultivation, the tenant can plant any trees, he is to be entitled to the produce and the wood of such trees during the continuance of his tenancy and on the termination of his tenancy, he is also entitled to such compensation for the said trees as may be determined by the government. However, if in such lands there are any trees naturally growing thereon, the tenant is entitled to two-thirds of the produce of the trees and the *bhatkar* to the remaining third. Tenants are also entitled to erect farmhouses with the consent of the *bhatkar* and without detriment to the area of cultivation. If the *bhatkar* refuses to give consent within a period of 60 days from the date of request or where the *bhatkar* unreasonably refuses to give such consent, the tenant is entitled to erect the farmhouse with the consent of the mamlatdar who gives permission after hearing the parties. Tenants also had the right to operate sluice gates (*manoos*) and enjoyed fishing rights.

If it appears to the government that for any two consecutive years including any period before the commencement of this Act, any land has remained uncultivated through default either of the *bhatkar* or of the tenant, or that cultivation of any land has seriously suffered for any other cause whatsoever, or that any land capable of being used, if reclaimed or otherwise improved, howsoever, has not been so reclaimed or otherwise improved and cultivated, or that any land is remaining as a pasture land in excess of the ordinary grazing requirements of the cattle of the person entitled to graze cattle thereon, the government may, after such enquiry as may be prescribed, declare by notification that the management of such land shall be assumed, and such declaration shall be conclusive. A land which is cultivable both during the *kharif* and *rabi* season in a year, is not cultivated during anyone of the said season during any year it is deemed to have remained uncultivated for that year.

Conclusion

Following Goa's liberation there have been many positive changes in the agrarian sector. The Goa, Daman and Diu Agricultural Tenancy Act, 1964, was a legislation enacted to secure tenure of agricultural tenants, to limit the rent payable by the tenants to the owners and to provide for common obligation of the cultivating tenants and their joint responsibilities of maintaining protective bunds, sluice gates, ponds and fisheries, water resources, etc. The Act was further amended to vest ownership rights of the tenanted land to the cultivating tenants by fixing price of the land deemed to be purchased by the tenant. The tenants deemed to have purchased the tenanted lands are required to apply for certificate of purchase and to pay the price as a lump sum or in instalments.

The government move to vest rights of tenanted land upon the tenants has largely remained unimplemented due to many factors. The revenue records of rights prepared under the Land Revenue Code provide that the entries in the Form No. 1 and 14 are presumed to be true until proved otherwise. This has led to a conflict between the *bhatkars* and tenants as the former normally refuse to accept the entries in the Record of Rights and force the tenant to prove the tenancy under the Agricultural Tenancy Act.[25] Even after four-and-half decades following enactment of Agricultural Tenancy Act, many tenants do not enjoy fully secured rights to the land that they hold. Suitable amendments should be made to the existing laws granting full rights to tenants who constitute a substantial section of the Goan populace. This would be a step in the right direction to give a push to the stagnating agricultural sector in Goa.

NOTES

1. The other members of the LRC included: Dr. Antonio Furtado (Judge, Goa High Court, Panaji), Narayan Naik (Secretary, Shetkari Parishad, Goa), Madhav Bir (Sarpanch, Nerul Gram Panchayat), Narsing

Damodar Naik (Chairman of the Executive Committee of the Association of Proprietors), Pedro Correia Afonso (Benaulim). Subsequently on April 6, 1963, A.F. Couto (IAS and Development Commissioner) was appointed Secretary to the Commission. In place of Pedro Correia Afonso and Narcinva Damodar Naik, who tendered their resignations on grounds of health, were appointed Gopal Appa Kamat on May 31, 1963 and Nicolau Menezes on December 5, 1963, respectively.

The LRC was to make a general survey of the existing system of land tenures and land revenue administration in Goa. In particular, it was to ascertain and report to the government the then position with regard to: (i) land tenures and their incidents; (ii) community lands and their management and administration by Comunidades; (iii) relationship subsisting between the owner of the land and the cultivator in respect of security of tenure; (iv) levy and recovery of rent by *bhatkar* from the tenant; (v) extent of waste land available for grant to landless persons; (vi) agricultural land holdings; and (vii) survey and assessment of land to land revenue and the maintenance of records of rights in land.

With a view to the ultimate realisation of the objectives of land reforms, as laid down in the Five-Year Plans, the Commission was also to recommend to the government measures for the improvement of the existing system of land tenures and land revenue administration and providing, in particular, for: (i) security of tenure to the tenant; (ii) levy of fair rent on agricultural lands; (iii) regulating the management and administration of community lands by Comunidades; (iv) prevention of indiscriminate resumption of land by the *bhatkar*; (v) prevention of fragmentation and consolidation of holdings; and (vi) the survey and assessment of agricultural land and maintenance of record of rights in land.

The LRC had to also indicate the extent to which Comunidades were to be relieved of their financial liability in respect of functions such as repair of bunds and maintenance of irrigation schemes, which they were then under an obligation to undertake, should its recommendations regarding fair rent result in a substantial reduction in their income".

The Commission held 18 sittings in Goa on March 20, 1963; April 3, 8 and 25, 1963; May 8, 17 and 18, 1963; September 11, 1963; November 14, 1963, December 27, 28, 30 and 31, 1963; January 1 and 2, 1964; and February 20-21 and 29, 1964. The Chairman visited various villages in Goa to examine conditions on the spot. On some of these occasions he was accompanied by members of the

annual rent of a paddy field exceeds 50 per cent of the gross produce the owner of the field shall not collect any rent in excess of 50 per cent of the gross produce;(2) In cases of doubt regarding the gross produce of any paddy field the gross produce of the field shall be fixed by the common accord of the owner and the tenant and in case of disagreement between them the gross produce shall be fixed by the *Administrador do Concelho* whose decision on the dispute shall be final; (c) In case the rent of any paddy field is payable to the owner in cash the tenant shall be entitled to a reduction of 20 per cent as is provided by article 3 of the Legislative Diploma No. 1628 dated the March 15, 1956 regarding Comunidades.

12. See BOGG. 1962. Series I, No. 37, November 8, 239-40; and BOGG. 1962. Series I, No. 38, November 15, 259-60. The government was of the considered opinion that: the economic stability of the cultivator and his continuity in the tenancy of the lands under his cultivation will contribute to an increase in agricultural production. The maintenance of such stability and continuity raised in the territory of Goa instant agrarian problems which required a careful study by a committee of experts to be appointed in due course. However, it was necessary to take urgent steps to prevent for the time being the arbitrary eviction of tenants by the *bhatkars.* The following was stipulated: (a) No tenant shall be evicted from the land under his cultivation merely on the ground that his tenancy in respect of the said land has expired by the efflux of time; (b) No surrender or relinquishment of any tenancy shall be valid unless it is made in writing before the *Administrator do concelho* within whose jurisdiction the subject matter of the tenancy lies. Such surrender or relinquishment shall state the reasons why the surrender of relinquishment is made; (c) This order shall apply only to leases in respect of paddy fields and areca groves valid and subsisting on or after July 1, 1962, and shall apply to suits in respect of such leases filed or pending on or after July 1, 1962, and to those filed hereafter.
13. The balance was to be paid by December 31, 1962. BOGG. 1962. Series II, No. 36, September 10, 518.
14. BOGG. 1962. Series II, No. 4, January 25, 15. However, often in the post-liberation period Comunidade lands have been taken over/ acquired by the government in public interest. See: BOGG. 1962. Series I, No. 40, November 29, 277; and BOGG. 1963. Series I, No. 35, September 5, 297-8.
15. Constitutionally, the Acts which paved the way for a democratically elected government in Goa included: Constitution (12th Amendment) Act 1962 integrating Goa into the Indian Union (passed on June 29,

1962, but effective from December 20, 1961) as a Union Territory; nomination of two Goan freedom fighters Dr. Antonio Colaco and Dr. Pundalik Gaitonde to the Lok Sabha in August 1962; and Union Territories (Amendment) Act, 1963 (passed on May 4, 1963) providing for 30 elected MLAs (of which one each for Daman and Diu) and two elected MPs to the Lok Sabha. It also sought the delimitation of constituencies to make way for the December 9 elections. The Act provided that the Chief Minister was to be nominated by the President of India on the advice of the Prime Minister. The Chief Minister and not the Lt. Governor would preside over the cabinet meetings, according to the Act. Three MLAs could be nominated by the Central government. The Act, however, did not provide for any SC/ST reservations in Goa Assembly due to the negligible presence of these communities in Goa. See: Fernandes 1997, 1; Couto 2002, 25-26.

16. The December 9, 1963, elections, the first ever democratic exercise in Goa after four and-a-half centuries of autocratic rule, witnessed an unprecedented 75 per cent voting. In an astonishing result, the MGP emerged as the single largest party with 14 seats (two short of majority), the UGP won 12 seats, the Praja Socialist Party won two seats, the Congress won one seat and one seat was won by an independent. See: Couto 2002, 28.
17. Other factors which contributed to MGP victory were: (a) the charismatic leadership of its president D.B. Bandodkar, his tremendous organisational abilities and his mass popularity and personal contact with the people in this small territory; (b) the backing of parties and leaders from Maharashtra in terms of trained electioneering manpower, vehicles and finances from that state (Nath Pai, N.G. Gore, S.M. Joshi, S.K. Patil and other seasoned politicians who participated in Samyukta Maharashtra Agitation backed the MGP); (c) a well organised propaganda unit and strategy with the backing of Marathi dailies *Pradeep, Gomantak* and *Kesari.* The *Navhind Times* backed the Congress while the UGP launched its own paper *Gomant Kiran;* and (d) the ability to successfully distribute party nominations for elections among dissident Congressmen, Jana Sangh, Praja Socialist Party and MGP members themselves, and resolve the conflicts arising out of this exercise. The conflict resolution mechanism guided by compromise was largely managed by Mr. Bandodkar—He was the cementing force of not only the party but the entire mass of depressed castes which identified with the party. See: Fernandes, 1997, 1-8.
18. These include: S.A. Nadkarni (Dir. of Civil Administration), Prabhakar Kamat (Dir. of Mines and Land Survey), K.G. Kholatkar (Dir. of Agriculture), Dr. Y.M. Karapurkar (Dy. Dir. of Agriculture), Carmo

de Noronha (Dir. of Fazenda), Maximo Menezes (Adminstrator of Comunidades, Tiswadi Taluka), J. Almeida (Dir. of Statistics), and A. da Costa (Engineer, Administration of Comunidades, Goa).

19. The Congress suffered the most humiliating defeat. Although it nominated 30 candidates, just one was elected in Daman. Eighteen Congressmen lost their deposits compared with five of the UGP and four of the MGP. The other parties in the fray, the Frente Popular and the Jana Sangh (pro-mergerists, that is, those who preferred the merger of Goa with the neighbouring State of Maharashtra), drew a blank.
20. BOGG. 1966. *The Agricultural Tenancy (Amendment) Act, 1966 (Act 10 of 1966)*. Series I, No. 32, November 10.
21. Subdivision or subletting of the land held by tenants was also not considered as valid in law.
22. In the event of his defaulting in payment of such loan in accordance with the terms on which such loan was granted it shall be lawful for the government or the cooperative society, as the case may be, to cause his interest in the land to be attached and sold and the proceeds to be utilised in payment of such loan.
23. Section 18A of the Tenancy Act provides that on the Tiller's Day (that is, 8.10.1976, the date of introduction of Goa, Daman and Diu Agricultural Tenancy (Fifth Amendment) Act, 1976 in the Legislative Assembly), every tenant shall subject to the other provisions of the Act, be deemed to have purchased from his *bhatkar* the land held by him as a tenant and such land shall vest in him free from such encumbrances on that day. Section 18E provides that on determination of the purchase price by the mamlatdar under section 18C, the tenant shall deposit the purchase price with the mamlatdar as provided in section 18E. Section 18H provides that on deposit of the purchase price the mamlatdar shall issue a certificate of purchase to the tenant-purchaser in respect of the land; and the purchase will be ineffective on tenant-purchaser's failure to pay the purchase price. Section 18J provides that where purchase of any land by the tenant under section 18A becomes ineffective under section 18C or 18H or where the tenant fails to exercise the right to purchase the land held by him within the specified period under section 18B, the mamlatdar may direct the land or part thereof, shall be disposed of in the manner provided therein. Section 18K of the Tenancy Act provides that no land purchased by a tenant under Chapter IIA of the Tenancy Act shall be transferred by sale, gift, mortgage, lease or assignment, without the previous sanction of the mamlatdar.
24. The tenant had the option to deposit the purchase price either as a lump sum or in 10 equal annual instalments. The first instalment of

the purchase price or where the purchase was payable in a lump sum the payment had to be done by the tenant within six months from the date of passing of the order by the mamlatdar in this regard. The second or subsequent instalments of the purchase price shall be paid within a period of one year from the date on which the previous instalment was due. Where the lump sum payment or any installment of the purchase price has not been deposited on the due date, the amount in default shall carry interest at the rate of 6 per cent per annum.

25. http://goalawcommission.gov.in/reports/report2. Accessed on July 26, 2013.

REFERENCES

Banerjee, Abhijit V. 1999. *Land Reforms: Prospects and Strategies*. Prepared for The World Bank's 11th Annual Bank Conference on Development Economics, Washington, in June.

Besley, Timothy and Robin Burgess. 2000. 'Land Reform, Poverty Reduction and Growth: Evidence from India', *The Quarterly Journal of Economics*, May, 115 (2).

Boletim Official Government Gazette. 1962. Series I, No 14, April 12.

_______. 1962. Series I, No 31, August 13.

_______. 1962. Series I, No 34, October 11.

_______. 1963. Series I, No 35, September 5.

_______. 1962. Series I, No 37, November 8.

_______. 1962. Series I, No 38, November 15.

_______. 1962. Series I, No 40, November 29.

_______. 1962. Series II, No 4, January 25.

_______. 1962. Series II, No 36, September 10.

_______. 1966. *The Agricultural Tenancy (Amendment) Act, 1966 (Act 10 of 1966)*. Series I, No 32, November 10.

_______. 1969. *The Agricultural Tenancy (Amendment) Act, 1968 (Act 13 of 1968)*. Series I, No 42.

_______. 1975. *The Agricultural Tenancy (Amendment) Act, 1975 (Act 18 of 1975)*. Series I, No 32.

_______. 1976. *The Agricultural Tenancy (Amendment) Act, 1976 (Act 17 of 1976)*. Series I, No 29.

_______. 1982. *The Agricultural Tenancy (Amendment) Act, 1982 (Act 2 of 1982)*. Series I, No 5.

_______. 1989. *The Goa Administration of Evacuee Property (Amendment) Act, 1989 (Act No. 19 of 1989)*. Series I, No 37.

Boletim Official Government Gazette. 1991. *The Agricultural Tenancy (Amendment) Act, 1991 (Act 4 of 1991)*. Series I, No 3.

_______. 1993. *The Agricultural Tenancy (Amendment) Act, 1993 (Act 23 of 1993)*. Series I, No 30 (Extraordinary).

_______. 2001. *The Agricultural Tenancy (Amendment) Act, 2001 (Act 29 of 2001)*. Series I, No 5.

Couto, Alban. 2002. "Administration Bridging Past & Future". In *Redefining Horizons – Goa Four Decades of Freedom*, edited by Mario Cabral e Sá. Panaji: Dept of Info & Publicity (Government of Goa).

da Costa, Joaquim Bernardino Catão. 1857. *O Triumpho da Verdade em Referencia a Varios Escriptos Publicados em Goa*. Nova Goa: Imprensa Nacional.

Deininger, Klaus & Hari Nagarajan. 2007. *Land Policies and Land Reforms in India: Progress and Implications for the future*. New Delhi: Brookings-NCAER India Policy Forum.

Deshpande, R.S. 2007. *Emerging Issues in Land Policy*. New Delhi: ADB.

Elkins, David J. 1975. *Electoral Participation in a South Indian Context*. Durham, N.C.: Carolina Academic Press.

Fernandes, Aureliano. 1997. *Cabinet Government in Goa (1961–1993)*. Panjim: Maureen & Camvet Pub.

Gomes, Francisco Luis. 1862. *A Liberdade da Terra e a Economia rural da India Portugueza*. Lisboa: Typographia Universal.

Government of Goa (Department of Information and Publicity). 1998. *Operation Vijay*. Corlim: Sahyadri Offset System.

Government of Goa, Daman and Diu. 1964. *Report of the Goa Land Reforms Commission*. Panjim: Govt. Printing Press

Pal, Debdatta, and Varsha Khandker. 2010. *Does Land Reform Matter? An Empirical Analysis of Indian States*. Ahmedabad: IIMA India.

Thimmaiah, G. 2001. "New Perspectives on Land Reforms in India". *Journal of Social and Economic Development*, III (2) (Bangalore).

Chapter 13

Negotiating Male Migration

The Experience of Women in Goa

Sachin Savio Moraes

Introduction

Migration as a social phenomenon is as old as human beings. The history of migration depicts that man has always moved from one place to another for greener pastures. Migration from Goa to different parts of the world is not something new and there is documented data from at least the 16th century (de Souza 1979, 54). M.N. Pearson also states that Goa had been open to the Arabian Sea and its littoral even before the Portuguese arrived. Nevertheless Goan migration has never been uniform; it has been in sporadic form (Gracias 2000). Gracias (2000) classifies Goan migration into three important phases. The early initial migration to the neighbouring kingdoms (16th to 17th century), migration to British India and Africa (19th to first half of 20th century), and the post-colonial migration to the Gulf, the West (Europe and America), Australia and New Zealand (1961 to 1990). In all these phases of migration in Goa, there is a striking point of Christian's migrating to a greater extent as compared to any other religious group (Mascarenhas-Keyes 1987; Gracias 1999 *et al.*). During the first two phases, customs, tradition, religion and food habits imposed restrictions on Hindu migration. The *Dharmashastras* imposed a ban on travel outside India for Hindus of upper classes. Travel across the salt seas was also considered polluting (www.goa-world.com/GOA/goanaway.htm). This ideology and thinking had far reaching effects on the third stage as most of the Hindus were faithfully following this ideology. On the other hand, Christians took advantage of the available opportunities in each phase. For example, in the first stage, a few Christians migrated to Portugal for educational purposes. In the second phase (19th and first half of the 20th centuries), Goan migration was of a socio-economic nature. It was the outcome of many factors. Among these was the British occupation of Goa and the Anglo-Portuguese Treaty of 1878.

During the Napoleonic wars Goa was occupied by the British. Their ships were anchored there and Goans went to work on them. When these ships left Goa for British India, the Goan staff went along. As a result of the Anglo-Portuguese Treaty, the British took the responsibility of building railways linking Goa with the rest of India, which improved the means of communication and transport and made travelling easy and fast. In addition, a high cost of living, unemployment, better job opportunities abroad, social problems and lack of educational facilities can be cited as some factors that forced Goans to migrate. Thus this gave birth to a new class of people called '*Tarvotis*' within the already existing caste system.

Goans migrated in large numbers in the 19th and early 20th centuries, and they did so mainly in two directions—to British India and Africa (www.goa-world.com/GOA/goanaway.htm. Significant to note here is that Portugal supported Goan migration because the remittances were invaluable to the stability of Goan economy (Brettel 2007, 157). In a way the Portuguese policy of using emigration as a safety valve rather than developing the region was responsible for the migration of Goans as there were shortage of opportunities. In India, Goans migrated primarily to Bombay, Karachi, Calcutta and Pune. A few Hindus also migrated to British India (Gracias 1999). Those who went to Africa were mainly Christians concentrated around East Africa (www.goa-world.com/GOA/goanaway.htm; see footnote 11). A small number went to Burma. A large number of Goans, again Christians, worked also as ship hands, sailors, stewards and cooks in passenger and cargo liners, which at present is the number one employment opportunity for the male members of Goan society. However, today non-Christians have also taken up to being a seaman (colloquially known as 'shippie') as over the years working on ships has redefined status—thus leading to the reinforcement of working on a ship. Of late female members have also taken up working on ships, mainly cruise liners.

In 1880, about 29,216 Goans, predominantly from the Old Conquests, left Goa (www.goa-world.com/GOA/goanaway.htm). By 1910 their number had gone up to 47,334. In 1935 around 38,788 Goan Catholics were absent from their homes (www.goa-world.com/GOA/goanaway.htm). Various events in the 19th and 20th centuries provided impetus to the migration of Goans from Goa. According to an estimate of 1954 about 180,000 Goans were away from their home (www.goa-world.com/GOA/goanaway.htm) (Gracias 1999; de Souza 1991). Another important point here is that because of the process of 'Christ-Westernisation' during Portuguese rule, Christians got westernised and thus could gain jobs in the West and westernised places such as Africa, as they could adjust easily to the culture and there was also no restriction based on religion (especially food) (Gracias 1999).

The third phase of Goan migration is the post-colonial period (1961–1991). This period is dominated by migration to the Gulf (Oman, Kuwait, the UAE, Saudi Arabia and Bahrain), and Western countries such as Portugal, the USA, the UK, Australia and Canada. The migration during this phase was driven by both sociological and economic factors. Thus, as stated earlier, Catholics have migrated to a greater extent as compared with Hindus. This is gleamed from the fact that every able-bodied Goan of whatever rank, educated or uneducated, regarded migration as a natural course and took advantage of every first available opportunity (Mascarenhas-Keyes 1987, 72). However, till the 1990s, Hindus did not consider international migration, which was the characteristic of the Catholics, as an option they would pursue; they did not consider it appropriate for husbands to leave their wives behind. They considered it unthinkable to spend most of one's life, or even a lifetime, away from their motherland. They also did not feel the need as they lived in joint families and most of their needs were met. Migration among Christians, especially males, has been and still continues to be prevalent, despite relative improvements in economic conditions. However, after the 1990s, non-Christians also started migrating as they saw the huge benefits migration brought with it.

Nevertheless, migration to the Gulf and for working on ships has dominated the psyche of a Goan; this is evident from the fact that that there have been a high number of Goans in the Gulf and working on a ship as compared with other parts of the world. In both of these cases there is a pattern of migration. In the first case (that is, to the Gulf), Goan migration is different from permanent Goan migration to the West, Australia and New Zealand. Goans migrate to the Gulf for certain periods of time. They cannot settle there permanently because of local laws that do not encourage permanent migration. Goans go to the Gulf as 'guest workers' on contractual jobs for a definite time period and return after the expiry of the period. Sometimes it is extended up to the entire working span of man's life and other times from 2 to 15 years. When their work is over, they generally return home to Goa, while others settle permanently elsewhere.

Goans who have migrated in recent times to the Gulf belong to all classes. The majority of those who migrate are from the age groups of 18 to 35 years. Unlike earlier migration to Africa, those who migrate to the Gulf countries are from all communities of Goa. However, in the early stages of migration to the Middle East, it was confined primarily to Christians. This could be due to reasons mentioned earlier, connected with restrictions imposed on them (Gracias, 1999). In the second case, Goans work on ships (cargo and passenger) for a period of six to nine months generally and join back when they receive a call. They usually spend 30 to 60 days at home. Thus in both cases the migration is not permanent.

Various studies on Goan migration have revealed that there has been a profound economic impact on those left behind, where the migrant and the migrants' family members have benefited. However, these studies of Goan migration have been limited in their scope as they have focused on the push and pull factors responsible for Goan migration, the economic benefits and the formation of a Goan Diaspora and Goan identity at the international level. There has been no comprehensive research study undertaken till date that focuses on or reveals the impact (sociological, psychological and political) of migration on those who have been left behind or that gives us a concrete picture of the changes in the Goan family *vis-à-vis* society due to migration. Further, the studies undertaken have limited the scope of development/progress only in economic terms. Probably that is because what the researchers felt was the ultimate goal of migration in Goa.

Migration has generally been gendered in nature. It is observed that males migrate to a larger extent as compared with females, though there have been exceptions to this trend. The main reason for this has been the patriarchal system, which was and still continues to be dominant.

Migration and Gender Sensitivity

Males have monopolised every sphere of life including migration. Consequently, the focus by political scientists, economists, anthropologists and sociologists has been on male migration. Despite the upsurge of interest and the large number of studies undertaken in the last few decades, an important limitation of migration studies has been the emphasis on male migration and gender issues being sidelined.

Feminists have rightly demonstrated the need for gender related issues in migration. One obvious question is: What impact does migration have on women left behind? The term 'impact' can be divided into two: first, those analysing the impact on migrants; and second, those analysing the impact on women left behind. Another category of migration is where women move out with their husbands or close relatives. However, my interest is confined to the impact that male migration has on the women left behind, which makes my research gender sensitive.

The Impact of Migration on Women

Studies focusing on the influence of migration on women have been few and those focusing on the impact of migration on women left behind have been even fewer. A UNESCO (1984) study reports about women whose male household members migrate, and who in their absence then have to take on more physical workload, emotional strain and financial burden as the male tasks are taken up by the women. Though other male relatives do provide help, management of kin ties becomes an important task for women. Even as women serve as temporary heads of households, for very long periods at times it does not substantially alter traditional norms concerning women's place or division of labour.

Elizabeth Gordon (1994), through her study on Lesotho women, brings to light the plight of these women who live their lives in reaction to the overwhelming out-migration of their husbands and live apart for much of their married lives, resulting in the erosion of family relationships. While men's absence promotes the independence of their wives, who enjoy their new emancipatory role, this impact is seen as further minimised by extended families. The study demonstrates that wives experienced significant strain, mostly in situations where there were greater responsibilities, fewer resources and longer exposure to their husband's migration.

In her study titled 'In the Absence of their Men,' Gulati (1993) demonstrates the positive influence on women in Kerala, whose men migrate to West Asia to improve their status. They regularly send home remittances, which is managed by the women (mothers, wives), making them dominant figures in their households. However, these women face many challenges and take on much more work than expected by the conventional gendered division of labour. These women also face life by taking on male tasks and mobilising male support from other networks. Through networking and managing relationships these women circumvent and overcome the handicap of illiteracy, work of households and familial interdependence, handling of finances, planning family size, engaging in income generation and similar activities.

Connell (1984) in the study titled 'Status and Subjugation? Women, Migration and Development in South Pacific' demonstrates how migration of a male may affect fertility, due to lack of proper contact with his wife, and also how migration has contributed to the increase in divorce rates, as male migration regards agricultural work as trivial and demeaning. Hence the value of rural life and rural wife also declines. However, both men and women experience loneliness and psychological pressures that direct them towards new partners, while others gain strength from their separation and prefer a single status.

Menon (1995) in her study titled 'The impact of migration on the work and status of tribal women in Orissa' demonstrates that when a migrant's income does not mitigate poverty or compensate in any form for the problems faced by women during the absence of men, it makes male migration problematic for women. Menon did not find women overtly favourable to male migration, and yet she found women also encouraging male migration, perhaps for the purpose of survival. She also observed men showing little concern for their young and pregnant wives.

Nagli (1990) in the study on Vietnamese immigrant community tries to explore the effects of migration on the gender roles and power. The women groups and networks play an important role in the exchange of social and economic resources among households and in the mediation of disputes between men and women in the family. This community forms an important source of informal power for women, enabling them to cope effectively with male authority in the family. Yet, despite their increased power, these women supported a patriarchal social structure, because it preserved their parental authority and promised greater economic security in the future.

Zachariah and Rajan (2001) proposed in their study on migration in Kerala, that a subtle transformation has occurred among the wives of migrants, leaving a lasting impact on Kerala society. Women are less capable of handling the pressures that arise due to their spouses' migration, leading to trauma-like situation. However, at the end of the day, the trauma is worth as they become well equipped to face the world on their own.

Mascarenhas-Keyes (1993) in the study 'International Migration: The changing identity of Catholics and Hindu Women in Goa', tries to examine the relationship between the different categories of female migrants, with particular emphasis on the processes which have led to changes in the socio-economic role and hence the identity of the two categories of women. In case of Catholic women the males have migrated abroad, while in the Hindu women's case it is the women who migrate from rural areas to urban areas. However, with regard to Catholic women she provides with three main patterns of migration. First, independent migration of unattached females, that is, invariably adult, generally low castes, have migrated to work as domestic servants and *ayahs* for families in India (Mehta 1960, quoted in Mascarenhas-Keyes 1989). A small contingent comprises upper caste women who migrate to work as teachers and office staff, usually because they had become the sole breadwinners of the house, owing to the death or desertion of their husbands or fathers.

Second, there is associational migration of women, since the probability of Catholic women marrying migrants is high, wives expect and are expected to be mobile. Many adult women have accompanied or joined their husbands abroad. Even when wives have joined migrant husbands, a period of conjugal separation has been inevitable for many because of tremendous emphasis placed on education of children and commitment necessary for ensuring access to appropriate facilities (Mascarenhas-Keyes 1990, 113). Third, for some there is a habitual residence in Goa: some wives only join their husbands for short holidays. Husbands who work in the Gulf and on a ship are rarely accompanied by their wives because the temporary uprooting of the family is expensive, inconvenient and, in particular, disruptive to the children's education.

Following the brief review of literature, I would like to shed light on some of the important questions that can be raised over here, and which the study will address in its due course. What impact does migration of a man have on the women left behind? Is the main question, associated with this question is: How do women cope with the responsibilities bestowed upon them? Can women's cooperation and sacrifice be seen as a means of success for male migration? What ways do women negotiate male migration? Why? Can migration of a male be seen as a means of perpetuation of gendered division of labour? What benefits do women enjoy due to male migration? Does male migration lay any hindrance on the movement and mobility of women? Apart from these questions that have been raised, the study specifically tries to bring to the fore the issue of male companionship and sexuality of women, which has always cried for sociological attention. Nevertheless, this issue has very often been made transparent through movies and novels. In Goa the folk theatre called 'tiatr' has very often shed some light on this issue. Thus these questions and the issue raised substantiate the scope and genuineness of my study. However, I am not forgetting those who have already worked on similar themes as mine and I know that their findings and insights would certainly be very useful.

Methodology and Design

To deal with the questions that I have raised, I adapted the qualitative method of research. I felt this method was best suited, which would help in the explanation and understanding of the issues that have been raised. Under the qualitative method I chose the 'life history', which is a new method and at the same time is interesting, challenging and provides a lot of information. In brief, life history is any retrospective account by an individual of his life in whole or part, in written or oral form that has been elicited or prompted by another person. The life history account may close at an earlier point of time or at the moment the subject is relating or writing it down. We use the term 'autobiography' by contrast to refer to a person's self-initiated retrospective account of his life, which is usually, but not always, in written form.

The study involved extensive interviewing in order to explore the lives of women left behind. Initially, though 10 women had agreed to share their experiences with me, later only five agreed. The place chosen for this study was Cuncolim, which is in the Salcette taluka of Goa. It is approximately 13 kilometres from Margao, the commercial capital of Goa. Cuncolim is a place where people of diverse religions consisting of Catholics, Hindus and Muslims co-exist in peace and harmony. Outward migration, especially to the Gulf, the western nations and on ships is a common phenomenon, not just in Cuncolim but in several other villages in Goa. However, this pattern of migration is generally seen to a greater extent among men and Christians. The study, as a result, is limited to the impact of migration of married Catholic men on their wives left behind.

Analysis/Findings

The cases that have been studied are varied and complex. Each case provides us with interesting and varied dimensions, of the impact that migration of a man has on the woman. All the cases, though varied, have one aspect in common, that is, all of the married men have migrated abroad. In such a situation all these women were faced with coping with the responsibilities in the absence of their men. The cases also show the manner in which each one managed the absence of her man, which was dependent on the situation in which each one of them was placed. On the basis of the five case histories and my empirical observation of women apart from these five, a few important issues have been observed and described here.

Marital Life Cycle

It has been evident that the marital life cycle follows the migration pattern of the husband. Let us start with the young brides. Their husbands migrate within a month of their marriage and they have not had time to conceive or bear a child. Even when they return, their duration of stay is just for four to eight weeks. This period is socially very hectic and emotionally draining. The wife in this case spends just a few weeks with her husband, who works on the ship, and the same process continues every time he comes, making her psychologically and emotionally weak and resulting in her becoming unfit to bear a child. In other cases of migration, most of the women had succeeded in bearing a child within a year or two. The condition of these women with children was comparatively better than the childless ones. Women with children felt more secure and also had a clear cut role to play in their husband's family.

Interdependence

In the absence of their men, women are bound to depend on their in-laws, parents, friends and neighbours in order to cope with different situations. In most cases the mothers-in-law had also gone through a situation similar to this, which in some cases helped them to have a better understanding of their daughters-in-law. Parents and in-laws played a vital role in providing support to bring up the children and in strengthening the emotional well-being of the women. Support from in-laws was based on whether the woman became a mother or not.

Friends and neighbours were very important to the woman to cope with the absence of her husband. The woman's life became difficult in cases where there was no help from relatives, whatever the reason. In some cases the woman tried to fulfil her emotional and other needs by developing extramarital relationships.

Marital Relationships

In the absence of the man, the wife's relationship with her husband was found to be positive or negative based on the following factors:

* The type of family members: whether the parents and in-laws are understanding and supportive.
* Proper communication with the husband.
* Support from husband.
* Ability to bear a child.

Marital relationships may become problematic if any of the above factors are in the negative.

Child Care and Education

In the absence of the father, responsible parenting becomes the duty of the mother. The women in my study found this duty challenging, rewarding and fulfilling the goal of motherhood. Children's education was given utmost importance and was easily managed by the women in the absence of their husbands. For working women, this task became easier when they received assistance from some other family members. For example, we see how well Anna in one of the cases managed different responsibilities with the help of her parents. Taking up children's lessons was also much easier when most of the members of the family were educated and my study showed that many of them enjoyed this task, which also kept them busy.

Communication

Communication with the husband was mainly through letters and more through phone calls. The frequency of communication differed from one family to another. A phone call or a letter always improved the emotional well-being of the wife and made her feel loved and cared. During the calls the wife discussed with her husband some of the problems she faced, while she avoided those things that would upset him. The frequency of phone calls reduced after the first year of marriage, while in some cases the wife initiated the reduction to lower costs.

Money Management

Another responsibility that a woman takes up in the absence of her man is managing the finances appropriately. Money management involves two aspects: managing money for household consumption and managing money as savings. Every month a major amount of the salaries go in savings. These savings are later used to enhance social status by building a new house, buying a new car or a bike, investing in land, etc. Money is also deposited in the children's name for their future, and for their education and medical expenses. Money is generally sent in the wife's name, though a small amount is also sent separately to the mother. All financial transactions are managed by the wife. However, in the case of building of a new house, we see how Priya, under the guidance of her husband, manages the money as she has to pay different people involved in building the house.

Mobility

The question of mobility of women whose husbands have migrated is a complicated one. The extra responsibilities that these women have to shoulder both within the private and public spheres compel them to be more mobile. The extent of shouldering various responsibilities among these women differ from family to family and so does the mobility of women. When it comes to social gatherings, weddings, parties and anniversaries, some of these women feel out of place without their husbands and also worry about what people would think about them. This forces them to be cautious and make sure some family members or their children, if they are grown up, accompany them to these functions. These women, however, have hardly any restrictions when she comes to shopping, taking the children to school, banking and visiting their parents. In some cases they may also stay with their parents whenever they want.

Negotiations and Compromise

In Cuncolim village in Goa the unique characteristic of male migration abroad is that the men have migrated before their marriage. This is evident from all my fieldwork. The women who married these men definitely negotiated and compromised for some benefits at the time of marriage. Women agreed to marry these men who were working abroad primarily for future security—for themselves, their children, children's education and career and old age. They also desired economic security, higher social status and upward mobility. But these women did not get what they desired so easily; they had to reckon with, and compromise, their own careers in some cases and their emotional, psychological and physical well-being. The economic benefits and the cooperation of women have been important factors for the success and reinforcement of male migration among the Catholics.

Conclusion

The conclusions that have been drawn are based on the questions and issues that have been raised and which seek explanation and understanding:

1. The impact that the migration of a man has on his wife, involves a process of negotiation, sacrifice and hardship both on the part of the husband and even more on the part of the wife, since she has to live with the various responsibilities that are thrust on her. Taking care of in-laws, children, maintenance of the household, organising the remittances in an appropriate way, etc., are some of the responsibilities (see also Gulati 1993). Migration of the head of the household abroad becomes a painful process when there is no one in the house, or there is no help from relatives or when there is neglect on the husbands' part of regularly sending remittances.
2. Women generally tend to adjust with the migration of their men for security purposes, both economic and social security concerning the present and the future well-being of the family, with top priority given to children's education and career.
3. In order to cope with male migration, women employ different strategies, which differ from person to person depending on the situation. One of the basic strategies employed by women is to confide with a friend or a close family member. Women are able to cope better with the

absence of their husbands when there is someone to share their joys and sorrows. In other words, family networks and friend's circle play an important role in coping with the absence of men (Gulati 1993).

4. Some women who are unable to cope with the absence of companionship and sexuality of their husbands, tend to get involved in extramarital affairs (Connell 1984), either to satisfy their own desires or sometimes for the sake of survival of their family members. In such situations of neglect by husband and other family members, the wife tends to cope with the stress and feeling of worthlessness by attempting suicide.
5. Migration of a husband in some cases hinders marital relationships. In some cases it also hinders the chances of bearing a child, which in turn stigmatises the wife, leading to her ostracisation and boycott in the family as well as in society.
6. Women also sometimes sacrifice their own career and well-being for the sake of their husband, children and family at large, thus contributing to the success of male migration. This in turn reinforces migration of a male for the welfare and security of the family, thus making male migration successful due to the cooperation and sacrifice of women (Nagli 1990; Menon 1995).
7. Migration of a male abroad also contributes, though unknowingly, to the gendered division of labour, as women are always supposed to look after the house and children.
8. Women of migrant households may or may not become mobile. However, my study reveals that the new and additional responsibilities women have to shoulder, both within and outside the house, compel them to be more mobile. The extent to which women have to take on new responsibilities differs from family to family (Gulati 1993; Mascarenhas-Keyes 1990).

To conclude, women have always been legally, politically, socially and psychologically subjugated by men. The establishment of capitalism and with it the emergence of wage labour, migration and greater individualism within nuclear families has tended to separate families from community and women from men. The migration of men physically emphasises this isolation and occasionally brings with it conflict and tension, leading families to deviate from the culture and values of their society. However, in general, economic remittances reinforce a traditional set of values and, through the inequality of migration tend to reinforce, rather than reject, the existing social hierarchy. Hence in this kind of situation, and there are certainly others, women are denied the opportunities to participate in a broadly based economic development *vis-à-vis* their own development.

Women's experience in the absence of men ranges from relative security to bitter frustration, acute personal stress and emotional dissolution as well as content and discontent. Women at the same time tend to negotiate the migration of men by supporting migration, in order to provide security for the future, both for them as well as their children. However, as in similar situations elsewhere in the world, the impact of male migration on women's life is complex and varied. On one hand women may gain independence, autonomy and competence in new skills and status as household heads, but on the other hand they may lose independence and status through overdependence on remittances, and also suffer poor health and welfare. However, the conclusions cannot be more precise because few such studies have been undertaken and many perceived effects are a function of time, apart from local and national, social and economic structures, and the perspectives of the researcher.

Limitations of the Study

1. The study is class restricted, in a sense it tends to focus on a given class and the conclusions that have been made may have been different with reference to other classes of women.
2. The study has a limited number of respondents, which number could have been more, and this may have added several other insights making the study more interesting and rich in its orientations.
3. The study is limited to the wives of male migrants, while it fails to see the other side with reference to what males go through in the absence of their family.

REFERENCES

Bolaria, Singh. 1997. *International and Labour Migration*. Delhi: Oxford University Press.

Brettel, C.B. 2007. "Portugal's First Post-Colonials: Citizenship, Identity, and the Repatriation of Goans". *Portuguese Studies Review*, 14 (2): 143–170.

Connell, John. 1984. "Status or Subjugation? Women, Migration and Development in South Pacific". *International Migration Review*, 24 (4): 964–983. http//:www.jstor.org

de Souza, T.R. 1979. *Medieval Goa: A Socio-Economic History*. New Delhi: Concept Publishers.

_______. 1990. *Goa through the ages*. New Delhi: Concept Publishing Company.

Elizabeth, Gordon. 1994. "The Plight of the Women of Lesotho Reconsideration with Decline of Apartheid". *Journal of Black Studies*, 2 (4): 435–441. http//:www.jstor.org.

Finch, Janet. 1984. "'It's great to have someone to talk to': the ethics and politics of interviewing women". In *Social Researching Politics, Problems, Practice*, edited by Bell and Roberts. London: Routledge and Kegan Paul.

Gracias, Fatima da Silva. 2000. "Goans away from Goa, Migration to the Middle East". *Losotopie*: 423–432.

Gulati, Leela. 1993. *In the Absence of their Men*. New Delhi: Sage Publications.

Lawrence, C. Watson.1985. *Interpreting Life Histories*. New Jersey: Reutgers University Press.

Mascarenhas-Keyes, Stella. 1986. "The Native Anthropologist: Constraints and Strategies in Research". In *Anthropology at Home*, edited by A. Jackson. London: Tavistock.

______. 1987. *Migration and International Goan Community*. Unpublished PhD thesis, SOAS.

______. 1990. *Goa through the Ages: International Migration: Its Development, Reproduction, and Economic Impact on Goa up to 1961*. New Delhi: Concept Publishing Company.

______. 1993. "International and Internal Migration: The Changing Identity of Catholic and Hindu Women in Goa". In *Migrant Women: Crossing Boundaries and Changing Identities*, edited by Gina Buijs. Delhi: Berg Publishers.

Menon, G. 1995. "The Impact of Migration on the Work and Status of Tribal Women in Orissa". In *Women and Seasonal Labour Migration*, edited by L. Schenk-Sandbergen. New Delhi: Sage Publications.

Nagli, Kebria. 1990. "Power Patriarchy and Gender Conflict in the Vietnamese Immigrant Community". *Journal of Gender and Society*, 4 (1): 9–24. http//:www.jstor.org

Osella, Gardener. 2004. *Migration, Modernity and Social Transformation in South Asia*. New Delhi: Sage Publications.

Pearson, M.N. 1990. *The Portuguese in India*. Hyderabad: Orient Longman, 156.

Premji, Mehandra. 1980. *Urban out Migration: A study of its Nature, Causes, and Consequences*. New Delhi: Sterling Publishers Pvt Ltd.

UNESCO. 1984. *Women in the Villages, Men in the Towns*. France: UNESCO.

Chapter 14

Elementary Education in Goa during Its Colonial Period (1821-1910) and Its Impact on Goan Society

Ricardo Cabral

A Brief Perspective of Education

According to the District Report Cards and Flash Statistics (Elementary Education in India, Arun C. Mehta, NUEPA, New Delhi) put out by the National University of Educational Planning and Administration (NUEPA), Goa has healthy education indicators outstripping many of the other Indian States. To cite just one example, the Pupil Teacher Ratio (PTR) is almost of international standards. As per the 2009-10 Educational Statistics, it was around 1:25. There are today 1,252 primary schools, 444 upper primary schools, 376 high schools and 82 higher secondary schools (Educational Statistics at a Glance, 2009-10). A survey conducted by Goa Sarva Shiksha Abhiyan in 2006-07 found that the total number of out-of-school children in the age group of six to 14 numbered around 2,000. Of these, 490 had never been enrolled in any school. Comparing this to the total number of children in school in that year up to the elementary level—which was 158,935—the dropout rate works out to be around two, whereas the all-India rate is around 32.

This is because, as far as access to educational institutions is concerned, there is a primary school in every 3-km radius serving a population of 1,076; an upper primary school at every 8.34 km radius serving a population of 3,035; a secondary school in every 9.85-km radius for a population of 3,584; and a higher secondary school in every 45.15-km radius for a population of 16,435. Though the enrolment ratio between boys and girls is a perfect 50:50 at all school levels, the male: female teacher ratio is heavily loaded in favour of the fairer sex—something like 70 : 30–as many ladies prefer teaching rather than clerical jobs.

In spite of the best efforts of the Central and the State governments it is seen that the enrolment figures at the all-India level have just managed to cross the 50 per cent mark. It has been realised that meeting the access and retention targets for universalisation of education is an uphill task in a country like India. All societies I suppose have to go through these growing pains because the situation was similar in 18th and 19th century Europe. Without any exception, Goa too went through that ordeal many years ago thanks to some of the well-meaning Portuguese rulers and Governors who brought out tremendous activities in the field of education in Goa.

Historical Background

I will limit myself here only to elementary education confined to the official schools called '*Escolas Primarias*' (Primary schools). Furthermore, the period of my discussion would be limited to 1821–1910. Though the impact of education may not have any time bar, this period has been taken because of its peculiar features. In 1836 a Constitutional Monarchy was in place in Portugal. As a fall-out of the 1821 Revolution, political rights had been granted to Goan Catholics—Catholicism was declared as the State religion though by the end of the 18th century the 'Novas Conquistas' had already been annexed—which enabled Goans to make their presence felt in the 'Cortes' the Portuguese Parliament. The Portuguese during the period mentioned above held sway over a small part of India—officially known as '*Estado da India Portuguesa*' (Indo-Portuguese State)—comprising Goa, Daman, Diu, Dadra and Nagar Haveli (Gune 1973). Since Goa was the largest portion of '*Estado da India Portuguesa*' the attention of the Portuguese was concentrated more on Goa than on the other territories. Hence I exclude the other areas and take Goa as representing the entire '*Estado da India Portuguesa*'.

Official primary education began in Goa in 1831 when the Governor, Dom Manuel de Portugal e Castro, set up six primary schools in places where the military regiments had been housed, namely Pangim, Ribandar, Margao, Bicholim, Ponda and Colvale. This was done mainly for two reasons: first, to provide learning facilities to the children of the military personnel who were at that time mostly Europeans; and second, to maintain a strict vigil as earlier experiments to provide instruction had failed because of the truancy of both teachers and students. Strategically, the Military Commander was made the Inspecting Authority of the school within his jurisdiction. But this was not the only master stroke of the Governor. After placing the schools in disciplined surroundings—in France, which was representative of continental Europe, the main objective of primary education was inculcation of discipline—he made them accessible also to all the other children from the neighbourhood. "*Panelichea nanvan shereak udok*" (In the name of the creeper the supporting plant too gets some water) goes the Konkani proverb. These schools were called '*Escolas de Primeiras Letras*' (School of basic education).

The Raison d'être

But why was the Government now interested in educating the people? The Portuguese had conquered Goa in 1510. Initially the possessions had to be guarded in sufficient numbers and by now the Portuguese were already short of hands. The miscegenation policy of Albuquerque had already died a natural death. Manpower requirement was becoming a teething problem for the colonialists. Hence, not unlike the British, the Portuguese decided to impart some literary and numerical skills to the locals so as to produce a class of people who would be able to man the administration.

But this was not the only reason. After having held Goa in its possession for more than 300 years, the political perception had changed and the Portuguese had no hesitation in calling it its own. Goa was no longer called a colony (though during the Salazar reign it was called so). Rather it was now addressed as an overseas province or a State. In Europe, national systems of education were being established. If that was the case then logically its citizens had to exhibit

Portuguese traits and manners. For this to happen there was an urgent need to integrate the people into the Iberian culture and the best way to do it was through the medium of education. Different approaches had been tried with limited success. Albuquerque's social engineering method had failed. Political hegemony too did not bring about any favourable transformation in Goan society. The proselytisation process was both limited and slow. But the immediate cause was the expulsion of the Jesuits; the same fate befell the other missionaries too, albeit in 1836, after the laws of Aguiar were enforced in Goa in 1772. Hence the political dispensation had to adopt a different approach to take care of its mounting needs.

The Governor, Dom Manuel de Camara, read the situation perfectly well and accordingly he wrote to the King in 1823 saying "Instruction (here) is almost nil. There isn't even a single school (*casa de educacao*) for a population of 260 thousand." (Gomes 1927). In 1829 the next Governor Dom Manuel de Portugal e Castro confirmed the aforesaid when he wrote to the King saying that the state of public instruction was in a lamentable situation. He was obviously referring to the fact that in spite of the '*Plano de Estudos*' (Plan of Studies) promulgated by the Marquis de Pombal in 1772 in Portugal, no development in the field of education had taken place in Goa.

Praiseworthy Initiatives

This set in motion a chain of significant events. The Missionaries were expelled and education became a State subject. Dom Manuel set up six schools of primary education besides the ones of Portuguese grammar. He was followed by the interim Governor, Lopes de Lima, who issued a *'Portaria'* (notification) with the intention of spreading education throughout the State and mandated the opening of over 40 schools, both village as well as Municipal, giving a quick shot in the arm for education. Though the next Governor, Conde de Antas, tried to reduce the number of schools to 25 due to financial constraints the spread and development of education continued unabated. At the close of the 19th century there were around 86 official primary schools for boys and eight schools for girls. Besides, there were many private schools and classes. By 1910, when Portugal became a Republic, there were around 4,000 students enrolled in various schools all over

Goa at the first level (*Primeiro grau*) and another 350 at the second level (*Segundo grau*) of primary education. Though the rise in numbers was modest, the system of education was in place.

Goans were fortunate that they started their educational journey along with most of the European nations. Goa perhaps was the first to experience Western style education. Whatever was happening in Europe was faithfully transplanted in Goa. Unlike today, Goans did not have to travel for studies to Europe. Instead Europe came to Goa. Official primary schools for the common people were established in France in 1833 after Victor Cousin's report and Guillaume Guizot's survey (Power 1970). Hence it is seen that in many areas Goans were almost on par with the Europeans. But the key point is to analyse the way/s in which Portuguese education impacted Goan society.

Value Additions to Goan Society

With a fillip being given to education, for the first time school buildings dotted the village skyline. Earlier classes were conducted in the parochial houses. The school building stood out amidst the thatched roofs and mud raised walls as it was also located in an elevated spot. It was built with stones and had a tiled roof. The design was either square or rectangular with a verandah all-round. The imposing structure, comparatively speaking, must have drawn many towards it, if not out of academic interest then at least out of curiosity. Later on this construction style with various modifications would be copied by the village folks to build their houses.

Initially getting the local children to enroll in these primary schools was a daunting task as there was all-round resistance. Everything was viewed with suspicion. People were simplicity personified and hence had no interest in academics. It was something alien to their culture. They could make neither head nor tail of what was being taught in school. Others were stubborn and refused to see any merit in the venture. It was an uphill task to get the children to school, similar to the struggle that the Government of India is going through at the moment. The colonial Government adopted various measures, such as giving incentives to the teachers (*Professores*), involving the local village authority, appointing local inspectors, giving free books and slates, providing free snacks, making education compulsory, and even threatening imprisonment for defaulting parents. Thanks to the Portuguese for their educational policy, as today the schooling culture is well set in Goa, with parents keen to enroll their wards in school as early as possible.

After sustained efforts there was widespread literacy and numeracy among the people of Goa. However, this literacy and numeracy was in the language of the colonial masters, which had both positive and negative results. They learnt a foreign script and a foreign language to the detriment of the local language. But conversely it helped them to express themselves scripturally in their own language as they smartly adapted the foreign script to the local language. It also helped in counting and gradually the barter system came to be replaced with currency. The gradual acquisition of language skills threw up a cornucopia of literature both in the Portuguese language and the Konkani language. The most productive period was the second half of the 19th century with over 50 periodicals and magazines (Da Costa 1997) published both in Goa and in Bombay either in Portuguese or Konkani or both (bilingual). But the most important development was the maintaining of records. Learning of the script helped in maintaining records. Perhaps Goa is the only Indian State where everything is found very well recorded including births and deaths. Hence no controversies!

To some extent, elementary education also helped in migration. Initially the educated people opened schools in places outside Goa such as Bombay, Belgaum, Calcutta, Karachi, etc. The school masters appointed in these schools were usually from Goa. Apart from the qualified staff, others were required for upkeep and maintenance. These again had to be from Goa. These could have been either literate or illiterate. However, all of them had to communicate with their loved ones at home and hence they had to learn to write a letter at least. This would be in the Roman script. The language used in the letters too would be a mixture of Konkani and Portuguese words since Portuguese, being taught in the classrooms, had freely intermingled with the local language leading to its enrichment.

Going to school meant wearing a uniform. Uniforms initially were given free of cost to the students. The uniform comprised a half shirt and half pant. This same pattern came to be replicated while tailoring other clothes. People started cultivating sartorial habits as fabric material was gradually made available.

As time went by, school became not only an academic centre but also an educational centre. A keen observer to Goa might have noticed that unlike the rest of the country *paan* (betal leaf with some other ingredients) eating and spitting is much less in Goa (Souza 1879). This is due to the fact that in the primary schools a spittoon had been kept and children were trained to spit in the spittoon, which makes us assume that some of the students too—the maximum admission age in Class I was 13—might have been eating *paan.* However, as time went by, either by design or by default, the habit of spitting in public died out.

At home everybody either squatted on the low floor or sat on the low stool called *bankin.* In school there were benches to sit on and the teacher had a table and a chair. Replicas of these pieces of furniture started appearing in houses as more and more people learnt to sit at a table.

To attract children to school one of the measures adopted was of starting canteens where the underprivileged were given free snacks. Usually it was '*pao e manteiga*' (bread and butter) and a nice cup of coffee. Some old timers still recollect nostalgically the overpoweringly appetizing smell of the butter. Goans gradually cultivated such habits of having bread and butter, tea and coffee, biscuits (*bolacha*), etc.

Every now and then the government takes credit for Goa having some of the best health indicators in the country. It all started at least a couple of centuries ago. Everyday the school master would check on the cleanliness of the clothes. The students had to also pare their nails regularly. At the time of admission the candidate had to produce a certificate from the Health Officer stating that he had been inoculated against all the contagious diseases. But even before that the location itself of the school was chosen in such a way that all pedagogical principles were strictly observed, such as cross-ventilation, ample light availability and distance from obnoxious places. The spot had to be approved by the Portuguese Health Authorities, who went to great lengths to maintain proper health and hygiene.

Education imparted in these primary schools was truly value-based. Moral education was stressed. Comprehensive rules and regulations were strictly enforced. Punishment was severe though, by 1831, the '*palmatorio*' (a flat but thick wooden contraption used to hit the students on their palms) had been banned (Souza 1879).

This led to a strong sense of discipline and consequently a certain respect for law and law enforcement authorities.

In Conclusion

The outcome of the entire Portuguese education system has been succinctly and comprehensively summed up by Dr. J. Benedito Gomes (Preface to the Annual Magazine of Primary Schools, 1927): "And thus with the pedagogy or with hygiene, with discipline or with morals, with the cultivation of work habits and modernisation, the student was prepared to be independent and conform to a moral superiority which would give him balance and justice."

It can be summed up as 'comprehensive education'. Forgive me for stating here only some of the educational indicators that impacted Goan society during the period of the Constitutional regime. There could be more. But whether it is openly admitted or not, the fact remains that certain mannerisms and competencies that were acquired during the last two centuries of Portuguese rule are still visible.

Unfortunately Goans have not been able to capitalise on the lead given to them by the colonial rulers. Instead they have allowed others to catch up with them while they have been busy nitpicking and hairsplitting. The charge that Portuguese education was elitist may not be wholly true since the rulers did try to be fair and square. It was mostly the landed Goan gentry that tried to keep the masses illiterate for their own vested interests. Yet the illumining effects of education did manage to escape through the cracks and chinks of the barricade erected by the Goan elites and spread its glow all over Goa. Honestly Goan society does owe a lot to the Portuguese education system.

REFERENCES

Annuario do Estado da India. Imprensa Nacional, Nova Goa, 1926.

Cabral, Ricardo. *Primary Education in Portuguese Goa*, Concept Publishing Company, New Delhi, 2013.

Da Costa, Aleixo Manuel. 1997. *Dicionario de Literatura Goesa*. Instituto Cultural/Fundacao Oriente, Macau, 1997.

Da Costa, J.A.J. *A History of Goa*, (self-published) Saligao, 1982.

Directorate of Education, Government of Goa. *Educational Statistics at a Glance, 2009–10.*

Goa Sarva Shiksha Abhiyan. *Household Survey Report*, 2006–07.

Gomes, J. Benedito. *Um Prefacio Historic-Pedagogico* in *Annuario das Escolas Primarias*, Tip. Rangel, Bastora, 1927.

Gune, V.T. *A Guide to the Collection of Records in the Goa Archives*, Imprensa Nacional, Nova Goa, 1973.

Mehta, Arun C.*Elementary Education in India.* NUEPA, New Delhi, 2007.

Power, Edward J.*Main Currents in the History of Education.* Tata McGraw, New York, 1970.

Souza, Felipe Nery Thomas Caetano de Rosario. *Noticia Historico e Legislacao da Instruccao Publica, Primaria, Secundaria e Superior na India Portugueza*, Imprensá Nacional, Nova Goa, 1879.

CHAPTER 15

From *Caminhão to Avião*

A Study on the System of Public Transportation in Goa

SHARMILA PAIS

Introduction

A study of transportation down the ages tells us that this subject spans the entire history of human civilisation. Throughout history, researchers have recognised its significance in understanding the economic development of a region and the military prowess of a ruler. It has allowed opportunities to harness natural resources, promote trade and regulate the lives of people.

The system of transportation in Goa has come a long way over the years. The physical features of the State, its river systems and location have contributed to its development. The 19th century, in particular, was witness to several worldwide advancements in transportation. Consequently, Goa too was exposed to these changes under the colonial regime. The technological feats of the 20th century and the introduction of new modes of transport allowed Goans to travel long distances with much ease and speed.

Public transportation refers to a system of vehicles which operate at a regular interval on a fixed route and are used by the public. An uphill task confronting the government after liberation was the restoration of public transport and its infrastructure disrupted by the retreating Portuguese forces in 1961. Today, 50 years since the liberation from colonial rule, Goa has all major modes of public transport: roadways, waterways, railways and airways. Since 1961, every passing decade has been witness to reform, better and faster means of travel, sometimes rendering the existing modes obsolete.

Road Transport

Roadways and road transport have played a crucial role in connecting different parts of Goa. The idea of 'walk ability' for good health is making a great come back in recent times, but walking was a popular mode of transport after liberation. Throughout the 1960s and 1970s, people in Goa walked long distances to reach their destination. Goans have travelled from villages to towns, to ferry points and within city limits to reach work, the market, schools and other destinations.

Bullock Cart

The bullock cart, once a popular mode of transportation, has almost been driven into oblivion in Goa. Locally termed *gaddo,* or the *boilam gaddo*, it is a two-wheeled cart drawn by oxen. The *gaddekar* (bullock cart driver) was as popular as the *voddhekar* (canoe driver) and highly in demand in society. During the 20th century, bullock carts were widely used to transport people as well as a variety of goods including manure, salt, rice and coconuts. The carts were privately owned and were often hired by people, particularly the rich, to commute long distances. One cart could accommodate up to eight people and had seats on its either side. For people arriving from overseas or Bombay, hiring a bullock cart after having crossed the rivers was a common mode of transport in the 1960s. There were 1,532 bullock carts registered in Goa during 1964-65; in 1965-66 their number had come down to 1,226. The downward trend continued further during 1966-67 to 1,197 bullock carts (NCAER *Development Programmes for Goa, Daman and Diu* 1970, 150).

In the late 1970s, the bullock cart was still seen as an important mode of transportation in many parts of India. The Central government had set up a steering group to study the problem connected with the bullock cart system in the country and even draw up a plan for its modernisation within a short span of time (*Goa Today* April 1979, 12). However, in Goa their use as a means of public transport had increasingly diminished with every passing decade. Very few carts are in operation in Goa now and are still required to pay a tax to the village Panchayat.

Horse Drawn Carriages

A few horse drawn carriages or *trens* were seen on Goan roads after 1961. They were gradually phased out on account of the alternative means of travel on the anvil. The *trens* were quite popular in several parts of the state prior to liberation. It was a convenient mode of travel within city limits, particularly for residents of Panaji, Mapusa, Vasco and Margao. They were driven by one or more horses, accommodating four to five people comfortably in the carriage. Carmo Miranda writes, "The seating arrangements in the *trens* were similar to that of the *machila* of the *caderinhas* type. Three persons of average weight were accommodated at the back of the vehicle. The *Lugar do Honra* was an esteemed seat and reserved for the privileged occupant. Few Goans though had private horses with a saddle, one among them being Dr. Rozendo Ribeiro in Bardez" (Miranda 1989, 56).

Caminhão

For more than a decade after liberation, the *Caminhão* served as the popular means of long distance travel till they were replaced by the 'modern' type buses. The generation of Goans who have travelled by it have nostalgic memories of the vehicle. The automobiles powered by internal combustion engines had ushered in an age of fast travel in Goa during the early 20th century. It was during this period that the *caminhãonetas* were introduced for public transport, generating a frenzy of sorts usually accompanying a novel phenomenon. The first service of the *caminhão* was established by the Costa Colaco family from its head office in Margao, commuting between Margao and Loutolim, and charging 12 *tangas* per passenger (Miranda 1989, 62). For a long time, it was the only mode of public transport for any one undertaking a long distance journey in Goa.

The *caminhão* would suddenly come to a screeching halt with a "*roa re*" to every passenger that had reached his doorstep (N. Souza 1986). It was also called the *carreira* and it became an integral part of Goan society. The vehicle was a low tin-plated bus that proved surprisingly resilient and weathered many a storm. It could complete a journey of 60 kilometres in a record time of over four hours. The slow pace of travel was attributed to the innumerable unscheduled stops undertaken *en route* (V. Souza 1983, 63). The *caminhão* was a convenient mode of transportation for regular commuters. Any halt by a *bhatkar* (landlord) from his balcony was sufficient to make the gate of his house a regular stop, much to the irritation of other passengers in the vehicle (V. Souza 1983, 63). Generally, they were owned privately by people and varied in size. Its journey commenced from a prime destination. The loud *pomnk-ponk,* the honking of its horn, announced its arrival and departure. Tony Fernandes in his work, *Goa: Memories of My Homeland,* states that some of these vehicles were assembled in Goa on imported Bedford and Dodge chassis.

According to the Motor Vehicles Department, the number of these old type of vehicles carrying passengers during 1960 was 445. They plied on different routes, with their centre of operation being the principal towns of Panaji, Mapusa, Cortalim, Agassaim, Betim, Sanvordem and other places. The buses operated on a licence issued by the government. A licence fee of Rs. 40 was charged by the authorities (NCAER *Techno-Economic Survey of Goa, Daman and Diu* 1964, 125). The last of these *caminhãoes* were completely phased out of service by the mid 1970s (Miranda 1989, 64).

Buses

The 'modern type' of buses gradually replaced the *caminhão* in the state. During the second half of the 20th century, these buses made their appearances on Goan roads ushering in a faster and comfortable means of travel. In 1952, the first bus was introduced in Goa by Xamba Phaterpekar which plied from Betim to Mapusa (D'Mello and Pinto 2008, 30).

By 1960 the Motor Vehicles Department had registered 85 'modern type' of buses which could carry from 29 to 43 passengers. They paid an annual amount of Rs. 272 as licence fee. By 1966-67 there were about 140 of these bus routes under operation. Nearly 565 buses (old and new type) plied along these routes and their operations were in private hands. It was anticipated that the needs of the future would increase at a faster pace (assuming an accelerated rate of 8 per cent in passenger transport). Therefore, it was felt that an additional fleet of 226 buses would be needed in the future. The number of buses in 1968 had risen to 630. The life of the vehicle was assumed to be nine to 12 years (NCAER *Development Programmes for Goa Daman and Diu* 1970, 89).

By January 1965, motorised public transport in Goa, Daman and Div were governed by the Motor Vehicle Rules of January 1965 replacing the existing decrees and rules under Portuguese rule. The Directorate of Transport was created to head the Motor Vehicles Department. Since then, it has been regulating all activities related to transportation in the State.

By 1971-72, the number of vehicles engaged in passenger transport across different parts of the State was about 440. The Maharashtra State Corporation as well the Karnataka State Corporation were also engaged in interstate transport services as per the agreements signed between these States (Gune 1979, 431-32).

Kadamba Transport Corporation

The monopoly of private bus operators in the state came to an end with the establishment of the Kadamba Transport Corporation Limited in October 1980. The government had aimed at providing regular and reliable service to the public and simultaneously connecting the far-flung villages to the urban centre of the state. It was during the 5th Five-Year Plan that the long pending plans of nationalisation of transport services were considered by the state government. On October 19, 1980, the Corporation launched its first bus from Dhavem to Panaji.

Three of its major routes have been nationalised: Panaji-Margao, Vasco-Margao and Panaji-Vasco. The services provided by the Corporation run parallel to those provided by private operators. The Corporation has also been operating Non-Stop Shuttle services along several routes in Goa (DPSE 2006, 43). During 2005-06, the Corporation had a fleet of 416 vehicles. An air-conditioned luxury shuttle service also operates along the Panaji-Margao route. The Corporation has introduced various schemes which include 50 per cent concession to *bona fide* students and physically challenged people,

50 per cent concession in bus fare to senior citizens and monthly passes to daily commuters (DPSE 2006, 44). Since March 2011, the Corporation has provided an online booking service in the state.

Table 15.1: Buses/minibuses of the Kadamba Transport Corporation

Year	*Registered for the year*	*Total*
2005–06	422	5,556
2006–07	687	6,376
2007–08	533	6,909
2008–09	706	7,644
2009–10	688	8,332
2010–11	575	8,907

Source: Directorate of Transport, Government of Goa.

Bicycles on Hire

Along with motorised transport, bicycles made their presence felt on Goan roads, initially with simple pedals and then followed by motorised ones, during the early 20th century. Besides privately owned cycles, they were also given on hire according to demand. There were several individuals who were involved in this business. The names of Xec Ismail, Mamod Yacub, Daud Mamod Aga and several others were well known in Panaji (*Anuario do Estado da India Portugueza* 1953a, 269).

A cycle had to be registered with the Panchayat in the village and the Municipality in the town for a stipulated fee. A seal was affixed on it after registration. People found it convenient to hire a cycle and travel long distances, than wait for a *carreira* whose frequency was limited and arrival sometimes uncertain. By 1966, the number of cycles on hire was 3,466; in 1967 their number had risen to 3,903 (NCAER *Development Programmes for Goa, Daman and Diu* 1970, 150). In the 1970s and 1980s bicycles were commonly owned by many households in Goa. The increasing popularity of motorcycles gradually sidelined the importance of cycles in the State.

Motorcycle Pilots

Goa has a unique tradition of black and yellow motorcycle taxis bearing a yellow mudguard with black number plates. They are operated by the famous 'pilots of Goa', a name which still baffles many a researcher. It is said that the motorcycle culture dates back to the days of the Portuguese *Estafeta* or the dispatch rider, the official messenger of the Portuguese period. During the early 20th century motorcycles made their appearance in the State and several brands such as Niele Scooter, Honda Benly, BSA Motorcycles and others were advertised in the press (Costa 2008, 84).

There was a time when powerful BMWs and Hercules were shipped from Germany and added to the Portuguese forces. The middle level officials would hitch rides with the *Estafetas* and non-commissioned officers, because of their lower rank, had to make do with two-wheeler mobility. Several riders began operating from a self-devised stand near the Church Square in Panaji. The large deployment of troops from Angola and Mozambique in Goa in 1955, after the *Satyagraha,* helped in the prosperity of the *baddem* business (Sequeira and De Souza 1986, 22).

Their nomenclature, 'pilot', has defied a proper explanation. One version narrates: "It's because they do more flying than riding." Others associate the riders to the business of prostitution where the latter would "pilot the customers to the prostitutes" (Sequeira and De Souza 1986, 22-23). Life for the motorcycle pilots was quite challenging during the early years of the liberation. They had to battle all odds, including a fierce struggle with the transport authorities. On registration of their vehicles with the government, the pilots were given badges (Sequeira and De Souza 1986, 24). In January 1969 the Goa government granted an extension of one year to the motorcycle taxi transport operators, after which they would be required to operate auto-rickshaws (*Goa Today* February 1969, 28). The motorcycle taxis were not legalised until another seven years later. It was under the Chief Ministership of Dayanand Bandodkar, in September 1976, that legal recognition came to them. The yellow and black motorcycle taxis have become almost an institution in the State. During the 1970s and 1980s, their services were sought after chiefly by the men, but today, changes in attitudes towards the pilots among the general public has encouraged their business and helped them prosper.

Table 15.2: Number of Motorcycle Pilots

Year	*Registered for the year*	*Cumulative*
2005–06	195	6,448
2006–07	1,543	8,081
2007–08	969	9,050
2008–09	2,154	11,204
2009–10	1,959	13,163
2010–11	2,242	15,405

Source: Directorate of Transport, Government of Goa.

Auto-rickshaws

Auto-rickshaws, the three-wheel vehicles, operated by a single driver were introduced in Goa a decade after liberation. They were chiefly hired for travelling within city limits or short distances rather than long distance travel. At regular intervals, the government has tried to enforce regulations on auto-rickshaw operators for the benefit of the public. The auto-rickshaw, as a means of public transportation, has mostly been preferred by tourists rather than locals, unlike other States where it serves as an efficient and a cheap mode of transportation. The operators do not go by the meter and most of them lament the sporadic business they get from tourists visiting the State. However, many operators acknowledge the rising trend among Goans of hiring auto-rickshaws for public travel, during the last decade.

Table 15.3: Number of Auto-rickshaws

Year of registration	*Registered for the year*	*Total-Cumulative*
2005–06	77	3486
2006–07	89	3586
2007–08	21	3607
2008–09	51	3659
2009–10	50	3709
2010–11	63	3772

Source: Directorate of Transport, Government of Goa.

Taxis

Motorcars surfaced on Goan roads at the dawn of the 20th century. For a long time, cars of brands such as Ambassador and Fiat were employed in business as taxis. In 1966, the number of taxis registered in Goa stood at 670; two years later their number had increased to 826. In a press note issued on September 1, 1969, the Government of Goa directed all taxis and auto-rickshaws to be fitted with meters from October 1, 1969–a decision which was resented by the vehicle owners (*Goa Today* October 1969, 30). A number of taxis were suspended in Panaji, Margao and Mapusa by police for not complying with the government directive to install meters (*Goa Today* November 1969, 30).

Shared taxis were also operational along important routes of Goa: Panaji–Mapusa; Mapusa–Calangute; Panaji–Agassaim; Cortalim–Margao; Margao–Colva; Panaji–Dabolim (airport); Mapusa–Colvale ("Tourist Guide" 1983, 93). Shared taxis are still popular along the Colva–Margao route till this date and are increasingly being used by local residents.

The yellow and black taxis have received several benefits from the State government unlike the white cabs operating in the market. A new trend visible in the market is the replacement of old brands of vehicles by brands such as Maruti, Tata, Hyundai and others. Besides these, there are other motorcars which are registered as commercial vehicles and can be hired on demand. The pre-paid meter counters set up at distinct places has been a great boon to tourists visiting the State.

Table 15.4: Taxis in Goa

Year	*Registered for the year*	*Total–Cumulative*
2005–06	325	9,314
2006–07	880	10,241
2007–08	1,644	11,885
2008–09	867	12,768
2009–10	904	13,672
2010–11	171	13,843

Source: Directorate of Transport, Government of Goa.

Waterways

Waterways are an important means of transportation in Goa on account of its river system and the long stretch of coastline. Its popularity finds a reflection in the local lore: "*Ghantar ghode ani Ghoyant voddhem*" (horses in the Ghats and canoes in Goa). Goan folk songs are replete with words like *tar*, *tariamama*, *vhodekhara* and *tarikodde*, all of which signify boats and boatsmen and are associated with the sea and sea transport. Waterways have helped people travel distances within the State, across the neighbouring regions and even long distance journeys across continents. Despite advancements in public transportation, people still rely on waterways as a means of travel in some parts of Goa.

Bombay to Goa Steamers

Travel by sea from Goa to Bombay was much sought after, for more than two decades after liberation. The Mogul Lines operated passenger ships between Bombay and Panaji during fair weather (September to May). There was a daily service, six days a week, whose arrivals and departures were subject to tides ("Tourist Guide" 1983, 92). In Bombay, the steamer service would commence from the Bhaucha Dhakka wharf in Mazagon and complete its journey in Panaji. It embarked at the ports of Raigad, Vengurla, Malwan and Ratnagiri.

Throughout the 1970s, the steamer service attracted the Goan public. In view of its popularity, the Union Cabinet and the Maharashtra government cleared the decks for the resumption of passenger sea service on the Bombay–Konkan–Goa route by the state-owned Mogul Lines after the monsoons (*Goa Today* September 1979, 9).

During this decade, the rise in oil prices had upset the economy of bus transport, and the authorities desired to make available a less expensive mode of travel for the benefit of the middle classes who used the service most. It had, therefore, prompted the officials to run this service on a long-term basis instead of reviewing the position yearly after the monsoon. A five-year plan was thus drafted to place the service on a sound basis. It was also proposed that the Mogul Lines would acquire new ships equipped with modern engines and chair cars instead of the prevailing bunks (sleeping berths). The speed of the new ships would be about 17 knots, which would help them reach optimum fuel efficiency and reduce the journey time considerably (*Goa Today* September 1979, 9).

The inaugural journey after the monsoons usually generated much excitement in the capital. On October 2, 1979, the Governor Pratap

S. Gill and his wife, Vasudev Rao Dempo and others assembled at the Panaji jetty to welcome Mogul Line, M.V. Konkan Sevak which after three months' hibernation sailed into the Mandovi river (*Goa Today* November 1979, 8).

Gradually, serious fears were expressed by the Central government on the feasibility of running the services on account of the losses incurred. The Centre had maintained that the service would be continued only if Goa and Maharashtra were prepared to bear the full burden of losses suffered by Mogul Lines. Hitherto the losses were shared by Maharashtra, Goa, Central government and Mogul Lines (32 per cent, 28 per cent, 20 per cent and 20 per cent, respectively). The steamer services found a staunch supporter in the Governor. Pratap S. Gill, who made a forceful plea to the former Union Transport and Shipping Minister Chand Ram that the Konkan service be retained at least for one year even if it meant incurring losses (*Goa Today* August 1979, 34). The interstate steamer service's death knell came in 1988, and the sea revellers lamented its end. An attempt to revive travel by sea saw the Catamaran service in 1999, but it could not continue for long on account of alternate means of travel available as well as the high cost of travelling by sea.

Domestic Waterways

Domestic waterways have served as a means of public transportation for a very long time in Goa. Mechanisation of boats introduced in the State by the last quarter of the 19th century had revolutionalised journey by sea. The *Vapor* and the *Lancha* gradually replaced boats and canoes as better alternatives. During the early 20th century, the *Navegacao Fluvial,* established by the decree of March 1906 regulated the Navigation of waterways (*Anuario do Estado da India Portugueza* 1932, 242). The government also encouraged private enterprise to run motor-operated launches after paying the requisite dues to the Department of Navigation by the legislative decree of July 13, 1934 (Noronha 1936, 36).

After 1961, the Department of River Navigation took over the responsibility of domestic waterways and operated ferry as well as launch services in the State. The then Governor Pratap S. Gill affirmed the requirements of additional ferry boats to enable people for crossing the rivers. A suggestion of building passenger sheds at ferry points to relieve people from the scorching sun was also considered by him. The administration had kept the interest of the public at heart and several government officers had been debarred from crossing on priority (*Goa Today* September 1979, 30). The total number of ferries owned by the Department during 1979 stood at 16 (*Goa Today* September 1979, 30).

The Water Navigation Department also provided launch services from Panaji Central jetty–Aldona (once a day), Panaji–Britona, Panaji–Naroa (twice a day) and Panaji–Verem. The Mormugao–Dona Paula launch services were usually suspended during the monsoons and resumed from September. During the late 1970s, the travelling public was provided with two additional launches, in keeping with increasing demand along the above route (*Goa Today* October 1979, 30). The launch services were in operation during the early 1990s, after which they were discontinued.

The Nehru bridge across the river Mandovi, inaugurated by Union Defence Minister Jagjivan Ram, collapsed on July 5, 1986, inviting national disgrace and severing a vital link on National Highway 17. However, the ferry and the launch services came to the rescue of the Goan public at this crucial juncture. Betim, at peak hours, was described as the 'theatre of the absurd'. By 1986, the River Navigation Department had a fleet of 10 launches in operation (*Goa Today* September 1986, 10).

Currently the River Navigation Department operates regular ferry services on 19 routes in the State, including an interstate service, along the Aronda–Kiranpani route. It renders valuable service mainly to islanders and places not connected by bridges. Foot travellers as well vehicular traffic are ferried across the rivers. Heavy vehicles are also permitted along different routes with restrictions on the load. People as well as two-wheelers are exempt from toll charges from April 1, 2000, and from January 1, 2006, respectively. The Department allows priority crossing for wedding vehicles, ambulances, sick patients and hearse vans (River Navigation Department 2009, 4). Buses and heavy vehicles with or without goods are not allowed along the following routes: Pomburpa–Chorao, Panaji–Betim, Cumbarjua–Gandaulim, Sarmanas–Tonca, Volvoi–Surla–Maina, Vanxim–Amboi and Cortalim–Marcaim. Special permission is required from the

Department to transport heavy loads (10 tonnes). The oldest ferry boats in service of the Department are F/B Pomburpa and F/B Amona manufactured during 1961 and 1962, respectively. A motor launch M/L Tiracol also belongs to the fleet of vessels. Plans are in the offing to replace the deteriorated launch with a new one (River Navigation Department 2009, 11-13).

Waterways as a means of public transportation are here to stay for a long time. Places not connected by bridges depend solely on river navigation. In April 2011, in a memorandum to the Captain of Ports, the Chorao Panchayat demanded four ferry boats along the Chorao–Ribandar route, highlighting the problems faced by the passengers due to the inadequacy of the two ferries 'Pednem' and 'Colva' plying on this route (*Heraldo* April 2011, 7).

Railways

Goa is today connected by the South Western and the Konkan Railways. During the 19th century the dawn of a new era in transportation was ushered into Goa with the introduction of a railway line linking the *Estado da India* with British India. It pioneered an exposure of Goa to a wider network of transportation system outside the State.

Before 1961, regular passengers could avail of rail concessions. A journey from Vasco da Gama to Castle Rock by first class cost Rs. 8 and 14 *tangas*; Rs. 4 and 7 *tangas* by second class and Rs. 1 and 4 *tangas* by third class. Monthly and quarterly passes could also be purchased at concessional rates (*Anuario do Estado da India Portugueza* 1953b, 380).

During the economic blockade, diplomatic relations with British India were severed and railway services between India and *Estado da India* came to a grinding halt. The *Junta Autonoma dos Portos e Caminhos de Ferro* looked after the administration. Rail traffic in 1961 was entirely local and consisted of 967,532 passengers. Heavy passenger bookings were recorded in the stations of Margao and Sanvordem. Three passenger trains, a Poona-bound and two locals ran both ways (NCAER 1964, 126).

A decade into the liberation and Goa had a meter gauge railway from Castle Rock to Mormugao. The system was also linked to the adjoining State of Mysore in Londa. Traffic density during 1966–67 was around 960,000. There had been representations to convert the existing meter gauge to broad gauge to speed up the trains and increase capacity. But it was observed that the density of passengers had comparatively declined since 1961 on account of the developments in road transport.

Certain divisions of erstwhile South Central Railways and the South Railways have been now reorganised into the South Western Railway. It was an important link connecting Goa with the rest of the country by rail till the Konkan railway entered the arena. Currently, the rail line operates six local trains from Culem to Vasco.

Konkan Railway

The Konkan coast-based Konkan railway line connecting the ports of Mumbai and Mangalore, with a stretch of 740 kilometres was formally inaugurated in January 1998. Four months later, the train service along the entire route was fully in operation. The construction of the railway line in Goa had its own share of conflicts. The original plan had aligned the railway route through the middle section of Goa, with the route passing through Ponda, but the final alignment with several modified changes would enter Goa from the North in Pernem, and proceed to Karmali. The route continued coast-wards, after crossing the parallel railway bridge along the Zuari river, along several villages of Salcette. It would then exit through Canacona (Alvares 1999, 122). Battling all odds and agitations, the Konkan railway commenced its full-fledged service in the middle of 1998. Today the Konkan railway completes 15 years of existence. It has been quite popular with the Goan public. It has train stations in Pernem, Tivim, Karmali, Margao and Canacona, with a central booking office in Panaji and headquarters in Navi Mumbai.

The railways offer monthly and quarterly passes to regular commuters and a fairly large number of Goans avail these services. The staff of Goa Shipyard and the Mormugao Port Trust residing along these rail routes journey to and fro by railways. The local trains running along the Konkan railway route also render valuable services to people residing in the neighbouring States of Goa.

Air Transport

Airways are employed for interstate and inter-national travel. Goa was introduced to air travel during the early 20th century when a small airstrip was built in Mangor hill in Vasco. With the introduction of the Avião or the airplane, Goans were excited about conquering the skies. In the 1950s an Air Agreement was concluded between Pakistan and Goa to facilitate flights between Portuguese India and Pakistan (Khera 1974, 51). Flights between Goa and Karachi were a common feature. By 1959, it had flown 7,223 passengers (Gune 1979, 445). The Dabolim airport prior to liberation was a civilian airport. It was not utilised by the Portuguese government for military purpose and neither was the FAP, *Força Aerea Portuguesa*, ever stationed in Dabolim.

The liberation of Goa from the Portuguese ushered in a new era in the aviation industry. The triumphant Operation Vijay resulted in the hand-over of the airport to the Indian Navy in April 1962 and thus, the air traffic control has since then been in its hands. Two months after liberation, air services were resumed once again. All types of passenger aircrafts with the Indian Airlines (Fokker Friendship, Viscount and others) could land in Goa. There were reservations of three seats each on Bombay-Goa-Cochin and Cochin-Goa-Bombay flights. The statistics of air passengers since 1961 show increasing air travellers in the State. The seats rose to 48 in 1966, and to 68 seats in 1968. These seats were distributed between 48 seats on Viscount flights, and 10 seats each were reserved by Fokker Friendship planes to Cochin and Bombay. Air traffic was popular between Bombay to Goa on account of convenience. The air journey to Bombay took one hour, compared to the rail or roadways which took 24 hours. The number of passengers travelling by air rose to 20,473 in 1968-69 as compared to 16,164 in 1967-68, an increase of 27 per cent (NCAER 1970, 90).

It was observed that airways in Goa had a great potential for development on account of its location and importance as a tourist destination. In the 1970s there was no direct flight to Bangalore. Till 1966-67, there was a flight between Bombay and Bangalore *via* Belgaum, Goa and Mangalore. It was subsidised by the Mysore government. Since the withdrawal of the subsidy the Indian airlines have stopped this flight (NCAER 1970, 90).

Indian Airlines–created on August 1, 1953, by Pandit Jawaharlal Nehru by nationalising eight private airlines by an Act of Parliament in 1953–began operating from Dabolim from 1966. Indian Airlines operates direct flights to 10 different destinations, namely Mumbai, Mangalore, Kochi, Calicut, Pune, Chennai, Agathi, Delhi, Kuwait and Sharjah.

Table 15.5: Air Traffic in Goa

Year	*Number of passengers*
1962–63	7,567
1963–64	10,355
1964–65	25,527 (exposition of the body of St Francis Xavier)
1965–66	14,076
1966–67	15,551
1967–68	16,164

Source: Development Programmes for Goa, Daman and Diu.

Currently the Goa International Airport has two terminals operated by the Airports Authority of India: the Domestic (1983) and the International (1996). Since the government decision to encourage privatisation of airways in 2003, a number of private players have entered the air rat race. The airlines flying to Goa are IndiGo Air, Jet Airways Ltd., Air India, GoAir, Air Arabia, Kingfisher Airlines, Qatar Airways, Jet Light and SpiceJet. There are other seasonal airlines such as Air Italy Polska, Condor Flugdienst, Monarch Airlines and several others. On an average, 30 to 40 flights are operated on a daily basis.

The airport ranks among the top 10 in the country. INS Hansa Commanding Officer Commodore has stated that Dabolim airport is the only one of its kind in the country to handle maximum civilian aircrafts, despite being a military air base, with a record 12,440 flights in 2010-11 (*Heraldo* September 2011, 5). Civilian aircraft operates for 19 hours, with 30-45 civilian flights arriving in Dabolim civil enclave each day, depending on the season (*Heraldo*, September 2011, 3). The control of the airport by the Indian Navy has been a matter of passive discontentment in the State. Since 2000, the Goa government has been considering the setting up of an international airport in Mopa in North Goa. A six-member Committee was appointed in January

2006 to study the feasibility of operating two parallel airports in Goa. The Ministry of Civil Aviation has already given in principle an approval to this project. It may not be a long wait to see this idea being translated into reality.

Conclusion

Five decades since liberation, and there is no denying the achievements made by the State in public transportation, yet many problems still prevail. Public transport remains the primary mode of travel for most people in Goa. The network of buses operated by the government and private operators is among the most utilised. The modes of travel in Goa are fairly extensive. The government claims to have been making attempts at improving the efficiency of public transportation and redressing the inequities of the past. However, the public in Goa as well as the substantial numbers tourists visiting the State express dissatisfaction over the services offered. Bus strikes by private operators are frequent and cause a nuisance to the public.

The State-run Kadamba Transport Corporation has its share of complaints. Accusations of neglect of its fleet of buses, improper maintenance, inadequate buses along the nationalised routes, and water seepage during monsoons along with corruption have tarnished the image of the Corporation. Complaints about the exorbitant fares charged by taxi and auto-rickshaw operators are not uncommon. Overcrowding of buses, poor services offered and other factors have forced the public to use their own modes of transport, with a resultant increase in road congestion.

Growing vehicular traffic and inadequate parking space have also become major concerns in the State. The vehicular population during the statistical year 2005–06 had crossed 5 lakh. The number of vehicles operating as tourist vehicles in the State had increased so tremendously that the government had to issue a regulatory policy to keep them under control. A moratorium on the issue of tourist permits was enforced from March 2005 for a period of one year to be extended for a period of one year up to February 2007 (DPSE 2006, 42). The officials of the Directorate of Transport have expressed concern about the rising number of vehicles, both in the transport and the non-transport category.

Nonetheless, as we rejoice in 50 years of liberation from foreign rule, we can also reflect on the positive changes obtained and hope for more advancements in the future, more so when public transportation in Goa will entice more commuters to leave their private vehicles at home to ease traffic congestion and battle the escalating fuel rise.

REFERENCES

1969. "A News Report". *Goa Today*. February.

1969. "Meters for Taxis". *Goa Today*. October.

1969. *Goa Today*. November 30.

1979. *Goa Today*. April.

1979. "A News Report". *Goa Today*. August.

1979. *Goa Today*. September.

1979. "Resumption of Steamer services". *Goa Today*. September.

1979. *Goa Today*. October.

1979. "A News Report". *Goa Today*. November.

1983. "Tourist Guide". In *This is Goa*, edited by Sarto Esteves and Vatsala de Sousa, 89–100. Bombay: Source Publishers Pvt. Ltd.

1986. "Post Collapse Blues". *Goa Today*. September.

2011. "A News Report". *Heraldo*, April 16.

2011. "A News Report". *Heraldo*, September 3.

Alvares, Claude. 1999. *The Politics of Environment Abuse*. In *Transforming of Goa*, edited by Norman Dantas. Mapusa: Other India Press.

Anuario do Estado da India Portugueza. 1932. "Navegação Fluvial". Nova Goa: Imprensa Nacional.

_______. 1953a. "Bicicletas de Aluguer". Nova Goa: Imprensa Nacional.

_______. 1953b. "Tabelas das differentes Carreiras". Nova Goa: Imprensa Nacional.

Costa, Lourdes Bravo. 2008. *Life Styles in Goa 1910–1961*. Panaji: Goa Chamber of Commerce and Industry.

De Sousa, Vatsala. 1983. "*Caminhão*". In *This is Goa*, edited by Sarto Esteves and Vatsala de Sousa, 63. Bombay: Source Publishers Pvt. Ltd.

D'Mello, Audrick, and Jason Pinto. 2008. *Transportaire*. A project report, St Xavier's College, Goa University.

DPSE (Directorate of Planning Statistics and Evaluation). 2006. "Infrastructure". *Economic Survey 2005–2006*, Government of Goa. Panaji: Government Printing Press.

Gune, V.T. (ed.). 1979. *Gazetteer of the Union Territory, Goa, Daman and Diu*. Panaji: Government Printing Press.

Khera, P.N. 1974. "Operation Vijay – *The Liberation of Goa and Portuguese colonies in India*. Delhi: Government India Press.

Miranda, Carmo Gonzaga.1989. "Os transportes Dos Goeses Dos Tempos Passados". *Purabhilekh Puratatva*, Journal of the Directorate of Archives and Museum, & Archaeology, Vol II, May–June. Panaji: Government Printing Press.

NCAER (National Council of Applied Economic Research). 1964. "Transport". *Techno-Economic Survey of Goa, Daman and Diu*. New Delhi.

_______. 1970. "Transport". *Development Programmes for Goa, Daman and Diu*. New Delhi.

Noronha, Tomaz. 1936. "*Carreiras Nos Rios de Goa*". *Boletim Official 58 – Extracto Alfabëtico-Remissivo Cronológico*. Nova Goa: Imprensa Nacional.

RND (River Navigation Department). 2009. "Services offered by the River Navigation Department". *Citizen's Charter*. Panaji: Government Printing Press.

Sequeira, Devika, and P. De Souza. 1986. "Pilots of the Road". *Goa Today*, April.

Souza, Nora. 1986. "Nostalgic transport". *The Navhind Times*, January 12.

CHAPTER 16

The Goa Ancient Monuments and Archaeological Sites and Remains Act, 1978 With Special Reference to the Role Played by the Goa Heritage Action Group in Preserving Goan Heritage

PRAJAL SAKHARDANDE

During the Shashikala Kakodkar regime (1973–79), some landmark legislations were passed. One such legislation was the much-needed 'The Goa Ancient Monuments and Archaeological Sites and Remains Act, 1978'.

The Bill to this effect was introduced in the Legislative Assembly of Goa, Daman and Diu in 1978 and passed in the same year. On January 25, 1979, it was assented to by the President of India. This was a historic Act to provide for the preservation of ancient heritage monuments, archaeological sites, remains of historic value other than those declared by or under any law made by Parliament to be of national importance, for the regulation of archaeological excavations and for the protection of sculptures, carvings and other similar objects which are antiquities. This 1978 Act pertained to historical monuments, sites, remains and antiquities of state-level importance under the Government of Goa. Monuments of national-level importance, such as the Kadamb era Tambdi Surla temple or the Adilshahi era Safa Masjid, do not come under the purview of this Act. These two and 19 other monuments are notified by the Archaeological Survey of India (ASI), Goa Circle. Under the 1978

Act, the State Archaeology Department has notified 50 odd historical monuments, sites since the Act came into force with effect from February 1, 1980.

This original Act of 1978 is very important to the preservation and very survival of Goa's history and heritage. Running into eight chapters, the Act included clauses which stood for the preservation and conservation of Goan heritage. Clause No. 7 defines the term 'maintain' with its grammatical variations and cognate expressions including the fencing, covering in, repairing, restoring and cleaning of a protected monument and the doing of any act which may be necessary for the purpose of preserving a protected monument or for securing convenient access thereto. Section 30 of this original Act mentions the penalties for whoever destroys, removes, injures, alters, defaces, imperils or misuses a protected monument, removes from a protected monument any sculpture, carving, image, bas-relief, inscription or other like object shall be punishable with imprisonment which may extend to three months, or with fine or with both. Forts like Cabo de Rama, Chapora, Khorjuvem, Juvem, ancient Saptakoteshwar temple tank, the Saptakoteshwar of Opa-Khandepar, the Khandepar Caves, the Uzgallimall-Pansaimall petroglyphs, British Cemetry, Vichundrem Narayandeo temple, Chapel of Our Lady of Monte, Cudnem Jain temple, Adilshahi masjid of Surla-tar, Namazgah of Bicholim, Chapel of St. Francis Xavier, Church of St. Peter, Frontispices of Sancoale Church, Alorna or Halarn fort, Jain basti of Bandoda, Kundai cave, Shigao cave, Rivona cave, Reis Magos fort and church, among others, are some of the many monuments under the 1978 State Archaeology Act.

Maintaining the originality and original material of any monument is crucial to the preservation of history and this original 1978 Act took care of preserving history and our valuable heritage in its original form. However, these important clauses and sections of the said Act have been drastically amended through the new bill passed by the present Goa State Legislative Assembly through the Goa Ancient Monuments and Archaeological Sites and Remains (Amendment) Bill, 2010, which substitutes some of the original clauses, especially Clause 7, to include new expressions such as **reconstruction** and **re-erection of a historical monument** and the penalties to be imposed on whoever defaces, destroys or alters any monument have been all struck off in the new amended bill. Thus the new Amendment bill threatens the very existence of our valuable history and heritage of Goa.

The Goa Daman and Diu Ancient Monuments and Archaeological Sites and Remains Act, 1978 (Amendment)

The following issues raise concern:

(A) The Act is to be amended so as to allow the government to undertake restoration, renovation, re-erection and reconstruction of ancient monuments without affecting their basic character, archaeological, historical and heritage value.

These monuments are notified by the State Archives and Archaeology Department and should be Grade A buildings which require preservation. As such, reconstruction and re-erection leaves much scope for misuse.

In addition, the internationally accepted definition of 'conservation' is action taken to prevent decay. It embraces all acts that prolong the life of our cultural and natural heritage, the object being to present to those who use and look at historic buildings the wonder of the artistic and human messages that such building possess. The international charters for conservation of historic buildings decree that the minimum effective action is always the best; if possible, the action should be reversible and not prejudice possible future interventions. Further, conservation must preserve and, if possible, enhance the messages and values of cultural property. The values help systematically to set overall priorities in deciding proposed interventions, as well as to establish the extent and the nature of the individual treatment. Thus documentation and identification of values—historic, architectural, social, etc.—of a cultural resource are a must and the degree of interventions is guided by the identified significance and impact on it. The seven degrees of interventions as accepted worldwide are: (1) Preservation of deterioration (indirect conservation); (2) Preservation of existing state; (3) Consolidation (or direct conservation); (4) Restoration; (5) Rehabilitation; (6) Reproduction; and (7) Reconstruction.

'Degree of intervention' is a matter of conservation policy ar specific to a site and should vary as per the value and significance of the site. Attempting to legislate a part of a policy is beyond any accepted norms. Thus, the specific amendment to the Goa Ancient Monuments Act with focus on 'reconstruction' and 're-erection' devoid of any mention of the detailed process that must be undertaken while developing the conservation plan raises major concern. In the Goa Ancient Monuments and Archaeological Sites and Remains Act, 1978, one fails to understand the need for the specific amendment and the incorporation of the words reconstruction and re-erection.

(B) It says that no government officials, benefactors, consultants, etc., can be tried in a court of law for any wrongdoing in such projects and the public has no right to interfere in such projects.

This means that there is no accountability and the people who are responsible for such projects are above the law. Moreover, since the monuments are "public property", citizens of the state definitely should have the right to ask questions and take legal action if improprieties are found.

(C) It comes into effect retrospectively from March 1, 2007, as per the bill introduced in the Assembly in 2007 titled the Goa Ancient Monuments, Archaeological Sites and Remains Amendment Act, 2007.

It is not possible to pass laws with retrospective effect. What is the need for this?

Heritage Movement led by the Goa Heritage Action Group Since 2000

Prior to the foundation of the Goa Heritage Action Group (GHAG), preservation and protection of Goan heritage was never a movement. The Goa State Archaeology Department and the Archaeological Survey of India, Goa circle, were doing their job as custodians of Goan heritage. We should place on record the contributions made by some of the Directors, archaeologists, deputy superintending archaeologists and some of the staff of these two state and central government bodies. During the Shashikala Kakodkar regime, the Goa Ancient Monuments and Archaeological Sites and Remains Act, 1978, was passed. Mr. K.T. Satarawala, ex-Governor of Goa, ex-Town Planner Deshpande, Sarto Almeida and The Indian Heritage Society (a Delhi-based non-governmental organisation [NGO]) had a chapter in Goa under the leadership of Mr. Percival Noronha since 1982, contributing to the preservation of Goan heritage.

However, a movement for the preservation and protection of Goan heritage truly began with the foundation of the first Goa-based independent NGO called the GHAG, founded on September 30, 2000, by Ms. Heta Pandit, Ms. Poonam Verma Mascarenhas, Mr. Prajal Sakhardande, Mr. Raya Shankhwalker, Mr Dean D'Cruz, Mr. Jorson Fernandes, Mr. Bismarck Martins, Mr. Ricardo Rebello, Mr. Sylvester D'Souza, Mr. Amit Modi, Mr. Sarto Almeida, Mr. K.D. Sadhale and Mrs. Anju Sakhardande at the Unitech City Centre in Panaji in their first foundation meeting held on the same day, at 4 pm. Since then, the GHAG has organised campaigns to preserve and protect historical monuments, heritage sites; organised heritage festivals such as the Fontainhas festival of the Arts; and brought out an annual publication called *Parmal* on the theme of preserving Goan heritage. It has also moved the court on many heritage issues; sowed the seed of the Goa Bachao Abhiyan in 2006 to save Goa's natural heritage; organised the Folk Utsav of folk dances, songs and folk music; brought out the heritage map of Goa; organised heritage walks; helped in the preparation of heritage markers in Old Goa; spread awareness through newspaper columns on the history and heritage of Goa titled 'Pages from the Past' (in the 'Sunday Panorama' section of *The Navhind Times*, written by Mr. Sakhardande since May 7, 2000, till date) and in other papers; created awareness of Goa's history and heritage through the Kushawati Heritage Trail, the Mhadei Heritage Trail designed by Mr. Sakhardande as well as an audio-visual presentation titled 'History through Heritage: Goa' mainly for college and school students and for other interested people.

The GHAG has brought out a book titled *Walking In and Around Panaji*, in 2005, documenting the heritage of Panaji, Taleigao, Ribandar and Dona Paula. Apart from its above-mentioned founder members, the GHAG has a nine-member executive body. Over the years, its executive members have been Ms. Pandit, Mr. Sakhardande,

Chapter 17

Concluding Panel Discussion

Rudolf C. Heredia and Rowena Robinson

Rudolf C. Heredia's Comments: Whether it is land or place or identity it must go with a realistic critique otherwise it freezes this all into a *status quo*. Somebody mentioned the romance of land, very true—but at the end someone said land has become a commodity. This will happen as an agricultural society gradually transforms itself into an urban industrial one. Land has a different meaning. Place will have a different meaning. We cannot, so to say, live in an anachronism, we have to look at it a little more carefully, but simply to live in the real is to limit ourselves. If we live only in the real without romance, poetry and imagination, we also lose. So what we need to do is to be realistic about our romance. But we also must keep in our understanding of this realism some romance that will open a horizon of hope. This is precisely what oppressed people need more than anything else, a horizon of hope. I think that this seminar has done a lot for that and I could see that many of the issues immediately became activists' concerns. For example: "We want this document, we want to do this, why was this not done, etc." This horizon of hope is what a true and critical understanding of history can open up. Thank you.

Rowena Robinson's Comments: It would be nice to know what your expectations were from this seminar and whether and to what extent they have been met. I came with very few preconceived ideas of what to expect and, in some ways, my expectations have been more than met, but there are other ways where there has been a deficit. Of course, I now feel I have received an enormous amount of information and it is very difficult to process all that. Though, it is a cool day there was a lot of heat in the room generated over questions on language, dialect, culture and identity. I was interested in the questions on language, culture and identity that came up in the morning and questions on land, identity and law that came up in the afternoon because they are intrinsically inter-linked.

Though we tend to think of culture and identities related to culture as something, as Dr. Heredia would put it, from the perspective of the romantic, these questions are very deeply implicated in question of law. From the moment we are born today as modern subjects of independent nation states we are subjects, citizens by law, and we have identities given to us by law. These identities may be mismatched with the identities we create and that we feel at the emotional level and which we felt. Sometimes the state can strip us of identities or overlay identities upon us and then those become lived identities. They are identities, or as someone was saying yesterday, labels by which we are identified and we will have to live with it and come to terms with it, even if that identification does not match with our lived reality, our sense of ourselves or our own understanding of our community, our history and our being.

In some sense this question of identity or how boundaries are drawn among groups begins from the moment a child learns to distinguish between I and you, first learning to distinguish between I and me. From that moment onwards the creation of boundaries is intrinsic to us as social beings, cultural beings. At all levels we will create boundaries, but the fact that all societies create that I-Thou and that Us-Them does not necessarily mean that these boundaries have to be constituted in a hierarchical perspective or from a perspective of inequality. There is a possibility of an I and Thou or Us and Them being constituted as different but equal. Therefore, taking up this question of how we construct boundaries and why we are constantly talking in the binaries of boundaries, for example, this community versus that community, this language versus that language, I refer to what Dr. Heredia said about how language divided the Hindus from the Muslims in north India. Of course, language is intrinsic to community identity and so therefore, we speak of language of ethnicity and it seems somehow that this identity seems to be more primeval than religious identity. Thus, when Pakistan was separated from India and East Pakistan came into being based apparently on the idea of religion, suddenly that identity then broke down when language became more important than religious identity. But even linguistic identity can be fluid and let this be a terrain of contesting possibilities rather than seeing which comes first and therefore is more original or pure than the other. Boundaries should not be made rigid, especially those based on linguistic or religious divide or even worse a divide based on both.

These ideas of identity and boundary and how to draw them in the context of communities that are extremely hierarchised is important from the point of how we look at land. The attachment to land has taken a great deal of space in sociological literature and we have built on a whole notion of the idea of the peasantry in political economy and sociology. The idea of the peasant at a certain period of time seemed to have become quite a romantic idea with people like James Scott and others espousing the idea of the moral economy of the peasant. It is this idea of an innate attachment of the peasant to the land which constitutes a space that involves equality, interdependence and face-to-face communication. It implies a moral economy that is more innocent of ideas of commodification, profiteering, all the evil things that we associate with capitalism. This is to an extent true, but when we think of attachment to land from the point of view of the idea of the moral economy of the peasant it becomes difficult to understand a number of contexts especially in India. We live in highly hierarchical societies and societies that have been hierarchical for a very long time, not just before the colonial period but much before the colonial period. And in such a hierarchical context when we think of land structurally and ideologically we need to understand the relation between land, caste and gender/patriarchy for much of India. We need to understand how caste and patriarchy come together in certain ways and are linked to land to create a certain kind of hierarchical social structure in Indian society, which did not disappear with a change of religion neither to Islam in certain parts of north India, nor with a change of religion to Catholicism.

Some of our romantic ideas regarding similarity of culture or syncretism of culture across communities in Goa is nothing but an inevitable attachment of these three associates—land, caste and patriarchy. These three will not disappear even if you change religion. It is not just syncretic religion that is manifesting itself. The hard reality of the cultural deep rootedness is because of these linkages among caste, patriarchy and land. They remain even if the Catholic Church replaces the temple as the space of worship and rituals are altered in certain ways.

Keeping with this idea of how we construct boundaries and in relation to the later papers on tribal history, the tribal in relation with Indian history has always been a problematic idea from the time and even before, when ideas such as what constitutes tribal identity, what is the relation of tribal identity with mainstream identity, etc. were popularised by Ghurye and the early sociologists. There has been this whole discourse in Indian social sciences concerning this fight about whether tribals are just backward Hindus. In relation to writings on history some very important questions were raised, 'who writes history', 'for whom is this history written', 'whose history is being written for', 'should communities write their own history', 'what is the legitimacy of these histories'.

This should be connected with what happened in Indian history in the last 25-30 years, *viz.* the idea of the subaltern that was born in Indian history and that tried to understand a contested terrain of the making of identities that may not fit in with the nationalistic identity or the nationalist discourse that is part of the making of Indian historiography. When the early subalterns began to talk of different histories and local histories they created the space wherein all of us could begin to talk about them, even though they did not fit preformed categories of Hindu or Muslim identity or that of the Indian Nationalist Congress. They created the space to think of the local or different trajectories of history. They also began to talk in terms of community, like the moral community of Scott, a particularly homogenised idea taking on all the ideas that I have been talking of so far, viz. innocent economy of the village, where there was harmony, syncretism, etc., which was innocent of political interests, the political economy, but which was impinged upon by outside forces that bring on evil distinctions of a kind.

But this idea begins to break when the subaltern project began to see all kinds of divides and groups. For a long time there was almost nothing written in subaltern studies on popular religion. India went through a very difficult phase in the 1980s. All that began to impact on the making of the subaltern project and we began to see not only that there were very different histories, but also very unequal histories and these histories had been unequal since very long time. Between writing a nationalist narrative where every community has to be included and taking it to a completely different direction where every community writes its own history and therefore, it can communicate only with itself, we have to draw some kind of mediating point, create some space where these conversations can dialogue with each other. And, that is the space that was perhaps mentioned in the morning and we agree that it is a contested space and there are going to be different and competing identities, but we can still talk to each other. It is not going to be a space where we create rigid boundaries. Both psychologists and sociologists will tell you that all societies and communities everywhere are built on a distinction between us and them. But we have this option that Dr. Heredia mentioned, do we make the boundary rigid or do we accept the boundary is fluid? And, secondly, the agreement that we can have boundaries but our boundaries need not be unequal and hierarchical but they can be boundaries of difference but equal.

This will then bring us to that question of law and identity, how do we understand this space when the law creates rigid boundaries. Alito [Sequeira] was saying that we should not wait for law to create rigid boundaries when we are forced to choose, but in the space of the popular we can play with these identities, we do not have syncretism in terms of harmony, but we have the space where we can work out differences. That is a much better option than to work towards the space of legalising everything, of instituting everything in law because law will create extreme rigidity. It will force us to converse and claim rights only in a certain kind of language, the language of evidence, the language of the court room, which will then restrict us because we have to produce a particular kind of document from a particular kind of file in a particular year in order to make a certain kind of claim on a public space. Therefore, those areas that we can keep out of the space of law should be kept, which are very few anyway since modernity inscribes us by law, by birth virtually. I would like to conclude by saying that we need to think of a creative way in which we can deal with identities in the space of the popular and the public without having recourse to the legal and the written, because they will come in turn to dominate us.

Thank you.